TEST ITEM FILE

WILLIAM D. SCOTT, III

CHEMISTRY
for Changing Times

NINTH EDITION

JOHN W. HILL
DORIS K. KOLB

Upper Saddle River, NJ 07458

Executive Editor: Kent Porter Hamann
Project Manager: Kristen Kaiser
Special Projects Manager: Barbara A. Murray
Production Editor: Benjamin St. Jacques
Supplement Cover Manager: Paul Gourhan
Supplement Cover Designer: PM Workshop Inc.
Manufacturing Buyer: Lisa McDowell

Printed in the United States of America

10 9 8 7 6 5 4 3 2 1

ISBN 0-13-089605-5

Prentice-Hall International (UK) Limited, London
Prentice-Hall of Australia Pty. Limited, Sydney
Prentice-Hall Canada, Inc., Toronto
Prentice-Hall Hispanoamericana, S.A., Mexico
Prentice-Hall of India Private Limited, New Delhi
Pearson Education Asia Pte. Ltd., Singapore
Prentice-Hall of Japan, Inc., Tokyo
Editora Prentice-Hall do Brazil, Ltda., Rio de Janeiro

Table of Contents

Prentice Hall: Instructor Support for Test Item Files

This hard copy of the test item file is just one part of Prentice Hall's comprehensive testing support service, which also includes:

- **Prentice Hall Custom Test:** This powerful computerized testing package is designed to operate on the DOS, WINDOWS, and MACINTOSH platforms. It offers full mouse support, complete question editing capabilities, random test generation, graphics, and printing capabilities.

Prentice Hall Custom Test has a unique two-track design—*Easytest*, for the novice computer user and *Fulltest*, for those who wish to write their own questions and create their own graphics.

In addition to traditional printing capabilities, Prentice Hall Custom Test offers the On-Line Testing System—the most efficient, timesaving examination aid on the market. With just a few keystrokes, the instructor can administer, correct, record, and return computerized exam results over a variety of networks.

Prentice Hall Custom Test is designed to assist educators in the recording and processing of results from student exams and assignments. Much more than a computerized gradebook, it combines a powerful database with analytical capabilities so the instructor can generate a full set of statistics. There is no grading system easier to use.

- **Prentice Hall Test Manager:** This powerful computerized testing package is designed for Windows 95, Windows 98, and Windows NT. It offers full mouse support, complete question editing capabilities, random test generation, graphics, and printing capabilities.

Prentice Hall Test Manager has removed the guesswork from your next move by incorporating "Screen Wizards" in all five databases. Each one will walk you through the important tasks from start to finish.

In addition to traditional printing capabilities, Prentice Hall Test Manager offers the On-Line Testing System—the most efficient, timesaving examination aid on the market. With just a few keystrokes, the instructor can publish a test to a local area network, correct, record and return computerized exam results over a variety of LANs.

Prentice Hall Test Manager is designed to assist educators in the recording and processing of results from student exams and assignments. Much more than a computerized gradebook, it combines a powerful database with analytical capabilities so the instructor can generate full sets of various class and individual statistics that allow you to analyze the performance of: test questions, students, an individual class or section, a course with multiple sections, and assessment types such as homework and on-line tests.

- The Prentice Hall Custom Test and Test Manager are free. To order a specific Prentice Hall Custom Test or Test Manager, you may contact your local sales representative or all our Facilities Support Services Department at 1-800-526-0485. Please identify the main text author and title.

Toll-free **technical support** is offered to all users at **1-800-550-1701**.

For those instructors without access to a computer, we offer the popular Prentice Hall Telephone Testing Service: It's simple, fast, and efficient. Simply pick the questions you'd like on your first test bank, and call the Testing Service at 1-800-550-1701; outside the U.S. and Canada, call 612-550-1705.

Identify the main text and test questions you'd like as well as any special instructions. We will create the test (or multiple versions if you wish) and send you a master copy for duplication within 48 hours. Free to adopters for the life of the text.

Chapter 1: Chemistry

TRUE/FALSE

1. There are some things you eat that are not chemicals.

   Answer: False Key 1: A Section: 1

2. Everything you wear is a chemical.

   Answer: True Key 1: A Section: 1

MULTIPLE CHOICE

3. Which science is **primarily** concerned with the study of matter and the changes it undergoes?
   a) biology
   b) chemistry
   c) geology
   d) physics

   Answer: b Key 1: A Section: 1

4. What is natural philosophy?
   a) a belief in natural foods
   b) an experimental approach to philosophy
   c) an experimental approach to the study of nature
   d) theoretical speculation about nature

   Answer: d Key 1: C Section: 1

SHORT ANSWER

5. The "Aristotelian philosophy" is generally non-productive. What does that mean?

   Answer:
   Aristotle was a natural philosopher who contemplated nature, but did no experiments to support his speculations.

   Key 1: C Section: 1

MULTIPLE CHOICE

6. The ancient Greek philosophers were probably the first to consider the behavior of matter in an organized fashion. Which is the major distinction between the "Greek philosophers" and "modern scientists"?
   a) observation
   b) hypotheses
   c) experimentation
   d) logic

   Answer: c Key 1: C Section: 1

7. Which developed first?
   a) Technology
   b) Chemistry
   c) Alchemy
   d) Natural Philosophy

   Answer: a Key 1: C Section: 1

8. Chemistry is
   a) the mystical search for the elixir of life.
   b) the study of matter and the changes it undergoes.
   c) speculation about the nature of matter.
   d) none of these.

   Answer: b Key 1: C Section: 1

TRUE/FALSE

9. The **technology** of smelting metals into ores was performed long before the **science** of metallurgy evolved.

   Answer: True Key 1: A Section: 1

ESSAY

10. What is alchemy? Give an example.

    Answer: Key 1: C Section: 2

FILL-IN-THE-BLANK

11. The impact of antibiotics on infectious disease is a 20th century example of the ________________ dream.

    Answer: Baconian Key 1: A Section: 2

MULTIPLE CHOICE

12. The leading cause of death in 1900 was infectious disease. The discovery, investigation and use of antibiotics, a class of chemicals that kill bacteria associated with infectious diseases, has dramatically reduced this cause of death. This is an example of the
    a) Baconian dream
    b) Carsonian dream
    c) Baconian nightmare
    d) Carsonian nightmare

    Answer: a Key 1: C Section: 2

FILL-IN-THE-BLANK

13. The negative impact of the overuse of pesticides on plant and animal life is an example of the _________________ nightmare.

    Answer: Carsonian Key 1: A Section: 2

MULTIPLE CHOICE

14. Chlorofluorocarbons (CFCs) are synthetic chemicals that find a variety of important applications. Probably the widest use of CFCs is as refrigerants in refrigerators and air conditioners. CFCs have been implicated in the destruction of the ozone layer. This is one example of the
    a) Baconian dream
    b) Carsonian dream
    c) Baconian nightmare
    d) Carsonian nightmare

    Answer: d Key 1: C Section: 2

FILL-IN-THE-BLANK

15. Science is testable, explanatory, and ____________________.

    Answer: tentative Key 1: D Section: 3

MULTIPLE CHOICE

16. Science is tentative, explanatory, and
    a) absolute
    b) testable
    c) unpredictable
    d) mystical

    Answer: b Key 1: D Section: 3

17. To be useful, a scientific hypothesis must be
    a) absolute
    b) complex
    c) simple
    d) tentative

    Answer: d Key 1: C Section: 3

18. Scientific results must be verified by
    a) constructing plausible theories
    b) consulting noted scientific authorities
    c) further experiment
    d) government agencies

    Answer: c Key 1: C Section: 3

19. A brief statement summarizing many observations of a physical phenomenon is called a
    a) scientific theory
    b) hypothesis
    c) fact
    d) law of nature

    Answer: d Key 1: D Section: 3

20. Tangible items used by scientists to represent invisible processes are
    a) theories
    b) models
    c) laws
    d) experiments

    Answer: b Key 1: D Section: 3

21. Kim Chemist proposes that increasing the proportion of butadiene in her glue formulation will make the glue stickier. Her proposal is called a(n)
    a) theory
    b) experiment
    c) law
    d) hypothesis

    Answer: d Key 1: D Section: 3

22. One method of rating complexity in scientific disciplines is with respect to the number of variables that are involved in experiments. Using this method, which of the following disciplines is the most complex?
a) biology
b) chemistry
c) mathematics
d) physics

Answer: a Key 1: A Section: 4

23. One method of rating complexity in scientific disciplines is with respect to the number of variables that are involved in experiments. Using this method, which of the following disciplines is the **most complex**?
a) biology
b) chemistry
c) mathematics
d) psychology

Answer: d Key 1: C Section: 4

ESSAY

24. The words science and technology are often used incorrectly as synonyms. Distinguish these two terms. Use an example of each.

Answer: Key 1: C Section: 5

MULTIPLE CHOICE

25. Archaeological evidence indicates that ancient Egyptians were brewing beer and other fermented beverages over 4000 years ago. In the mid-19th century, French scientist Louis Pasteur discovered and explained the source of fermentation (yeast). This example illustrates that
a) scientific knowledge may come before technological knowledge.
b) technological knowledge may come before scientific knowledge.
c) science and technology mean the same thing.
d) science and technology are not related.

Answer: b Key 1: A Section: 5

26. Methapyrilene, once an active ingredient in certain over-the-counter sleeping pills, was found to be a potent carcinogen (a substance that causes cancer). The pills were also found to be about as effective as placeboes in promoting sleep. The desirability quotient (DQ) for methapyrilene is
    a) low
    b) moderate
    c) high
    d) uncertain

    Answer: a Key 1: A Section: 5

ESSAY

27. Use the automobile and automobile travel to explain risk-benefit analysis.

    Answer: Key 1: C Section: 5

MULTIPLE CHOICE

28. Saccharin is used in some artificial sweeteners. Saccharin has been shown to be a very weak carcinogen (a substance that causes cancer) in animal tests, but there is little evidence of carcinogenicity in humans. Studies have also shown that artificial sweeteners provide little benefit to those who want to lose weight. The DQ for saccharin is
    a) low
    b) moderate
    c) high
    d) uncertain

    Answer: d Key 1: C Section: 5

29. The evaluation of societal risk includes all of the components of individual risk plus
    a) the probability that an incident will occur
    b) the degree of severity of the incident
    c) the number of people affected by the incident
    d) the benefit associated with the incident

    Answer: c Key 1: C Section: 5

30. When doing a risk-benefit analysis and determining DQ, which situation is often the most difficult to evaluate from both an individual and societal perspective?
    a) small benefit and high risk
    b) large benefit and high risk
    c) large benefit and low risk
    d) all are equally difficult to evaluate

    Answer: b Key 1: C Section: 5

31. A Biochemist is hired by a pharmaceutical firm to synthesize a medical remedy for cancer. This person in engaged in
    a) applied research
    b) basic research
    c) natural speculation
    d) medical technology

    Answer: a Key 1: C Section: 7

TRUE/FALSE

32. One engages in **basic research** to discover knowledge for the sake of knowing, while one engaged in **applied research** is usually directing that research toward a specific goal.

    Answer: True Key 1: C Section: 7

MULTIPLE CHOICE

33. Mass is
    a) the measure of the amount of space that matter occupies
    b) the measure of the amount of matter
    c) the measure of the force of gravity on matter
    d) the measure of the volume of matter

    Answer: b Key 1: D Section: 8

FILL-IN-THE-BLANK

34. Mass is ____________________ no "matter" where you are in the universe.

    Answer: constant ("conserved" would work, too) Key 1: C Section: 7

MULTIPLE CHOICE

35. Both mass and weight provide a measure of the amount of matter. Mass is the preferred measure of the amount of matter because
    a) mass is dependent upon location
    b) mass is independent of location
    c) mass is easier to measure
    d) mass is measured using the metric system

    Answer: b Key 1: C Section: 8

36. On Mars gravity is one-third that on Earth. What would be the weight on Mars of a person who has a weight of 150 pounds (lb) on Earth?
   a) 50
   b) 100
   c) 150
   d) 200

   Answer: a Key 1: A Section: 8

37. On Mars gravity is one-third that on Earth. What would be the mass on Mars of a person who has a mass of 60 kilograms (kg) on Earth?
   a) 20
   b) 60
   c) 80
   d) 180

   Answer: b Key 1: A Section: 8

FILL-IN-THE-BLANK

38. The production of hydrogen gas by the electolysis of water is a ____________ process.

   Answer: chemical Key 1: A Section: 8

39. The purification of water by distillation is a ____________ process.

   Answer: physical Key 1: A Section: 8

40. The melting of ice is an example of a ________________ change.

   Answer: physical Key 1: A Section: 8

MULTIPLE CHOICE

41. Which of the following is a **physical** change?
   a) carbon combines with oxygen to form carbon dioxide
   b) ice melts at 0° C
   c) a red substance is decomposed by heat to mercury and oxygen
   d) water is decomposed by electricity into hydrogen and oxygen

   Answer: b Key 1: A Section: 8

42. Which of the following is a **chemical** property?
   a) sodium reacts with water to form sodium hydroxide
   b) salt dissolves in water
   c) sugar is a solid at room temperature
   d) oil and water do not mix

   Answer: a Key 1: A Section: 8

43. Which of these is a chemical change?
    a) the hair stylist cuts your hair
    b) bleaching powder dissolves in water
    c) silkworms convert mulberry leaves into silk
    d) wool is spun into yarn

    Answer: c Key 1: A Section: 8

44. Which of these **DOES NOT** involve a chemical change?
    a) cocaine causes the release of norepinephrine from nerve cells
    b) red delicious apples taste sweet
    c) antacids often help an upset stomach
    d) mercury is used in barometers because it has a large density

    Answer: d Key 1: C Section: 8

45. A mixture of iron, salt and sand can be separated using a magnet, water, a filter and a hot plate. Think about this separation. The separation of this mixture
    a) uses physical changes or processes
    b) uses chemical changes or processes
    c) uses chemical and physical changes or processes
    d) can not be done with the materials listed

    Answer: a Key 1: A Section: 8

46. A chemical change always involves a change in the __________ of a piece of matter.
    a) state
    b) composition
    c) volume
    d) temperature

    Answer: b Key 1: D Section: 8

47. As water flows over a dam,
    a) kinetic energy increases and potential energy decreases
    b) kinetic energy decreases and potential energy increases
    c) kinetic energy and potential energy remain constant
    d) kinetic energy and potential energy increase

    Answer: a Key 1: C Section: 12

48. The **ultimate source** for almost all of the energy on Earth is
    a) fossil fuel
    b) the moon
    c) the sun
    d) the oceans

    Answer: c Key 1: C Section: 12

TRUE/FALSE

49. Temperature is a measure of the amount of heat an object contains.

    Answer: False Key 1: D Section: 12

MULTIPLE CHOICE

50. The physical state that retains both shape and volume is
    a) solid
    b) liquid
    c) gas
    d) element

    Answer: a Key 1: D Section: 9

51. A gas is characterized by
    a) definite shape and volume
    b) definite shape and indefinite volume
    c) indefinite shape and definite volume
    d) indefinite shape and volume

    Answer: d Key 1: D Section: 9

52. The label on a can of sparkling mineral water lists the following ingredients: carbonated water and natural lime flavor. Which one of the following best classifies the beverage?
    a) mixture
    b) element
    c) compound
    d) pure substance

    Answer: a Key 1: A Section: 9

53. The label on a bottle of shampoo lists many ingredients, such as water, sodium laureth sulfate, lauramide DEA, sodium chloride, etc. From this information, shampoo is best classified as
    a) a pure substance
    b) an element
    c) a compound
    d) a mixture

    Answer: d Key 1: A Section: 9

54. Pure water is an excellent substance for dissolving many other substances. Given this, the tap water that you drink is best classified as a(n)
a) pure substance
b) mixture
c) element
d) compound

Answer: b Key 1: A Section: 9

55. Vinegar is composed of approximately 5% acetic acid and 95% water. Which one of the following is the best classification of vinegar?
a) pure substance
b) element
c) compound
d) mixture

Answer: d Key 1: A Section: 9

56. Refined white table sugar is usually derived from either sugar cane or sugar beets. Irrespective of the source of table sugar, after refining it always has the same composition of carbon, hydrogen and oxygen. Sugar is most specifically classified as which one of the following?
a) ideal mixture
b) element
c) compound
d) mixture

Answer: c Key 1: A Section: 9

57. Molasses is a by-product of the refining of sugar from sugar cane. The specific composition of molasses varies depending upon the source of the sugar cane. Which one of the following is the best classification of molasses?
a) pure substance
b) element
c) compound
d) mixture

Answer: d Key 1: A Section: 9

58. A substance that can not be broken down by chemical means into simpler substances is called a(n)
a) solid
b) element
c) compound
d) mixture

Answer: b Key 1: D Section: 9

59. Which one of the following statements concerning the relationship between the number of elements and the number of compounds is correct?
   a) The number of elements and compounds are approximately the same
   b) The number of elements is much larger than the number of compounds
   c) The number of compounds is much larger than the number of elements
   d) The number of elements must equal the number of compounds

   Answer: c Key 1: A Section: 9

60. The number of known elements at this time is approximately
   a) 50
   b) 100
   c) 200
   d) infinite

   Answer: b Key 1: D Section: 9

61. Which one of the following can **not** be the chemical symbol for an **element**?
   a) Co
   b) Cf
   c) B
   d) CU

   Answer: d Key 1: A Section: 9

62. What is the chemical symbol for potassium?
   a) P
   b) Po
   c) Pu
   d) K

   Answer: d Key 1: D Section: 9

63. What is the chemical symbol for calcium?
   a) C
   b) Ca
   c) Cl
   d) Cm

   Answer: b Key 1: D Section: 9

64. What is the chemical symbol for sodium?
   a) Na
   b) K
   c) S
   d) Sm

   Answer: a Key 1: D Section: 9

65. What is the chemical symbol for iodine?
    a) I
    b) Id
    c) In
    d) Io

    Answer: a Key 1: D Section: 9

66. What is the chemical symbol for iron?
    a) Fe
    b) I
    c) In
    d) Ir

    Answer: a Key 1: D Section: 9

67. What is the name of the element with the symbol N?
    a) neon
    b) nitrogen
    c) sodium
    d) nickel

    Answer: b Key 1: D Section: 9

68. What is the name of the element with the symbol Ag?
    a) silver
    b) gold
    c) mercury
    d) antimony

    Answer: a Key 1: D Section: 9

69. What is the name of the element with the symbol Hg?
    a) silver
    b) gold
    c) mercury
    d) antimony

    Answer: c Key 1: D Section: 9

70. What is the name of the element with the symbol Au?
    a) silver
    b) gold
    c) mercury
    d) antimony

    Answer: b Key 1: D Section: 9

71. Which one of the following symbols represents an element?
    a) CO
    b) He
    c) HF
    d) NO

    Answer: b Key 1: D Section: 9

72. Which one of the following represents a compound?
    a) Co
    b) He
    c) CO_2
    d) Na

    Answer: c Key 1: A Section: 9

73. In the SI system of measurement, the unit of length is the
    a) kilogram
    b) meter
    c) liter
    d) yard

    Answer: b Key 1: D Section: 10

74. In the SI system of measurement the unit of mass is the
    a) kilogram
    b) kilometer
    c) liter
    d) yard

    Answer: a Key 1: D Section: 10

75. How many meters are in 5.0 cm?
    a) 0.0050
    b) 0.050
    c) .5
    d) 500

    Answer: b Key 1: A Section: 10

76. How many kilometers are in 500 m?
    a) 0.005
    b) 0.05
    c) 0.5
    d) 500

    Answer: c Key 1: A Section: 10

77. How many micrograms are in 0.010 mg?
    a) 10 μg
    b) 100 μg
    c) 10000 μg
    d) .000010 μg

    Answer: a Key 1: A Section: 10

78. A typical pain reliever tablet contains 325 mg of acetaminophen as the active ingredient. This mass may also be expressed as
    a) 325 μg
    b) 0.000325 g
    c) 0.325 g
    d) 32.5 μg

    Answer: c Key 1: A Section: 10

79. A female student has a mass of 120 pounds. Her mass in kilograms is approximately
    a) 30 kg
    b) 50 kg
    c) 100 kg
    d) 260 kg

    Answer: b Key 1: A Section: 10

80. The prefix **centi** means
    a) 10^{-3}
    b) 10^{-2}
    c) 10^{-1}
    d) 10^{2}

    Answer: b Key 1: A Section: 10

81. The prefix **centi** means
    a) 1/1,000
    b) 1/100
    c) 1/10
    d) 100

    Answer: b Key 1: D Section: 10

82. The prefix **centi** means
    a) 0.001
    b) 0.01
    c) 0.1
    d) 100

    Answer: b Key 1: D Section: 10

83. The prefix **milli** means
   a) 10^{-9}
   b) 10^{-6}
   c) 10^{-3}
   d) 10^{3}

   Answer: c Key 1: D Section: 10

84. The prefix **milli** means
   a) 1/1,000,000
   b) 1/1,000
   c) 1/10
   d) 1,000

   Answer: b Key 1: D Section: 10

85. The prefix **milli** means
   a) 0.000001
   b) 0.001
   c) 0.1
   d) 1000

   Answer: b Key 1: D Section: 10

86. The prefix **micro** means
   a) 10^{-9}
   b) 10^{-6}
   c) 10^{-3}
   d) 10^{3}

   Answer: b Key 1: D Section: 10

87. The prefix **micro** means
   a) 0.000001
   b) 0.001
   c) 100
   d) 1000

   Answer: a Key 1: D Section: 10

88. The prefix **kilo** means
   a) 0.000001
   b) 0.001
   c) 100
   d) 1000

   Answer: d Key 1: D Section: 10

89. The prefix **mega** means
  a) 10^{-6}
  b) 10^{-3}
  c) 10^{3}
  d) 10^{6}

  Answer: d Key 1: D Section: 10

90. The symbol for the prefix **micro** is
  a) M
  b) m
  c) mm
  d) μ

  Answer: d Key 1: D Section: 10

91. The prefix **kilo** means
  a) 10^{-9}
  b) 10^{-6}
  c) 10^{-3}
  d) 10^{3}

  Answer: d Key 1: D Section: 10

92. The symbol for the prefix Mega is____?
  a) M
  b) m
  c) mm
  d) μ

  Answer: a Key 1: D Section: 10

93. The SI unit for temperature is the
  a) Calorie
  b) Celsius
  c) Fahrenheit
  d) Kelvin

  Answer: d Key 1: D Section: 10

94. The freezing point of water on the **Celsius** temperature scale is
  a) -32 °C
  b) 0 °C
  c) 100 °C
  d) 212 °C

  Answer: b Key 1: D Section: 10

95. The boiling point of water on the **Celsius** temperature scale is
a) 100 °C
b) 212 °C
c) 273 °C
d) 373 °C

Answer: a Key 1: D Section: 10

96. The freezing point of water on the **Kelvin** temperature scale is
a) 0 K
b) 100 K
c) 273 K
d) 373 K

Answer: c Key 1: D Section: 10

97. The boiling point of water on the **Kelvin** temperature scale is
a) 0 K
b) 100 K
c) 273 K
d) 373 K

Answer: d Key 1: A Section: 10

98. The boiling point of ethanol is 78° C. What is this temperature on the **Kelvin** scale?
a) 351 K
b) 195 K
c) 78 K
d) -195 K

Answer: a Key 1: A Section: 10

99. The melting point of tungsten, W, is 3683 K. What is this temperature on the **Celsius** scale?
a) 3956 °C
b) 3583 °C
c) 3471 °C
d) 3410 °C

Answer: d Key 1: A Section: 10

100. The melting point of tungsten, W, is 3410 °C. What is this temperature on the **Kelvin** scale?
a) 3137 K
b) 3310 K
c) 3510 K
d) 3683 K

Answer: d Key 1: A Section: 10

101. The energy content of foods is stated on food labels in **Calories**. The Calorie is equal to
a) 1000 calories
b) 1000 kilocalories
c) 1000° C
d) 1000 joules

Answer: a Key 1: C Section: 10

102. The density of a certain type of steel is 8.1 g/cm^3. What is the **mass** of a 100 cm^3 chunk of this steel?
a) 0.081 g
b) 8.1 g
c) 12 g
d) 810 g

Answer: d Key 1: A Section: 11

103. The density of gold is 19.3 g/cm^3. What is the **volume** of a 100 g gold ingot?
a) 0.193 cm^3
b) 5.18 cm^3
c) 19.3 cm^3
d) 193 cm^3

Answer: b Key 1: A Section: 11

104. What is the **density** of a salt solution that has a volume of 10.0 mL and a mass of 22 grams?
a) 0.22 g/mL
b) 0.46 g/mL
c) 2.2 g/mL
d) 4.5 g/mL

Answer: c Key 1: A Section: 11

105. The density of lead is 11.3 g/cm^3. What **mass** of lead is required to make a 1 cm^3 fishing sinker?
a) 1.00 g
b) 1.13 g
c) 11.3 g
d) 113 g

Answer: c Key 1: A Section: 11

106. A train robber in a western movie steals two gold ingots, each of which has a volume of 1000. cm^3. The density of gold is 19.3 g/cm^3. What is the mass of the two ingots?
a) 38.6 g
b) 19,300 g
c) 38,600 g
d) 104 g

Answer: c Key 1: A Section: 11

107. A student working in the laboratory needs 200 g of a liquid chemical whose density is 0.69 g/cm^3. What volume of this liquid should he measure?
a) 138 cm^3
b) 69 cm^3
c) 200 cm^3
d) 290 cm^3

Answer: d Key 1: A Section: 11

108. The density of mercury is 13.6 g/cm^3. What **approximate mass** of mercury is required to fill a 1 ounce bottle? An ounce is approximately 30 cm^3.
a) 400 g
b) 130 g
c) 14 g
d) 0.5 g

Answer: a Key 1: C Section: 12

ESSAY

109. Between 1981 and 1991 the US chemical industry maintained a trade **surplus**. What does this mean? Is this good or bad for the US economy?

Answer: Key 1: A Section: 6

110. Explain the impact of the US chemical industry on trade with other nations.

Answer: Key 1: A Section: 6

111. Briefly describe the central role of chemistry in science. Use an example.

Answer: Key 1: C Section: 6

MULTIPLE CHOICE

112. Among 42 basic US industries ranked from highest to lowest with respect to worker safety by the National Safety Council during the 1980's, the chemical industry ranked in
a) the top 10%
b) the second 10%
c) the bottom 10%
d) last

Answer: a Key 1: D Section: 6

FILL-IN-THE-BLANK

113. A chemist is hired by a major petroleum company to do research into developing a gasoline mixture that burns more efficiently in automobile engines. This is best described as _________ research.

Answer: applied Key 1: A Section: 7

MULTIPLE CHOICE

114. A chemist employed by an airplane manufacturer investigates new adhesives for the purpose of building airplanes without rivets. She is engaged in
a) alchemy
b) applied research
c) basic research
d) risk-benefit analysis

Answer: b Key 1: C Section: 7

115. One of the hallmarks of science is the ability to think _______________.
a) often
b) constantly
c) critically
d) independently

Answer: c Key 1: C Section: 7

FILL-IN-THE-BLANK

116. The acronym FLaReS helps to remember four rules: Falsifiability, logic, replicability and ___________.

Answer:
Sufficiency
Critical thinking

Key 1: C

TRUE/FALSE

117. Science does not prove a theory or hypothesis to be true, it can only prove something false.

Answer:
True
Critical thinking

Key 1: C

118. A psychic claims he can bend a spoon using only the power of his mind. However, he says he can do so only when the conditions are right and there must be no one with negative energy present. This claim is falsifiable.

Answer:
False
Critical thinking

Key 1: A

119. The research work of Gertrude Elion is an example of basic research.

Answer: True Key 1: C Section: 7

MULTIPLE CHOICE

120. The woman who shared the 1988 Nobel prize in physiology and medicine, and in 1991 became the first woman inducted into the National Inventors Hall of Fame was ______.
a) Madame Curie
b) Rachel Carson
c) Gertrude Elion
d) Amelia Earhart

Answer: c Key 1: A Section: 7

Chapter 2: Atoms

MULTIPLE CHOICE

1. The Greek word **atomos** means
   a) atom
   b) indivisible
   c) invisible
   d) continuous

   Answer: b Key 1: D Section: 1

2. Leucippus and Democritus proposed the "first" atomic view of matter. They arrived at this view based on
   a) many experiments
   b) careful measurements
   c) philosophical and intuitive speculation
   d) all of the above contributed to their atomic view

   Answer: c Key 1: C Section: 1

3. The ancient Greeks believed that matter was composed of four basic elements. Which one of the following **WAS NOT** one of the four?
   a) gold
   b) fire
   c) water
   d) earth

   Answer: a Key 1: D Section: 1

4. An atomic **view** of matter was first proposed approximately how many years ago?
   a) 50
   b) 100
   c) 200
   d) 2000

   Answer: d Key 1: C Section: 1

5. Lavoisier performed many of the same experiments as his predecessors. The one thing that most distinguished Lavoisier's work was
   a) the results
   b) the mass measurements
   c) the chemicals
   d) the glassware

   Answer: b Key 1: C Section: 2

6. By measuring the mass of substances before and after chemical reactions, Lavoisier summarized his observations with a(n)
   a) hypothesis
   b) observation
   c) theory
   d) law

   Answer: d Key 1: C Section: 2

7. Which one of the following statements **is not** a correct statement of the Law of Conservation of Mass?
   a) The mass of a system is dependent upon chemical reactions that may occur.
   b) The mass of a system is conserved in a chemical reaction.
   c) Matter can not be created or destroyed.
   d) Atoms are conserved in chemical reactions.

   Answer: a Key 1: C Section: 2

8. A mixture containing 15 grams of carbon and 25 grams of oxygen is sealed in a flask. The total mass of the system is 140 grams. The flask is heated to cause the carbon and oxygen to react. The sealed flask is massed. What is the mass of the sealed flask?
   a) 40 grams
   b) 100 grams
   c) 125 grams
   d) 140 grams

   Answer: d Key 1: A Section: 2

9. A student measures 10.5 g of mercury(II) oxide into an open test tube and heats. The heat causes the mercury(II) oxide to decompose into mercury and oxygen. After reaction, the student finds the mass of the contents of the tube to be 9.7 g. Which one of the following describes these observations?
   a) The decomposition of mercury(II) oxide does not obey the Law of Conservation of Mass.
   b) 0.8 grams of oxygen gas are lost from the tube.
   c) There are errors associated with the student's measurements.
   d) Heating destroys some mass.

   Answer: b Key 1: A Section: 2

SHORT ANSWER

10. Antoine Lavoisier is often credited with doing more than anyone else to establish chemistry as a quantitative science. What was the significance of Lavoisier's work?

    Answer: Careful measurements on chemical reactions.

    Key 1: A Section: 2

ESSAY

11. What is the significance of the Law of Conservation of Mass in waste disposal?

    Answer: Key 1: C Section: 2

MULTIPLE CHOICE

12. The amount of carbon on the Earth, including the atmosphere,
    a) is essentially constant
    b) is decreasing due to consumption of carbon based fuels, such as coal and petroleum
    c) is increasing due to plant and animal growth on the planet
    d) fluctuates dramatically with the seasons

    Answer: a Key 1: C Section: 2

13. The amount of aluminum on the Earth today relative to the amount 100 years ago when Al was first commercially extracted from bauxite, an aluminum containing ore,
    a) is essentially the same
    b) is decreasing rapidly due to production of aluminum beverage containers
    c) is decreasing, but more slowly recently due to interest in recycling
    d) is actually increasing due to recycling efforts and more energy efficient production methods

    Answer: a Key 1: C Section: 2

14. Hydrogen peroxide decomposes into water and oxygen when exposed to heat or light. A tightly capped bottle of hydrogen peroxide is placed on a mass scale (a balance) and exposed to light for three weeks. The mass reading on the scale does not change. This is an example of
    a) the Law of Conservation of Mass
    b) the Law of Definite Proportions
    c) the Law of Constant Composition
    d) the Law of Multiple Proportions

    Answer: a Key 1: A Section: 2

15. Methane can be decomposed into two simpler substances, hydrogen and carbon. Therefore, methane
    a) is a gas
    b) can not be an element
    c) must be a mixture
    d) must have the formula CH

    Answer: b Key 1: D Section: 2

16. Which term best fits this definition: a statement that summarizes the data obtained from observations?
a) hypothesis
b) law
c) theory
d) model

Answer: b Key 1: D Section: 2

17. The ability to recycle aluminum (or glass, or plastic) is ultimately an illustration of
a) the law of the conservation of mass
b) the law of definite proportions
c) the ingenuity of chemists
d) the law of multiple proportions

Answer: a Key 1: C Section: 2

18. The Law of Definite Proportion was first stated by ________
a) Lavoisier
b) Galileo
c) Dalton
d) Proust

Answer: d Key 1: C Section: 2

19. ___________ was the first person to propose a consistent "modern" atomic theory.
a) Dalton
b) Democritus
c) Proust
d) Lavoisier

Answer: a Key 1: A Section: 2

20. Which discovery was **not** in conflict with Dalton's atomic theory?
a) the discovery of electrical charge
b) the discovery of the electron
c) the discovery of the element gallium
d) the discovery of the proton

Answer: c Key 1: A Section: 2

SHORT ANSWER

21. When 10.0 g of lead are heated with 1.6 g of sulfur, 11.6 g of lead sulfide are formed. How many grams of lead sulfide form when 10.0 g of lead are heated with 3.0 g of sulfur?

Answer: 11.6 g Key 1: A Section: 3

ESSAY

22. Distinguish a compound from a mixture.

    Answer: Key 1: A Section: 3

MULTIPLE CHOICE

23. When added to a sealed flask and heated, 6.0 g of carbon and 16.0 g of oxygen react to form 22.0 g of carbon dioxide. How much carbon dioxide is formed when 12.0 g of carbon is reacted with 100.0 g of oxygen?
    a) 22.0 g
    b) 28.0 g
    c) 44.0 g
    d) 112.0 g

    Answer: c Key 1: A Section: 3

24. The observation that 20 g of hydrogen gas always combines with 160 g of oxygen gas to form 180 g of water, even when there is more than 160 g of oxygen present in the reaction container, illustrates the law of
    a) definite proportions
    b) multiple proportions
    c) ideal gases
    d) excess reactants

    Answer: a Key 1: C Section: 3

25. No matter how much extra oxygen is available, 12 grams of carbon always combines with 32 grams of oxygen. This best illustrates the law of
    a) conservation of mass
    b) definite proportions
    c) multiple proportions
    d) conservation of energy

    Answer: b Key 1: C Section: 3

26. Heptane is always composed of 84.0% carbon and 16.0% hydrogen. This illustrates the law of
    a) conservation of mass
    b) definite proportions
    c) multiple proportions
    d) all of the above

    Answer: b Key 1: C Section: 3

27. When 10.00 g of lead and 1.56 grams of sulfur react, 11.56 g of lead sulfide is produced. Suppose 30.00 g of lead and 1.56 g of sulfur are allowed to react. Analysis of the reaction mixture would show
a) 31.56 g of lead sulfide
b) 34.68 g of lead sulfide
c) 11.56 g of lead sulfide and 20.00 g of lead
d) no reaction

Answer: c Key 1: A Section: 3

TRUE/FALSE

28. The Law of Constant Composition and the Law of Definite Proportions are different names for the same phenomenon.

Answer: True Key 1: C Section: 3

MULTIPLE CHOICE

29. After many observations, Proust stated that elements combine in definite proportions to form compounds. Dalton explained these observations by proposing that matter must consist of atoms. Dalton's explanation is called a(n)
a) law
b) theory
c) hypothesis
d) observation

Answer: b Key 1: C Section: 4

30. Nitrogen forms a number of different compounds with oxygen, depending upon the experimental conditions. This type of observation concerning the behavior of matter is summarized by
a) the law of conservation of mass
b) the law of definite proportions
c) the law of constant composition
d) the law of multiple proportions

Answer: d Key 1: C Section: 4

SHORT ANSWER

31. Describe what happens in a chemical reaction.

Answer: The arrangement of atoms changes. Key 1: D Section: 4

TRUE/FALSE

32. Ammonia and hydrazine are compounds composed of only hydrogen and nitrogen. These compounds illustrate the law of multiple proportions.

    Answer: True Key 1: A Section: 4

33. Dalton's atomic theory states that atoms may change into other atoms in a chemical reaction.

    Answer: False Key 1: C Section: 4

MULTIPLE CHOICE

34. Which one of the following **IS NOT** part of Dalton's atomic theory?
    a) matter is composed of atoms
    b) atoms of the same element have the same properties
    c) atoms of different elements have different properties
    d) atoms change into other atoms in chemical reactions

    Answer: d Key 1: D Section: 4

35. Although all parts (postulates) of Dalton's atomic theory are important, which one of the postulates is crucial to explain the observations summarized by the Law of Definite Proportions?
    a) Matter is composed of atoms
    b) Atoms of the same element have the same properties
    c) Atoms combine with other atoms in fixed, whole number ratios to form compounds
    d) Atoms are very small

    Answer: c Key 1: C Section: 4

36. Which one of the following DOES NOT occur in a chemical reaction?
    a) Matter is rearranged
    b) Matter is conserved
    c) Atoms react with other atoms
    d) Atoms are changed into other atoms

    Answer: d Key 1: C Section: 4

37. Dalton explained the law of conservation of mass by stating that atoms are neither created nor destroyed in a chemical reaction. Dalton's explanation is an example of a scientific
    a) theory
    b) law
    c) hypothesis
    d) experiment

    Answer: a Key 1: C Section: 4

38. When electricity is passed through molten potassium bromide, two simpler substances, potassium and bromine, are produced. Therefore, potassium bromide
a) can not be an element
b) must be a mixture
c) must be a compound
d) must have a formula PB

Answer: a Key 1: A Section: 4

39. Which set of compounds illustrates the law of **multiple proportions**?
a) NH_3, PH_3, AsH_3
b) NH_3, NF_3, NCl_3
c) NH_3, N_2H_4
d) all of these

Answer: c Key 1: A Section: 4

40. Which set of compounds illustrates the law of **multiple proportions**?
a) CH_4, C_2H_6, C_3H_8
b) NO, NH_3, NH_4Cl
c) H_2O, H_2
d) all of these

Answer: a Key 1: A Section: 4

41. Under conditions of limited oxygen, carbon burns to form carbon monoxide, a poisonous gas. In conditions with unlimited oxygen, carbon burns to form carbon dioxide. This illustrates the law of
a) conservation of mass
b) definite proportions
c) different chemical reactions
d) multiple proportions

Answer: d Key 1: A Section: 4

42. In plentiful air, 3.0 parts of carbon react with 8.0 parts of oxygen to form carbon dioxide. How much carbon is required to produce 2200 g of carbon dioxide?
a) 6600
b) 3300
c) 1200
d) 600

Answer: d Key 1: A Section: 4

SHORT ANSWER

43. In light of present day knowledge criticize Dalton's proposal that atoms are indivisible.

    Answer:
    Radioactive elements decompose into elements that are different from the parent element and emit particles in the process.

    Key 1: C   Section: 4

MULTIPLE CHOICE

44. Which set of compounds illustrates the law of **multiple proportions**?
    a) SO_2, SO_3
    b) N_2O, NO, NO_2
    c) H_2O, H_2O_2
    d) all of these

    Answer: d   Key 1: A   Section: 4

45. John Dalton discovered which of the following laws?
    a) The Law of Conservation of Mass
    b) The Law of Definite Proportions
    c) The Law of Constant Composition
    d) The Law of Multiple Proportions

    Answer: d   Key 1: C   Section: 4

46. Mendeleev organized the elements
    a) by increasing atomic number and similar properties
    b) by increasing atomic weight and similar properties
    c) alphabetically by name
    d) by number of electrons

    Answer: b   Key 1: C   Section: 5

SHORT ANSWER

47. Explain why Mendeleev left gaps in his periodic table of the elements.

    Answer:
    Mendeleev left gaps in his periodic table so that elements with similar properties could be grouped together. He correctly predicted that the gaps would correspond to elements that had not been discovered at that time.

    Key 1: C   Section: 5

MULTIPLE CHOICE

48. The unit of atomic weight is
    a) atomic weight unit
    b) atomic mass unit
    c) microgram
    d) the mass of an electron

    Answer: b Key 1: C Section: 5

49. The atomic masses for elements are
    a) actual masses determined by weighing individual atoms
    b) relative masses determined by comparison with a standard reference
    c) the same as the atomic number
    d) unknown

    Answer: b Key 1: C Section: 5

50. Perhaps the greatest triumph of Mendeleev's periodic table was
    a) the use of rows and columns to organize the elements
    b) the ability to predict electron configurations of elements
    c) the use of atomic numbers as an organizing criterion
    d) the prediction of the existence of undiscovered elements

    Answer: d Key 1: C Section: 5

51. The scientist who published a table of atomic weights in 1828 containing 54 elements was
    a) Dalton
    b) Berzelius
    c) Mendeleev
    d) Boyle

    Answer: b Key 1: C Section: 5

52. The Periodic Table is helpful in all of the following endeavors but one. Which is the exception?
    a) predicting formulas of compounds
    b) predicting chemical reactivity of elements
    c) predicting physical properties of elements
    d) predicting monetary values of elements

    Answer: d Key 1: A Section: 5

53. Mendeleev's statement of the **periodic law** is "the properties of the elements are periodic functions of their ____"
a) atomic weights.
b) atomic numbers.
c) both atomic weights and atomic numbers.
d) position in his periodic table.

Answer:
a

Key 1: D Section: 5

54. The modern periodic law of the elements states that the properties of the element are periodic functions of _____
a) atomic weights.
b) atomic numbers.
c) both atomic weights and atomic numbers.
d) position in the periodic table.

Answer: b Key 1: D Section: 5

55. What is the name of the Russian chemist who was a pioneer in the development of the periodic law?
a) Meyerovic
b) Mendeleev
c) Döbereiner
d) Newlands

Answer: b Key 1: A Section: 5

TRUE/FALSE

56. Scientists can observe computer enhanced images of atoms.

Answer: True Key 1: C Section: 6

MULTIPLE CHOICE

57. If drops of water are subdivided to the ultimately smallest drops possible, what is the smallest particle of water that retains the chemical and physical properties of water?
a) molecule
b) mixture
c) atom
d) micron

Answer: a Key 1: D Section: 7

Chapter 3: Atomic Structure

MULTIPLE CHOICE

1. Which statement best summarizes the general nature of investigations during the **1800's** related to the acquisition and development of knowledge concerning the atomic structure of matter?
   a) Qualitative observations, although often influenced by ideas related to magic and mysticism, provide glimpses of the structure of matter.
   b) Quantitative measurements, particularly those related to mass, lead to the formulation of fundamental laws leading to an atomic theory of matter.
   c) The development and use of electrical probes to study matter lead to experimental evidence for the existence of subatomic particles in atoms.
   d) The use of new experimental and mathematical techniques provide information concerning the organization of subatomic particles in atoms.

   Answer: c Key 1: C Section: 1

2. Electrolysis is
   a) the production of electrical currents from a battery
   b) the decomposition of compounds by electricity
   c) the production of cathode rays in vacuum tubes using electricity
   d) the conversion of elements into new elements by the use of electricity

   Answer: b Key 1: C Section: 1

3. The application of electricity to chemical systems provided much of the experimental evidence for the existence of subatomic particles. With respect to the use of electricity in probing matter, which one of the following scientists **WOULD NOT** be grouped with the others?
   a) Humphry Davy
   b) Michael Faraday
   c) J.J. Thomson
   d) Ernest Rutherford

   Answer: d Key 1: A Section: 1

4. Ions are
   a) charged atoms
   b) electrons
   c) neutrons
   d) electrodes

   Answer: a Key 1: D Section: 1

5. A **cation** is a
   a) negatively charged ion
   b) positively charged ion
   c) negative electrode
   d) positive electrode

   Answer: b Key 1: D Section: 1

ESSAY

6. Describe a cathode ray tube and its significance in determining the subatomic structure of atoms.

   Answer: Key 1: C Section: 1

MULTIPLE CHOICE

7. Electrolytes are important substances in the chemistry of living systems. An **electrolyte** is a compound that
   a) conducts electricity when melted or taken into solution
   b) generates light when electricity is applied
   c) contains electrons
   d) contains electrodes

   Answer: a Key 1: D Section: 1

FILL-IN-THE-BLANK

8. Scientists studying cathode rays determined that the rays must be **negatively charged** because the beam moved from the ___________ electrode to the _______________ electrode.

   Answer: negative, positive Key 1: C Section: 1

MULTIPLE CHOICE

9. Cathode rays are beams of
   a) anions
   b) electrons
   c) neutrons
   d) protons

   Answer: b Key 1: C Section: 1

10. By measuring the deflection of cathode rays in electrical and magnetic fields, J.J. Thomson was able to determine the
a) mass of the electron
b) speed of the electron
c) charge on the electron
d) ratio of mass to charge for the electron

Answer: d Key 1: C Section: 1

11. Which experimental observation led scientists to speculate that cathode rays contained particles that were constituents of all matter?
a) the rays were deflected by electrical fields
b) the rays were deflected by magnetic fields
c) the rays were independent of the type of gas in the vacuum tube
d) all of the above provided evidence of the "fundamental" nature of cathode rays

Answer: c Key 1: C Section: 1

12. The existence of **positively** charged particles in gas discharge tubes was first experimentally verified by
a) Lavoisier
b) Dalton
c) Faraday
d) Goldstein

Answer: d Key 1: C Section: 1

13. Millikan's "oil drop" apparatus allowed for the determination of which property of the electron?
a) mass
b) charge
c) ratio of mass to charge
d) speed

Answer: b Key 1: D Section: 1

14. When combined with Thomson's determination of the mass to charge ratio of the electron, Millikan's experimental work allowed for the determination of the
a) charge on the electron
b) mass of the electron
c) speed of the electron
d) all of the above

Answer: b Key 1: C Section: 1

TRUE/FALSE

15. Anions migrate toward the cathode.

    Answer: False   Key 1: A   Section: 1

16. Cations migrate towards the cathode.

    Answer: True   Key 1: C   Section: 1

17. The positive particles had varying masses in Goldstein's experiments using a gas discharge tube with perforated cathodes.

    Answer: True   Key 1: C   Section: 1

ESSAY

18. Compare and contrast fluorescence and radioactivity.

    Answer: Key 1: C   Section: 1

MULTIPLE CHOICE

19. An anion is a
    a) negatively charged ion
    b) positively charged ion
    c) negative electrode
    d) positive electrode

    Answer: a   Key 1: D   Section: 1

20. William Crookes passed an electric current through a tightly sealed tube. The current generated a green beam of light (due to fluorescence as the beam struck a zinc sulfide surface) which seemed to pass from one electrode to the other. This beam was called a cathode ray because
    a) it seemed to leave the anode and travel to the cathode.
    b) it seemed to leave the cathode and travel to the anode.
    c) it seemed to travel from the zinc sulfide screen to the cathode.
    d) it seemed to travel from the zinc sulfide screen to the anode.

    Answer: b   Key 1: C   Section: 1

21. A stream of electrons will behave in what way in an electric field?
    a) be unchanged
    b) be stopped
    c) be deflected toward the positive electrode
    d) be deflected toward the negative electrode

    Answer: c   Key 1: A   Section: 1

22. Radioactivity is
    a) the spontaneous emission of radiation from unstable elements
    b) the emission of light from certain substances after exposure to sunlight
    c) the spontaneous emission of radio waves from matter
    d) the emission of light from matter when exposed to radio waves

    Answer: a Key 1: C Section: 2

23. Which person(s) won two Nobel prizes (one in physics; the other in chemistry) for work with radioactivity?
    a) Antoine Henri Becquerel
    b) Marie Sklodowska Curie
    c) Pierre Curie
    d) Marie and Pierre Curie

    Answer: b Key 1: D Section: 2

24. Which **IS NOT** one of the three types of radiation emitted from radioactive elements?
    a) alpha, α
    b) beta, β
    c) gamma, γ
    d) lambda, λ

    Answer: d Key 1: D Section: 2

25. Which radioactive particle was used by Geiger and Marsden in their experiments with thin metal foils?
    a) alpha, α
    b) beta, β
    c) gamma, γ
    d) lambda, λ

    Answer: a Key 1: A Section: 3

26. The nuclear model of the atom was constructed from which fundamental experiment?
    a) alpha particle scattering by thin metal foils
    b) cathode ray behavior in electrical fields
    c) atomic spectra from gas discharge tubes
    d) electrolysis of water

    Answer: a Key 1: C Section: 4

27. Based upon the experiments of his co-workers, Rutherford proposed that
    a) atoms are mostly empty space
    b) most of the mass of atoms is located in a dense, small volume nucleus
    c) the nucleus is positively charged
    d) all of the above

    Answer: d Key 1: C Section: 4

28. Relative to the mass of the nucleus of an atom, the **mass of the electrons** is
    a) always much smaller
    b) always much larger
    c) about the same
    d) dependent upon the element

    Answer: a Key 1: A Section: 4

ESSAY

29. Explain the significance of the relatively few alpha particles that were deflected in Rutherford's experiments with thin metal films.

    Answer: Key 1: C Section: 4

30. Contrast the three subatomic particles with respect to mass and charge.

    Answer: Key 1: C Section: 4

MULTIPLE CHOICE

31. Who first proposed the nuclear nature of the atom?
    a) Rutherford
    b) Dalton
    c) Thomson
    d) Millikan

    Answer: a Key 1: C Section: 4

32. The proton has
    a) the same mass and charge as the electron
    b) a smaller mass and same charge as the electron
    c) a smaller mass and opposite charge as the electron
    d) a larger mass and opposite charge as the electron

    Answer: d Key 1: C Section: 5

33. The neutron has
   a) the same approximate mass and charge as an electron
   b) the same approximate mass and charge as a proton
   c) the same approximate mass as a proton, but no charge
   d) the same approximate mass as an electron, but no charge

   Answer: c Key 1: A Section: 5

34. The experiment that confirmed the existence of neutrons was performed
   a) before the discovery of the proton
   b) at about the same time as the discovery of the proton
   c) after the discovery of the proton
   d) has not been made as of 1991

   Answer: c Key 1: A Section: 5

35. The number of protons in an atom is called the
   a) atomic mass
   b) atomic number
   c) atomic weight
   d) mass number

   Answer: b Key 1: C Section: 5

36. Which is a correct description of the **organization** of subatomic particles in atoms?
   a) Protons and electrons are tightly packed into a small nucleus. Neutrons occupy the space outside the nucleus.
   b) Protons and neutrons are tightly packed into a small nucleus. Electrons occupy the space outside the nucleus.
   c) Neutrons and electrons are tightly packed into a small nucleus. Protons occupy the space outside of the nucleus.
   d) Electrons are tightly packed into a small nucleus. Protons and neutrons occupy the space outside of the nucleus.

   Answer: b Key 1: D Section: 5

37. Which is a valid definition of **atomic number**? Atomic number is
   a) the number of protons in an atom
   b) equal to the positive charge of an atom's nucleus
   c) equal to the number of electrons in a neutral atom
   d) all of the above are valid definitions

   Answer: d Key 1: A Section: 5

38. Isotopes are atoms of the same element with
    a) different numbers of neutrons
    b) different numbers of electrons
    c) different numbers of protons
    d) different atomic numbers

    Answer: a Key 1: A Section: 5

39. With the discovery of isotopes, which postulates of Dalton's original atomic theory must be modified?
    a) Matter is made up of atoms.
    b) Atoms combine with other atoms in whole number ratios to form compounds.
    c) Atoms of the same element are the same.
    d) In chemical reactions, the arrangement of atoms is changed.

    Answer: c Key 1: D Section: 5

ESSAY

40. How do the three isotopes of hydrogen differ?

    Answer: Key 1: A Section: 5

MULTIPLE CHOICE

41. The number of protons in a Mg atom is
    a) 12
    b) 13
    c) 24
    d) 25

    Answer: a Key 1: C Section: 5

42. How many protons are there in a calcium atom?
    a) 6
    b) 20
    c) 40
    d) 55

    Answer: b Key 1: A Section: 5

43. How many protons are there in a silver atom?
    a) 16
    b) 38
    c) 47
    d) 79

    Answer: c Key 1: A Section: 5

44. How many protons are there in a gold atom?
    a) 16
    b) 38
    c) 47
    d) 79

    Answer: d Key 1: A Section: 5

45. Which statement best summarizes the general nature of investigations during the **1900's** related to the acquisition and development of knowledge concerning the atomic structure of matter?
    a) Qualitative observations, although often influenced by ideas related to magic and mysticism, provide glimpses of the structure of matter.
    b) Quantitative measurements, particularly those related to mass, lead to the formulation of fundamental laws leading to an atomic theory of matter.
    c) The development and use of electrical probes to study matter lead to experimental evidence for the existence of subatomic particles in atoms.
    d) The use of new experimental and mathematical techniques provide information concerning the organization of subatomic particles in atoms.

    Answer: d Key 1: A Section: 5

46. The isotope of hydrogen that has two neutrons is called
    a) deuterium
    b) hydrogen
    c) dihydrogen
    d) tritium

    Answer: d Key 1: C Section: 5

47. If X can represent the chemical symbol of any element in the periodic table, then $^{238}{}_{92}X$ represents an isotope of
    a) Calcium
    b) Uranium
    c) Niobium
    d) Lead

    Answer: b Key 1: A Section: 5

48. The specific pattern of colors emitted by excited atoms is called a
    a) rainbow
    b) line spectrum
    c) continuous spectrum
    d) cathode ray

    Answer: b Key 1: C Section: 6

49. A line spectrum is to an element as a(n) ____________________ is to a person.
    a) brain
    b) eye
    c) fingerprint
    d) ear

    Answer: c Key 1: D Section: 6

50. Which **IS NOT** characteristic of the line spectrum of an element?
    a) continuous
    b) discrete
    c) unique
    d) energy profile

    Answer: a Key 1: A Section: 6

51. The line spectra of atoms provides experimental evidence for
    a) the organization of particles in the nucleus of atoms
    b) the number of protons
    c) the arrangement of electrons
    d) all of the above

    Answer: c Key 1: A Section: 6

52. In attempting to explain the line spectrum of hydrogen, Bohr suggested that the energy of electrons in atoms is
    a) zero
    b) infinite
    c) continuous
    d) quantized

    Answer: d Key 1: C Section: 6

53. The lines in an atomic line emission spectrum are due to
    a) nuclear transitions in atoms
    b) movement of electrons from lower energy states to higher energy states in atoms
    c) movement of electrons from higher energy states to lower energy states in atoms
    d) the presence of isotopes

    Answer: c Key 1: C Section: 6

54. As the energy level of an electron increases, the electron's distance from the nucleus, on average,
    a) increases
    b) decreases
    c) remains the same
    d) can not be predicted

    Answer: a Key 1: A Section: 6

55. The number of electrons in a neutral atom is equal to the
    a) atomic mass
    b) atomic number
    c) atomic weight
    d) line spectrum

    Answer: b Key 1: C Section: 6

56. When an electron in an excited atom "falls down" to a lower energy level, the excited atom emits a characteristic
    a) electron
    b) neutron
    c) photon
    d) proton

    Answer: c Key 1: C Section: 6

57. The **maximum** number of electrons that may reside in the n=3 energy level is
    a) 2
    b) 3
    c) 8
    d) 18

    Answer: d Key 1: D Section: 6

58. The **maximum** number of electrons that may reside in the n=2 energy level is
    a) 2
    b) 3
    c) 8
    d) 18

    Answer: c Key 1: D Section: 6

59. How many electrons are there in a potassium atom?
    a) 15
    b) 19
    c) 39
    d) 84

    Answer: b Key 1: A Section: 6

60. How many electrons are there in a phosphorus atom?
    a) 15
    b) 19
    c) 39
    d) 84

    Answer: a Key 1: A Section: 6

61. How many electrons are there in a sulfur atom?
    a) 16
    b) 38
    c) 47
    d) 79

    Answer: a Key 1: A Section: 6

62. In the quantum mechanical view of the atom, electrons are confined to charge clouds called
    a) orbits
    b) orbitals
    c) energy levels
    d) ions

    Answer: b Key 1: A Section: 6

ESSAY

63. Define electrolysis.

    Answer: Key 1: C Section: 6

MULTIPLE CHOICE

64. Which is a result of the mathematically based quantum view of electrons in atoms?
    a) The position of every electron in an atom is precisely known.
    b) All electrons have the same position in atoms.
    c) The most probable position of each electron can be predicted.
    d) The position of electrons in atoms is not important.

    Answer: c Key 1: D Section: 6

65. The model for the atom which has electrons in fixed orbits was developed by
    a) Rutherford
    b) Schrödinger
    c) Bohr
    d) Einstein

    Answer: c Key 1: A Section: 6

66. The designations s, p, d, f designate
    a) different electron energy levels
    b) different electron orbitals within an energy level
    c) different types of electrons
    d) valence electrons

    Answer: b Key 1: C Section: 7

67. Which is an **IMPOSSIBLE** electron configuration?
    a) $1s^2\ 2s^2$
    b) $1s^2\ 2s^2\ 2p^4$
    c) $1s^3\ 2s^2\ 2p^4$
    d) $1s^2\ 2s^2\ 2p^4\ 3s^1$

    Answer: c Key 1: C Section: 7

68. The ground state electron configuration for sodium is
    a) $1s^2\ 2s^2\ 2p^6\ 3s^2\ 3p^4$
    b) $1s^2\ 2s^2\ 2p^6\ 3s^1$
    c) $1s^2\ 2s^2\ 2p^8$
    d) $1s^2\ 2s^2\ 2p^6\ 3s^2\ 3p^6\ 4s^1$

    Answer: b Key 1: A Section: 7

69. The element with the ground state electron configuration of $1s^2\ 2s^2\ 2p^6\ 3s^2$ is
    a) Mg
    b) Ca
    c) Mn
    d) Ne

    Answer: a Key 1: A Section: 7

70. The element with the ground state electron configuration of $1s^2\ 2s^2\ 2p^6\ 3s^2\ 3p^5$ is
    a) F
    b) Cl
    c) Ar
    d) Br

    Answer: b Key 1: A Section: 7

ESSAY

71. Write the electron configuration showing the filling of sub-levels for potassium.

    Answer: Key 1: A Section: 7

72. Write the electron configuration showing the filling of sub-levels for Mg.

    Answer: Key 1: A Section: 7

73. Write the electron configuration showing the filling of sub-levels for bromine.

    Answer: Key 1: A Section: 7

74. Write the electron configuration showing the filling of sub-levels for carbon.

    Answer: Key 1: A Section: 7

MULTIPLE CHOICE

75. What is the maximum number of electrons that can occupy a single p orbital?
    a) 1
    b) 2
    c) 6
    d) 10

    Answer: b Key 1: A Section: 7

76. What is the maximum number of electrons that can occupy the 2p sublevel?
    a) 2
    b) 8
    c) 6
    d) 10

    Answer: c Key 1: C Section: 7

77. An f sublevel can hold a maximum of
    a) 2 electrons.
    b) 6 electrons.
    c) 10 electrons.
    d) 14 electrons.

    Answer: d Key 1: C Section: 7

78. A vertical column in the modern periodic table is called a
    a) period
    b) group
    c) branch
    d) valence

    Answer: b Key 1: C Section: 7

79. An element with electronic structure $1s^2\ 2s^2\ 2p^4$ is in which group of the periodic table?
a) II-A
b) IV-A
c) VI-A
d) VIII-A

Answer: c Key 1: A Section: 7

80. A horizontal row in the modern periodic table is called a
a) period
b) group
c) branch
d) valence

Answer: a Key 1: D Section: 8

81. Elements in the **same group** have
a) the same atomic number
b) the same number of neutrons
c) the same number of electrons
d) the same number of valence electrons

Answer: d Key 1: D Section: 8

82. Elements in the **same period** have
a) the same atomic number
b) the same number of neutrons
c) the same number of valence electrons
d) none of the above

Answer: d Key 1: C Section: 8

83. Which element is a **nonmetal**?
a) calcium
b) iron
c) iodine
d) mercury

Answer: c Key 1: C Section: 8

84. Which element is a **metal**?
a) Ca
b) Br
c) I
d) Si

Answer: a Key 1: C Section: 8

85. Which element is in the same group as carbon?
    a) B
    b) Ge
    c) Al
    d) P

    Answer: b Key 1: C Section: 8

86. Which element is in the same period as carbon?
    a) B
    b) Ge
    c) Al
    d) P

    Answer: a Key 1: A Section: 8

87. Which element is a noble gas?
    a) B
    b) Ge
    c) Ar
    d) K

    Answer: c Key 1: A Section: 8

88. Which element is an alkaline earth?
    a) Ca
    b) Cl
    c) Ar
    d) K

    Answer: a Key 1: A Section: 8

89. Which element is a halogen?
    a) Mg
    b) Hg
    c) Xe
    d) Br

    Answer: d Key 1: A Section: 8

90. Which element is a transition metal?
    a) Mg
    b) Hg
    c) Xe
    d) Br

    Answer: b Key 1: A Section: 8

91. Which element is a transition metal?
    a) Li
    b) Ca
    c) Fe
    d) Br

    Answer: c Key 1: A Section: 8

92. In which group do all atoms have seven valence electrons in the ground state?
    a) alkali metals
    b) alkaline earths
    c) halogens
    d) noble gases

    Answer: c Key 1: A Section: 8

93. In which group do all atoms have one valence electron in the ground state?
    a) alkali metals
    b) alkaline earths
    c) halogens
    d) noble gases

    Answer: a Key 1: A Section: 8

94. In which group do all atoms have two valence electrons in the ground state?
    a) alkali metals
    b) alkaline earths
    c) halogens
    d) noble gases

    Answer: b Key 1: A Section: 8

95. In which group do all atoms have eight valence electrons in the ground state?
    a) alkali metals
    b) alkaline earths
    c) halogens
    d) noble gases

    Answer: d Key 1: A Section: 8

96. Which element has the same number of valence electrons as phosphorus?
    a) Li
    b) As
    c) Al
    d) K

    Answer: b Key 1: A Section: 8

97. Which element has the same number of valence electrons as boron?
    a) Li
    b) As
    c) Al
    d) P

    Answer: c Key 1: A Section: 8

98. Which element has the same number of valence electrons as potassium?
    a) Li
    b) As
    c) Al
    d) P

    Answer: a Key 1: A Section: 8

99. Which element is classified as a metalloid?
    a) Li
    b) Si
    c) Cl
    d) Fe

    Answer: b Key 1: A Section: 8

100. A metalloid
    a) is the same as a metal
    b) is located on the left side of the periodic table
    c) has properties intermediate between metals and nonmetals
    d) is all of the above

    Answer: c Key 1: A Section: 8

101. Elements in the same group generally have
    a) different properties
    b) similar properties
    c) similar number of neutrons
    d) similar chemical symbols

    Answer: b Key 1: D Section: 8

102. Elements in the same period generally have
    a) different properties
    b) similar properties
    c) similar number of neutrons
    d) similar chemical symbols

    Answer: a Key 1: C Section: 8

103. The noble gases are a unique group of elements. They are recognized as unique due to the fact that they are
a) all gases at room temperature
b) extremely stable and unreactive
c) the most reactive member of their period
d) named after Nobel prize winners

Answer: b Key 1: C Section: 8

104. Carbon has ________ valence electrons.
a) one
b) two
c) three
d) four

Answer: d Key 1: D Section: 8

105. All noble gases have ________ valence electrons.
a) three
b) five
c) seven
d) eight

Answer: d Key 1: A Section: 8

106. Bromine has ________ valence electrons.
a) three
b) five
c) seven
d) eight

Answer: c Key 1: A Section: 8

FILL-IN-THE-BLANK

107. Calcium has ________ valence electron(s).

Answer: two Key 1: A Section: 8

108. Potassium has ________ valence electron(s).

Answer: one Key 1: A Section: 8

MULTIPLE CHOICE

109. The electrons in the outermost energy level of an atom are called
    a) group electrons
    b) core electrons
    c) valence electrons
    d) orbital electrons

    Answer: c Key 1: A Section: 8

110. Which of the halogens is a liquid at room temperature?
    a) Fluorine
    b) Chlorine
    c) Bromine
    d) Iodine

    Answer: c Key 1: D Section: 8

111. Which of the halogens is a solid at room temperature?
    a) Fluorine
    b) Chlorine
    c) Bromine
    d) Iodine

    Answer: d Key 1: D Section: 8

TRUE/FALSE

112. In the United States the letter A identifies the main group elements and the letter B indicates the transition metal elements of the periodic table.

    Answer: True Key 1: A Section: 8

113. Beryllium has properties that are typical of the alkaline earth metals family.

    Answer: False Key 1: A Section: 8

MULTIPLE CHOICE

114. How does the periodic table substantiate atomic theory?
    a) Both are theoretical and cannot support each other.
    b) Groups in the periodic table have similar properties based on similar features of atomic structure, namely, the same number of valence electrons per atom.
    c) All elements in a given period of the periodic table have the same number of valence electrons.
    d) Mendeleev declared consistency between the periodic table and atomic theory.

    Answer: b Key 1: C Section: 8

115. An element in the fourth period of the periodic table.
    a) C
    b) Cu
    c) Cs
    d) Cl

    Answer: b Key 1: A Section: 8

116. Which element is a very good conductor of electricity?
    a) arsenic
    b) boron
    c) sulfur
    d) silver

    Answer: d Key 1: A Section: 8

Chapter 4: Nuclear Chemistry

MULTIPLE CHOICE

1. If it were possible to obtain a cubic centimeter of pure atomic nuclei, it's mass would be approximately
   a) 1 g
   b) 19 g
   c) 1.2 x 1011 kg
   d) 1 kg

   Answer: c Key 1: C Key 2: I

2. The diameter of an atom is 100,000 times as great as the diameter of its nucleus. If an atom could be expanded to the size of a classroom the nucleus would be about the size of a
   a) BB
   b) marble
   c) basketball
   d) period at the end of a sentence

   Answer: d Key 1: C Key 2: I

3. Atoms that have the **same** atomic number but **different** numbers of neutrons are
   a) radioactive
   b) isotopes
   c) impossible
   d) ions

   Answer: b Key 1: D Section: 1

4. Nuclear physicists have discovered over 100 different particles that compose the nucleus of an atom. From a **chemistry perspective**, the nucleus is best described as being composed of
   a) protons and neutrons packed tightly into a very small volume
   b) protons and electrons packed tightly into a very small volume
   c) neutrons and electrons packed tightly into a very small volume
   d) protons, neutrons and electrons packed tightly into a very small volume

   Answer: a Key 1: C Section: 1

5. The difference in mass between protons and neutrons is generally regarded as
   a) significant
   b) insignificant
   c) unknown
   d) variable

   Answer: b Key 1: C Section: 1

6. Essentially all of the mass of an atom is due to the
   a) protons
   b) neutrons
   c) nucleons
   d) electrons

   Answer: c Key 1: C Section: 1

7. The mass of the electrons in atoms is generally regarded as
   a) significant
   b) insignificant
   c) comparable to the mass of the nucleus
   d) unknown

   Answer: b Key 1: C Section: 1

8. The mass of a nucleon is
   a) 1 gram
   b) 1 amu
   c) equivalent to the mass of the electron
   d) 0

   Answer: b Key 1: C Section: 1

9. Which statement comparing chemical and nuclear properties of isotopes is correct?
   a) Isotopes have similar chemical and nuclear properties.
   b) Isotopes have different chemical and nuclear properties.
   c) Isotopes have different chemical properties, but generally the same nuclear properties.
   d) Isotopes generally have the same chemical properties, but often different nuclear properties.

   Answer: d Key 1: C Section: 1

10. The charge on the nucleus of a sodium atom is
   a) 0
   b) 1+
   c) 11+
   d) 23+

   Answer: c Key 1: A Section: 1

11. The element tin (Sn) occurs naturally as ten isotopes. Each of these isotopes <u>has</u>
   a) 50 protons
   b) 50 electrons
   c) a different number of neutrons
   d) all of the above

   Answer: d Key 1: A Section: 1

12. The sum of protons and neutrons in an atom is called the
    a) atomic number
    b) atomic mass
    c) nuclear mass
    d) nucleon number

    Answer: d Key 1: D Section: 1

SHORT ANSWER

13. How many neutrons are in this isotope of chlorine?
    $^{37}_{17}Cl$

    Answer: 20 Key 1: A Section: 1

MULTIPLE CHOICE

14. How many neutrons are in this isotope of tin?
    $^{106}_{50}Sn$
    a) 50
    b) 56
    c) 106
    d) 156

    Answer: b Key 1: A Section: 1

SHORT ANSWER

15. How many protons are in this isotope of uranium?
    $^{235}_{92}U$

    Answer: 92 Key 1: A Section: 1

MULTIPLE CHOICE

16. How many nucleons are in this isotope of calcium?
    $^{36}_{20}Ca$
    a) 56
    b) 36
    c) 20
    d) 16

    Answer: b Key 1: A Section: 1

17. How many nucleons are in this isotope of tin?
$^{106}_{50}Sn$
a) 50
b) 56
c) 106
d) 156

Answer: c Key 1: A Section: 1

18. The isotope of carbon commonly referred to as "carbon-14" is
a) $^{14}_{6}C$
b) $^{12}_{6}C$
c) $^{13}_{6}C$
d) $^{28}_{14}Si$

Answer: a Key 1: A Section: 1

19. Which contains 14 neutrons?
a) $^{14}_{6}C$
b) $^{14}_{7}N$
c) $^{9}_{5}B$
d) $^{28}_{14}Si$

Answer: d Key 1: A Section: 1

20. Which contains 7 neutrons?
a) $^{14}_{6}C$
b) $^{14}_{7}N$
c) $^{9}_{5}B$
d) $^{28}_{14}Si$

Answer: b Key 1: A Section: 1

21. How many neutrons are there in the potassium-40 isotope?
   a) 59
   b) 40
   c) 21
   d) 19

   Answer: c Key 1: A Section: 1

22. How many nucleons are there in the sulfur-32 isotope?
   a) 16
   b) 32
   c) 48
   d) none of the above

   Answer: b Key 1: A Section: 1

23. The isotope $^{31}_{15}P$ is also called
   a) phosphorus-15
   b) phosphorus-16
   c) phosphorus-31
   d) phosphorus-46

   Answer: c Key 1: A Section: 1

24. Which is an isotope of uranium?
   a) $^{233}_{92}U$
   b) $^{235}_{93}Np$
   c) $^{235}_{91}Pa$
   d) all of these

   Answer: a Key 1: A Section: 1

25. The following nuclear reaction is an example of

   $$^{26}_{88}Ra \text{ -----> } ^{4}_{2}He + ^{222}_{86}Rn$$

   a) alpha decay
   b) beta decay
   c) gamma decay
   d) an impossible reaction

   Answer: a Key 1: A Section: 1

26. An alpha particle is the same as a
    a) helium-3 nucleus
    b) helium-4 nucleus
    c) helium-5 nucleus
    d) proton

    Answer: b Key 1: C Section: 1

27. Thorium-234 undergoes beta decay:

    $^{234}_{90}Th$ ---> $^{0}_{1-}e$ + Q. What is Q?
    a) $^{234}_{91}Pa$
    b) $^{234}_{89}Ac$
    c) $^{233}_{90}Th$
    d) $^{233}_{91}Th$

    Answer: a Key 1: A Section: 1

28. Uranium-238 decays by emission of an alpha particle. The product of this decay is
    a) $^{234}_{92}U$
    b) $^{234}_{91}Pa$
    c) $^{234}_{90}Th$
    d) $^{234}_{88}Ra$

    Answer: c Key 1: A Section: 1

29. $^{222}_{86}Rn$ decays by emission of an alpha particle.
    The product of this decay is
    a) $^{226}_{88}Ra$
    b) $^{218}_{84}Po$
    c) $^{218}_{88}Ra$
    d) $^{220}_{86}Rn$

    Answer: b Key 1: A Section: 1

30. $^{214}_{83}Bi$ decays by beta emission. The product is
    a) $^{214}_{84}Bi$
    b) $^{214}_{84}Po$
    c) $^{210}_{82}Pb$
    d) $^{212}_{79}Au$

    Answer: b Key 1: A Section: 1

31. The process of beta emission can be envisioned as the
    a) conversion of a proton to a neutron and electron. The electron is emitted.
    b) conversion of a neutron to a proton and electron. The electron is emitted.
    c) conversion of a neutron to a proton and electron. The proton is emitted.
    d) conversion of a proton to a neutron and electron. The proton is emitted.

    Answer: b Key 1: C Section: 1

32. Which of the following particles has a mass of 4 amu and a charge of 2+?
    a) alpha particle
    b) electron
    c) neutron
    d) proton

    Answer: a Key 1: A Section: 1

33. The atomic number increases by 1 during what type of radioactive decay?
    a) alpha
    b) beta
    c) gamma
    d) none of these

    Answer: b Key 1: C Section: 1

34. With the discovery of nuclear reactions, and particularly transmutation, which one of the following postulates of Dalton's atomic theory must be modified?
a) Matter is composed of atoms
b) Atoms of the same element are the same; atoms of different elements are different
c) Atoms combine with other atoms in fixed, whole number ratios
d) Atoms may not be changed into other atoms

Answer: d Key 1: A Section: 1

35. After three half-lifes, what fraction of the original radioactive isotope remains in a sample?
a) none
b) 1/16
c) 1/8
d) 1/4

Answer: c Key 1: A Section: 2

36. Nitrogen-13 has a half-life of 10 minutes. How much of a 16 mg sample would remain after 40 minutes?
a) 0.5 mg
b) 1 mg
c) 2 mg
d) 4 mg

Answer: b Key 1: A Section: 2

37. Sodium-24 has a half-life of 15 hours. How much of a 20 mg sample would remain after two half-lifes?
a) 0 mg
b) 2 mg
c) 5 mg
d) 10 mg

Answer: c Key 1: A Section: 2

38. The amount of a radioactive isotope that remains after two half-lives have passed is
a) 98%
b) 75%
c) 50%
d) 25%

Answer: d Key 1: A Section: 2

39. Exposure to radioactive material is considered safe after 10 half-lives because
    a) less than a tenth of 1% of the material remains
    b) less than 12.5% of the material remains
    c) ten is an even number
    d) all of the material will have decayed at that time

    Answer: a Key 1: A Section: 2

40. Plants incorporate carbon as long they live. Once a plant dies, it takes how many years for 99.9% of the carbon-14 to decay (half-life of C-14 is 5730 years)?
    a) 573 yrs
    b) 2865 yrs
    c) 5730 yrs
    d) 57300 yrs

    Answer: d Key 1: A Section: 3

41. Carbon-14 dating of ancient objects is particularly effective because c-14
    a) has the shortest half-life
    b) is continuously produced in the upper atmosphere and its ratio to c-12 in living systems and the environment is constant
    c) is a stable isotope and is therefore particularly easy to work with
    d) decays by a simple fission reaction

    Answer: b Key 1: C Section: 3

ESSAY

42. What is transmutation?

    Answer: Key 1: C Section: 4

MULTIPLE CHOICE

43. The bombardment of nitrogen-14 with alpha particles produces oxygen-17 and a proton. This process is called
    a) alpha emission
    b) transmutation
    c) isotopic enrichment
    d) fission

    Answer: b Key 1: C Section: 4

44. In 1932, James Chadwick bombarded beryllium-9 with alpha particles. One product was a neutron. This led to the direct experimental verification of the existence of neutrons. The other product of Chadwick's nuclear reaction was
a) nitrogen-14
b) carbon-12
c) boron-12
d) helium-4

Answer: b Key 1: A Section: 4

45. When potassium-39 is bombarded by neutrons, chlorine-36 is produced. What other particle is emitted?
a) alpha particle
b) electron
c) neutron
d) proton

Answer: a Key 1: A Section: 4

46. Phosphorus-30 decays by positron emission. The product is
a) silicon-30
b) phosphorus-29
c) sulfur-30
d) sulfur-29

Answer: a Key 1: A Section: 4

47. Which one of the following is most penetrating?
a) alpha particle
b) beta particle
c) gamma ray
d) visible light

Answer: c Key 1: C Section: 8

48. Which type of radioactive emission is very similar to x-rays?
a) transmutation
b) alpha particle
c) beta particle
d) gamma ray

Answer: d Key 1: C Section: 8

ESSAY

49. Rank the penetrating power of nuclear radiation from the least to most penetrating.

Answer: Key 1: C Section: 8

MULTIPLE CHOICE

50. Radioactive alpha emitters pose the greatest potential health risk when they are
    a) unshielded
    b) on the skin
    c) injested
    d) all of the above

    Answer: c Key 1: C Section: 8

51. Alpha particles can be stopped by a
    a) sheet of paper
    b) block of wood
    c) thin sheet of aluminum
    d) all of these

    Answer: d Key 1: A Section: 8

52. Gamma Rays can be stopped by
    a) a sheet of paper
    b) a thin aluminum sheet
    c) a block of wood
    d) several centimeters of lead

    Answer: d Key 1: A Section: 8

ESSAY

53. Discuss why radioisotopes are used as tracers in medical diagnostics and research.

    Answer: Key 1: A Section: 6

MULTIPLE CHOICE

54. The use of radioisotopes as tracers in medical and environmental research takes advantage of the fact that isotopes
    a) generally behave identically in chemical and physical processes
    b) generally behave differently in chemical and physical processes
    c) have different masses
    d) none of the above

    Answer: a Key 1: C Section: 6

55. The currently accepted mechanism of photosynthesis has been worked out by using which of the following isotopes?
a) phosphorus-32
b) carbon-11
c) carbon-14
d) cobalt-57

Answer: c Key 1: A Section: 6

56. Which one of the following radioactive isotopes is useful in the investigation of thyroid problems?
a) Uranium-235
b) Barium-120
c) Iodine-131
d) Cesium-145

Answer: c Key 1: A Section: 7

57. Positron emission tomography (PET) is a
a) therapy for cancer using positrons
b) diagnostic technique for monitoring dynamic processes in the body, such as brain activity
c) device for containing a nuclear fusion reaction
d) mechanism for transmutation of elements

Answer: b Key 1: C Section: 7

58. Technetium-99^m is a radioisotope used in a variety of diagnostic tests. Technetium-99^m has a short half life (6 hr). The advantage of a short half-life for diagnostic purposes is
a) the radioactivity is easier to monitor
b) the radioactivity does not linger in the body
c) the radioactivity lasts for a long time
d) the chemical reactions induced by the technitium are more rapid

Answer: b Key 1: A Section: 7

ESSAY

59. Comment on three peacetime uses of nuclear energy.

Answer: Key 1: A Section: 7

MULTIPLE CHOICE

60. The medical application of cobalt-60 is
    a) brain scans
    b) Blood volume determination
    c) determination of bone density
    d) radiation cancer therapy

    Answer: d Key 1: A Section: 7

TRUE/FALSE

61. Nuclear science has saved many more lives than have been destroyed by nuclear bombs.

    Answer: True Key 1: A Section: 7

MULTIPLE CHOICE

62. Gadolinium-153 is the most widely used radioisotope in medicine. It is used for the detection of
    a) heart disease
    b) tumors
    c) osteoporosis
    d) obstructions in blood flow

    Answer: c Key 1: A Section: 7

63. The radioisotope used to determine the size, shape and activity of the thyroid gland is
    a) gadolinium-153
    b) iron-59
    c) plutonium-238
    d) iodine-131

    Answer: d Key 1: A Section: 7

64. The radioactive decay of ^{99m}Tc to ^{99}Tc MUST occur with the emission of
    a) an alpha-particle alone
    b) two beta-particles
    c) a gamma-ray alone
    d) the combination of a beta-particle and a gamma-ray

    Answer: c Key 1: A Section: 7

65. In positron emission tomography (PET) a positron collides with an electron and the two particles disappear in a burst of
a) an alpha-particle and a gamma-ray
b) two beta-particles
c) a neutron and an alpha-particle
d) two gamma-rays

Answer: d Key 1: A Section: 7

66. In carbon-14 dating
a) the radioactivity of carbon is artificially induced
b) the radioactivity of carbon occurs naturally
c) radioactive carbon is added to the sample to be dated
d) none of the above

Answer: b Key 1: A Section: 3

67. The isotope of carbon that is used for radioisotopic dating of previously living objects is
a) carbon-11
b) carbon-12
c) carbon-13
d) carbon-14

Answer: d Key 1: C Section: 3

68. A piece of fossilized wood has a carbon-14 radioactivity that is 1/4 that of new wood. The half-life of carbon-14 is 5730 years. How old is the cloth?
a) 1 x 5730 = 5730 years
b) 2 x 5730 = 11,460 years
c) 3 x 5730 = 17,190 years
d) 0.25 x 5730 = 1432 years

Answer: b Key 1: A Section: 3

69. A piece of cloth is dated using carbon-14. The cloth is determined to be 1400 years old. The half-life of C-14 is 5730 years. The C-14 radioactivity in the cloth will be ________________ than the radioactivity in a new cloth.
a) greater
b) the same
c) less
d) can not be predicted

Answer: c Key 1: A Section: 3

70. Tritium is the common name for
    a) hydrogen-0
    b) hydrogen-1
    c) hydrogen-2
    d) hydrogen-3

    Answer: d Key 1: C Section: 3

71. Deuterium is the common name for
    a) hydrogen-0
    b) hydrogen-1
    c) hydrogen-2
    d) hydrogen-3

    Answer: c Key 1: C Section: 3

72. Although Albert Einstein is considered one of the greatest scientists of all time, his work generally did not involve much of an aspect that is traditionally associated with science. That aspect is
    a) creativity
    b) mathematics
    c) theories
    d) experiments

    Answer: d Key 1: C Section: 9

73. In the famous relationship: $E = mc^2$, the symbol m represents
    a) mass
    b) molecules
    c) momentum
    d) metastable

    Answer: a Key 1: C Section: 9

74. Nuclear fission is a process by which the nucleus of an atom
    a) splits into two or more fragments spontaneously
    b) is induced to split into two or more fragments by some external source
    c) combines with another nucleus to produce a larger nucleus
    d) loses a proton with the release of a large amount of energy

    Answer: b Key 1: C Section: 10

SHORT ANSWER

75. In the fission of uranium-235, which particle causes and propagates the chain reaction?

    Answer: neutron Key 1: C Section: 10

MULTIPLE CHOICE

76. In the fission of uranium-235, which particle causes and propagates the chain reaction?
    a) alpha particle
    b) beta particle
    c) neutron
    d) electron

    Answer: c Key 1: C Section: 10

77. Critical mass is
    a) the minimum amount of fissionable material that will sustain a chain reaction
    b) the maximum amount of fissionable material that will sustain a chain reaction
    c) the amount of fissionable material that produces the most energy when split
    d) the largest amount of fissionable material that can be obtained from isotopic enrichment

    Answer: a Key 1: D Section: 10

78. The U.S. president who ordered the dropping of atomic bombs on the Japanese cities of Hiroshima and Nagasaki was
    a) Franklin Roosevelt
    b) Harry Truman
    c) Dwight Eisenhower
    d) John Kennedy

    Answer: b Key 1: D Section: 10

ESSAY

79. What is isotopic enrichment and why was it a crucial step in the manufacture of the first atomic bomb?

    Answer: Key 1: A Section: 10

MULTIPLE CHOICE

80. Naturally occurring uranium contains approximately what percentage of uranium-235, the isotope that undergoes fission?
    a) 1%
    b) 10%
    c) 50%
    d) 100%

    Answer: a Key 1: D Section: 10

81. The nuclear synthesis of plutonium-239 was an important part of the effort to build an atomic bomb during WWII because
a) plutonium-239 is required to cause uranium-235 to fission
b) plutonium-239 is fissionable
c) plutonium-239 has a longer half-life than uranium-235
d) of all of these reasons

Answer: b Key 1: C Section: 10

82. The often tedious process by which a naturally occurring mixture of isotopes is separated and concentrated is called
a) isotopic transmutation
b) isotopic ionization
c) isotopic synthesis
d) isotopic enrichment

Answer: d Key 1: D Section: 10

83. Element 106 is named in honor of what scientist?
a) Albert Einstein
b) Niels Bohr
c) Enrico Fermi
d) Glenn Seaborg

Answer: d Key 1: D Section: 10

84. Stagg Field, at the University of Chicago, is where
a) nuclear fission was discovered
b) radioactivity was discovered
c) nuclear fusion was discovered
d) the first nuclear pile was built

Answer: d Key 1: C Section: 10

85. Strontium-90 from nuclear fallout is a potential major long term human health threat because
a) it is chemically similar to calcium and it has a relatively long half-life
b) it is chemically similar to calcium and it has a relatively short half-life
c) it is chemically similar to sodium and has a relatively long half-life
d) it is chemically similar to sodium and has a relatively short half-life

Answer: a Key 1: A Section: 11

86. Iodine-131 from nuclear fallout is a potential major short term human health threat because
    a) it is concentrated in the thyroid and has a relatively long half-life
    b) it is concentrated in the thyroid and has a relatively short half-life
    c) it is chemically similar to calcium and has a relatively long half-life
    d) it is chemically similar to calcium and has a relatively short half-life

    Answer: a Key 1: A Section: 11

87. Cesium-137 and Strontium-90 are both produced in nuclear fallout. Cesium-137 has a half-life of 30 years. Strontium-90 has a half-life of 28 years. Cesium-137 is considered less of a health threat because
    a) it is chemically similar to potassium and is more readily removed from the body than strontium
    b) it is chemically similar to potassium and builds up in the body to a greater extent than strontium
    c) cesium-137 has a longer half-life
    d) cesium-137 is not radioactive

    Answer: a Key 1: A Section: 11

88. Which scientist won a Nobel prize for chemistry in recognition of his work involving the structure of proteins, and the Nobel prize for peace for his efforts in controlling nuclear weapons?
    a) Albert Einstein
    b) Linus Pauling
    c) Enrico Fermi
    d) Glenn Seaborg

    Answer: b Key 1: C Section: 11

89. Which of the following isotopes produced in fission bomb explosions is of greatest health risk to humans?
    a) xenon-143
    b) strontium-90
    c) krypton-94
    d) barium-139

    Answer: b Key 1: A Section: 11

ESSAY

90. What is "nuclear winter"?

    Answer: Key 1: D Section: 12

MULTIPLE CHOICE

91. The hypothesis that debris and smoke from a large nuclear attack would block as much as 90% of sunlight and lead to a devastating impact on world climate is called
    a) nuclear fallout
    b) nuclear holocaust
    c) nuclear winter
    d) nuclear summer

    Answer: c Key 1: D Section: 12

92. The major part of the average exposure of humans to radiation comes from
    a) nuclear power plants
    b) diagnostic x-rays
    c) other humanmade sources
    d) naturally occurring sources

    Answer: d Key 1: C Section: 8

93. Cosmic rays are
    a) high energy radiation produced by the sun
    b) high energy radiation produced in the ozone layer
    c) high energy radiation produced by the earth's core
    d) none of these

    Answer: a Key 1: D Section: 8

94. Ionizing radiation
    a) is radiation of sufficient energy to produce ions
    b) is radiation of sufficient energy to remove electrons from atoms
    c) is radiation of sufficient energy to produce charged atoms
    d) is all of the above

    Answer: d Key 1: D Section: 8

95. The mass of a helium nucleus is slightly less than the sum of its parts (2 protons & 2 neutrons) because
    a) some of the mass is converted to binding energy
    b) some of the mass is given to electrons
    c) the mass of protons and neutrons are not precisely known
    d) nuclear scientists can't add

    Answer: a Key 1: C Section: 9

96. The commercial generation of power from a fusion reaction is not yet practical because of
    a) the danger of a nuclear explosion
    b) the disposal of radioactive by-products
    c) the high temperatures needed
    d) the high cost of the nuclear fuel

    Answer: c Key 1: C Section: 13

97. The original source of essentially all of the energy on the earth is
    a) plants
    b) oil
    c) coal
    d) the sun

    Answer: d Key 1: C Section: 14

98. The source of the energy produced by the sun is
    a) burning of fossil fuels
    b) fission of uranium-235
    c) fusion of primarily hydrogen
    d) unknown

    Answer: c Key 1: C Section: 14

ESSAY

99. Compare and contrast nuclear fission and nuclear fusion.

    Answer: Key 1: C Section: 14

MULTIPLE CHOICE

100. In nuclear fusion,
    a) large unstable nuclei are fused together, and then split with the release of binding energy
    b) large, relatively unstable, nuclei are split releasing binding energy
    c) small, relatively stable, nuclei are split releasing binding energy
    d) smaller, relatively stable, nuclei are forced together to create a larger nucleus with the release of binding energy

    Answer: d Key 1: C Section: 14

101. All of the elements beyond which atomic number are produced only by transmutation of other elements?
a) 55
b) 92
c) 100
d) 105

Answer: b Key 1: D Section: 14

102. The most serious technical problem in the commercial generation of electricity from nuclear power is
a) the design of the nuclear pile
b) the conversion of heat from the pile into steam
c) the design of the containment building
d) the disposal of radioactive wastes

Answer: d Key 1: C Section: 15

103. The factor that is NOT a detriment to the building of nuclear power plants is
a) the possibility of a "nuclear bomb-like" explosion
b) the scarcity of ^{235}U
c) the disposal of nuclear wastes
d) the high cost of the power produced

Answer: a Key 1: C Section: 15

Chapter 5: Chemical Bonds

MULTIPLE CHOICE

1. The element whose atoms have a unique ability to bond to each other and to other kinds of atoms is ________.
   a) sodium
   b) carbon
   c) sulfur
   d) nitrogen

   Answer: b Key 1: C Key 2: I

2. The nature of bonding forces in a piece of matter influences which observable property of the matter?
   a) chemical reactivity
   b) state of the matter at room temperature
   c) strength and rigidity
   d) all of the above

   Answer: d Key 1: C Section: 1

3. The noble gases are inert. This means they
   a) undergo very few chemical reactions
   b) exist as gases at room temperature
   c) undergo many chemical reactions
   d) lose and gain electrons easily

   Answer: a Key 1: C Section: 1

4. The inertness of the noble gases is due to
   a) the unique structure of their nuclei
   b) the special number of protons and neutrons
   c) the bonds they form with other elements
   d) the number and arrangement of their electrons

   Answer: d Key 1: C Section: 1

5. A sodium ion, Na^+, has the same electron configuration as a(n)
   a) sodium atom
   b) chlorine atom
   c) neon atom
   d) argon atom

   Answer: c Key 1: A Section: 1

6. A chloride ion, Cl^- has the same electron configuration as a
   a) sodium atom
   b) chlorine atom
   c) neon atom
   d) argon atom

   Answer: d Key 1: A Section: 1

7. The number of electrons in a chloride ion, Cl^-, is
   a) 16
   b) 17
   c) 18
   d) 35

   Answer: c Key 1: A Section: 1

8. The number of protons in a chloride ion, Cl^-, is
   a) 16
   b) 17
   c) 18
   d) 35

   Answer: b Key 1: A Section: 1

9. The number of electrons in a sodium ion, Na^+, is
   a) 10
   b) 11
   c) 12
   d) 23

   Answer: a Key 1: A Section: 1

10. The number of protons in a sodium ion, Na^+, is
    a) 10
    b) 11
    c) 12
    d) 23

    Answer: b Key 1: A Section: 1

FILL-IN-THE-BLANK

11. The number of protons in a cation must always be ____________ the number of electrons.

    Answer: greater than Key 1: A Section: 1

12. The number of protons in an anion must always be ____________ the number of electrons.

    Answer: less than Key 1: A Section: 1

MULTIPLE CHOICE

13. When magnesium reacts with chlorine, magnesium ions, Mg^{2+}, and chloride ions, Cl^-, are formed. In this reaction, magnesium atoms
    a) lose electrons
    b) gain electrons
    c) lose protons
    d) gain protons

    Answer: a Key 1: A Section: 1

14. When magnesium reacts with chlorine, magnesium ions, Mg^{2+}, and chloride ions, Cl^-, are formed. In this reaction, chlorine atoms
    a) lose electrons
    b) gain electrons
    c) lose protons
    d) gain protons

    Answer: b Key 1: A Section: 1

15. When atoms lose or gain electrons in chemical reactions they form
    a) new atoms
    b) noble gases
    c) nucleons
    d) ions

    Answer: d Key 1: C Section: 1

16. Which molecule is not likely to exist?
    a) H_2
    b) Cl_2
    c) CH_4
    d) Ne_2

    Answer: d Key 1: A Section: 1

17. Noble gases are unreactive because of their electronic structures. The kind of reasoning that states "if other elements could be made to achieve noble gas electronic structures they would be more stable" is called _____.
    a) logic
    b) inductive reasoning
    c) deductive reasoning
    d) critical thinking

    Answer: c Key 1: C Section: 1

18. Mg2+ has the same electronic structure as
    a) Ne
    b) Mg
    c) C
    d) Ar

    Answer: a Key 1: A Section: 1

19. The number of electrons in a sulfide ion, S^{2-}, is
    a) 16
    b) 14
    c) 18
    d) 32

    Answer: c Key 1: A Section: 1

20. Which of the following molecules is not likely to exist?
    a) N_2
    b) F_2
    c) CCl_4
    d) He_2

    Answer: d Key 1: A Section: 1

21. With respect to chemical bonding, which particles play the most active role?
    a) protons
    b) neutrons
    c) valence electrons
    d) core electrons

    Answer: c Key 1: A Section: 2

22. An electron-dot structure is a convenient method of representing
    a) valence electrons of an atom
    b) core electrons of an atom
    c) all electrons of the atom
    d) the complete electron configuration of the atom

    Answer: a Key 1: A Section: 2

23. From the periodic table, the number of valence electrons for most of the main group elements may be determined directly from the
    a) atomic number
    b) group number
    c) period number
    d) nucleon number

    Answer: b Key 1: A Section: 2

ESSAY

24. Write the electron dot symbol for potassium.

    Answer: Key 1: A Section: 2

25. Write the electron dot symbol for nitrogen.

    Answer: Key 1: A Section: 2

26. Write the electron dot symbol for carbon.

    Answer: Key 1: A Section: 2

MULTIPLE CHOICE

27. Which is the electron dot structure of magnesium?
    a) Mg
    b) Mg·
    c) ·Mg·
    d) ·Mg:

    Answer: c Key 1: A Section: 2

28. Which is the electron dot structure of sulfur?

    a) $\cdot\dot{\underset{\cdot}{S}}\cdot$

    b) $:\dot{\underset{\cdot}{S}}:$

    c) $:\underset{\cdot}{S}:$

    d) :S:

    Answer: b Key 1: A Section: 2

29. Which is the electron dot structure of oxygen?
    a) $\cdot\dot{\underset{\cdot}{O}}\cdot$

    b) $:\dot{\underset{\cdot}{O}}:$

    c) $:\underset{\cdot}{O}:$

    d) :O:

    Answer: b Key 1: A Section: 2

30. Which is the electron dot structure of nitrogen?
    a) :N· (with one dot above and one dot below N)
    b) :N: (with one dot above and one dot below N)
    c) :N:
    d) ·N:

    Answer: a Key 1: A Section: 2

31. Which is the electron dot structure of calcium?
    a) Ca
    b) Ca·
    c) ·Ca·
    d) ·Ca:

    Answer: c Key 1: A Section: 2

32. Where does an element X with the electron dot structure

    ·X· (with one dot above X)

    fit in the periodic table?

    a) Group IA
    b) Group IIA
    c) Group IIIA
    d) Group VA

    Answer: c Key 1: A Section: 2

33. Which of the noble gases **DOES NOT** have an octet of electrons in its outer shell?
    a) He
    b) Ne
    c) Ar
    d) Kr

    Answer: a Key 1: C Section: 2

34. In a Lewis formula the dots represent
    a) all the electrons in the atoms
    b) the valence electrons in all the atoms
    c) only the electrons that are being transferred or shared
    d) whatever number of electrons are needed to satisfy the octet rule

    Answer: b Key 1: C Section: 2

35. With respect to chemical bonding, which particles play the least active role?
a) nucleons
b) core electrons
c) valence electrons
d) all play equal roles

Answer: a Key 1: A Section: 2

36. How many dots will appear in the Lewis dot structure for an element from VIII-A of the periodic table?
a) one
b) five
c) eight
d) three

Answer: c Key 1: A Section: 2

37. Why do chemists use the Lewis symbols to represent chlorine and sodium rather than drawing the electron diagrams of each element before and after the reaction?
a) Lewis symbols are easier to use
b) Lewis symbols are more scientific
c) Lewis symbols are more accurate
d) Lewis symbols are more abstract

Answer: a Key 1: C Section: 3

38. When a freshly cut piece of sodium metal, Na, is dropped into a flask with chlorine gas a violent reaction takes place creating a compound. This compound
a) has properties that are more like Na than Cl
b) has properties that are totally unlike either Na or Cl
c) has properties that more like Cl than Na
d) has properties that are like both Cl and Na

Answer: b Key 1: A Section: 4

TRUE/FALSE

39. Ionic compounds generally form between metals and non-metals.

Answer: True Key 1: A Section: 5

MULTIPLE CHOICE

40. A lithium ion is
    a) Li^+
    b) Li^{2+}
    c) Li^-
    d) Li^{2-}

    Answer: a Key 1: A Section: 5

41. A fluoride ion is
    a) F^+
    b) F^{2+}
    c) F^-
    d) F^{2-}

    Answer: c Key 1: A Section: 5

42. An oxide ion is
    a) O^+
    b) O^{2+}
    c) O^-
    d) O^{2-}

    Answer: d Key 1: A Section: 5

43. A nitride ion is
    a) N^+
    b) N^{3+}
    c) N^{2-}
    d) N^{3-}

    Answer: d Key 1: A Section: 5

44. Potassium forms ions with a charge of
    a) 1^+
    b) 2^+
    c) 3^+
    d) 3^-

    Answer: a Key 1: A Section: 5

45. Oxygen forms monatomic ions with a charge of
    a) 2^+
    b) 3^+
    c) 1^-
    d) 2^-

    Answer: d Key 1: A Section: 5

46. Which atom is least likely to form an ion?
    a) chlorine
    b) sodium
    c) carbon
    d) oxygen

    Answer: c Key 1: A Section: 5

47. Which atom is least likely to form an ion?
    a) bromine, Br
    b) phosphorus, P
    c) aluminum, Al
    d) carbon, C

    Answer: d Key 1: A Section: 5

48. Calcium reacts with chlorine to form
    a) $CaCl$
    b) $CaCl_2$
    c) Ca_2Cl
    d) Ca_2Cl_3

    Answer: b Key 1: A Section: 5

49. Magnesium reacts with oxygen to form
    a) MgO
    b) Mg_2O
    c) Mg_2O
    d) Mg_3O_2

    Answer: a Key 1: A Section: 5

50. Sodium reacts with chlorine to form
    a) $NaCl$
    b) Na_2Cl
    c) $NaCl_2$
    d) Na_2Cl_3

    Answer: a Key 1: C Section: 5

51. When magnesium combines with oxygen, the bond formed is best classified as
    a) ionic
    b) nonpolar covalent
    c) polar covalent
    d) metallic

    Answer: a Key 1: A Section: 5

52. When magnesium combines with oxygen, the reaction involves a
    a) transfer of electrons from Mg to O
    b) transfer of electrons from O to Mg
    c) sharing of electrons between Mg and O
    d) conversion of protons into electrons

    Answer: a Key 1: A Section: 5

53. When magnesium reacts with chlorine, the reaction involves a
    a) transfer of electrons from Mg to Cl
    b) transfer of electrons from Cl to Mg
    c) sharing of electrons between Mg and Cl
    d) creation of electrons

    Answer: a Key 1: A Section: 5

54. When calcium reacts with chlorine, the reaction involves a
    a) transfer of electrons from Ca to Cl
    b) transfer of electrons from Cl to Ca
    c) sharing of electrons between Ca and Cl
    d) creation of electrons

    Answer: a Key 1: A Section: 5

55. In reactions to form ionic compounds, metals generally
    a) lose electrons
    b) gain electrons
    c) become non-metals
    d) do not react

    Answer: a Key 1: C Section: 5

56. In reactions to form ionic compounds, non-metals generally
    a) lose electrons
    b) gain electrons
    c) become metals
    d) do not react

    Answer: b Key 1: C Section: 5

57. Which substance has ionic bonds?
    a) O_2
    b) CaO
    c) H_2O
    d) OF_2

    Answer: b Key 1: A Section: 5

58. Which substance has ionic bonds?
a) Cl_2
b) NH_3
c) H_2O
d) KBr

Answer: d Key 1: A Section: 5

59. Which substance has ionic bonds?
a) K_2S
b) SO_3
c) CCl_4
d) N_2

Answer: a Key 1: A Section: 5

60. Which pair of atoms would form an ionic bond?
a) K and Na
b) Mg and S
c) Cl and Br
d) O and O

Answer: b Key 1: A Section: 5

61. The cation formed when a sodium atom loses an electron is called the
a) sodide ion
b) sodate ion
c) sodium ion
d) soda ion

Answer: c Key 1: C Section: 5

62. The anion formed when oxygen gains two electrons is called the
a) oxygen ion
b) oxyide ion
c) oxide ion
d) oxy ion

Answer: c Key 1: C Section: 5

63. The anion formed when nitrogen gains three electrons is called the
a) nitride ion
b) nitrite ion
c) nitrogide ion
d) nitro ion

Answer: a Key 1: C Section: 5

64. For which atom is it difficult to predict the most probable ionic charge using the periodic table?
a) Co
b) Na
c) Al
d) Cl

Answer: a Key 1: A Section: 5

65. For which atom is it difficult to predict the most probable ionic charge using the periodic table?
a) N
b) Fe
c) S
d) Br

Answer: b Key 1: A Section: 5

66. The name of the compound with a formula $AlCl_3$ is
a) aluminum(III) chloride
b) aluminum trichloride
c) monoaluminum trichlorine
d) aluminum chloride

Answer: d Key 1: A Section: 6

67. The formula of aluminum oxide is
a) AlO
b) AlO_2
c) AlO_3
d) Al_2O_3

Answer: d Key 1: A Section: 6

68. The formula of magnesium nitride is
a) Mg_3N_2
b) Mg_2N_3
c) Mg_2N
d) MgN

Answer: a Key 1: A Section: 6

69. The chemical formula for silver sulfate is
a) $AgSO_4$
b) Ag_2SO_4
c) $Ag(SO_4)_2$
d) Ag_3SO_4

Answer: b Key 1: A Section: 6

70. The correct formula for lithium acetate is
    a) $LiC_2H_3O_2$
    b) $Li_3C_2H_3O_2$
    c) $LiC_2O_3H_2$
    d) $Li(C_2H_3O_2)_2$

    Answer: a   Key 1: A   Section: 6

71. The correct formula for the nitrite ion is
    a) NO_3^-
    b) NO_3^{2-}
    c) NO_2^{2-}
    d) NO_2^-

    Answer: d   Key 1: A   Section: 6

72. The correct formula for iron(III) carbonate is
    a) $FeCO_3$
    b) Fe_2CO_3
    c) Fe_3CO_3
    d) $Fe_2(CO_3)_3$

    Answer: d   Key 1: A   Section: 6

73. The formula for the compound magnesium fluoride is
    a) MgF
    b) Mg_2F
    c) MgF_2
    d) Mg_3F_2

    Answer: c   Key 1: A   Section: 6

74. A covalent bond is formed when a pair of electrons is
    a) transferred
    b) shared
    c) split
    d) destroyed

    Answer: b   Key 1: C   Section: 7

75. An ionic bond is formed when electrons are
    a) transferred
    b) shared
    c) split
    d) destroyed

    Answer: a   Key 1: C   Section: 7

76. Hydrogen is a diatomic molecule, H_2. The bond holding the hydrogen atoms together is
    a) ionic
    b) nonpolar covalent
    c) polar covalent
    d) metallic

    Answer: b Key 1: C Section: 7

77. Covalent bonds generally form between
    a) ions
    b) metals
    c) metals and non-metals
    d) non-metals

    Answer: d Key 1: C Section: 7

78. Octet means
    a) stable electrons
    b) valence electrons
    c) eight
    d) filled shell

    Answer: c Key 1: C Section: 7

79. In a nonpolar covalent bond, electrons are
    a) shared equally
    b) shared unequally
    c) transferred
    d) uncharged

    Answer: a Key 1: C Section: 8

80. Which term fits this definition? A measure of the tendency of an atom in a molecule to attract electrons to itself.
    a) ionization
    b) electronegativity
    c) polar
    d) nonbonding

    Answer: b Key 1: D Section: 8

81. Which one of the following has the **LOWEST** electronegativity?
    a) sodium
    b) oxygen
    c) chlorine
    d) fluorine

    Answer: a Key 1: C Section: 8

82. In the hydrogen chloride molecule, HCl, the chlorine end of the molecule is more negative than the hydrogen end because
    a) chlorine is more electronegative than hydrogen
    b) hydrogen is more electronegative than chlorine
    c) hydrogen and chlorine have the same electronegativity
    d) hydrogen transfers an electron to chlorine

    Answer: a Key 1: A Section: 8

83. In a covalent bond, the shared electrons are sometimes referred to as
    a) core electrons
    b) bonding pairs
    c) nonbonding pairs
    d) neutral pairs

    Answer: b Key 1: D Section: 8

84. Which substance has nonpolar covalent bonds?
    a) O_2
    b) NO_2
    c) NaCl
    d) CO

    Answer: a Key 1: C Section: 8

85. Which substance has polar covalent bonds?
    a) SO_2
    b) N_2
    c) Cl_2
    d) CaO

    Answer: a Key 1: A Section: 8

86. Which substance has polar covalent bonds?
    a) O_2
    b) NH_3
    c) Cl_2
    d) Ca_2C

    Answer: b Key 1: A Section: 8

87. When two chlorine atoms combine with each other, the bond that forms is
    a) ionic
    b) polar covalent
    c) nonpolar covalent
    d) ionic-covalent

    Answer: c Key 1: C Section: 8

88. The attraction of an atom for a pair of shared electrons is called its
    a) polarity
    b) electronegativity
    c) valence
    d) covalence

    Answer: b Key 1: C Section: 8

89. When a fluorine atom reacts with a chlorine atom, the bond that forms between them should be
    a) ionic
    b) polar covalent
    c) nonpolar covalent
    d) ionic-covalent

    Answer: b Key 1: C Section: 8

90. Which substance has covalent bonds?
    a) LiCl
    b) NaCl
    c) $MgBr_2$
    d) CO_2

    Answer: d Key 1: A Section: 8

91. If two atoms from the same element share three pairs of electrons in forming a molecule the bond is called a
    a) single covalent bond
    b) double covalent bond
    c) triple covalent bond
    d) coordinate covalent bond

    Answer: c Key 1: D Section: 8

92. Hydrogen and carbon react to form
    a) CH
    b) CH_2
    c) CH_3
    d) CH_4

    Answer: d Key 1: A Section: 9

93. Hydrogen and nitrogen react to form
    a) NH
    b) NH_2
    c) NH_3
    d) NH_4

    Answer: c Key 1: A Section: 9

94. Hydrogen and sulfur react to form
 a) HS
 b) H_2S
 c) HS_2
 d) H_4S_2

 Answer: b Key 1: A Section: 9

95. Ammonia is the common name for which formula?
 a) NH_3
 b) CH_4
 c) HCl
 d) CCl_4

 Answer: a Key 1: A Section: 9

96. Methane is the common name for which formula?
 a) NH_3
 b) CH_4
 c) HCl
 d) CCl_4

 Answer: b Key 1: A Section: 9

97. In a molecule of nitrogen, N_2, the nitrogen atoms are bonded to each other by
 a) an ionic bond
 b) a single covalent bond
 c) a double covalent bond
 d) a triple covalent bond

 Answer: d Key 1: A Section: 10

98. Which is the electron dot structure for nitrogen?
 a) : : :N:N: : :
 b) : :N: :N: :
 c) :N: : :N:
 d) N: : : :N

 Answer: c Key 1: A Section: 10

SHORT ANSWER

99. What is the formula of sodium sulfate?

 Answer: Na_2SO_4 Key 1: A Section: 10

MULTIPLE CHOICE

100. What is the formula of ammonium nitrate?
    a) NH_4NO_3
    b) $(NH_4)_2NO_3$
    c) $NH_4(NO_3)_2$
    d) NH_4N

    Answer: a Key 1: A Section: 10

101. Sodium hydroxide is commonly known as lye. The formula of sodium hydroxide is
    a) $NaOH$
    b) Na_2OH
    c) $Na(OH)_2$
    d) SOH

    Answer: a Key 1: A Section: 10

102. Chalk is composed of primarily calcium carbonate. The formula of calcium carbonate is
    a) $CaCO_3$
    b) Ca_2CO_3
    c) $Ca(CO_3)_2$
    d) $Ca_3(CO_3)_2$

    Answer: a Key 1: A Section: 10

SHORT ANSWER

103. What is the formula of iron(III) phosphate?

    Answer: $FePO_4$ Key 1: A Section: 10

MULTIPLE CHOICE

104. The formula of iron(II) phosphate is
    a) $FePO_4$
    b) Fe_2PO_4
    c) $Fe_2(PO_4)_3$
    d) $Fe_4(PO_4)_2$

    Answer: d Key 1: A Section: 10

105. What is the name of NaH_2PO_4?
a) sodium hydrogen phosphate
b) sodium dihydrogen phosphate
c) monosodium dihydrogen monophosphate
d) sodium(II) dihydrogen monophosphate

Answer: b Key 1: A Section: 10

106. In the formula for copper(II) phosphate, the number of phosphorus atoms is
a) one
b) two
c) three
d) four

Answer: b Key 1: A Section: 10

107. In the formula for ammonium nitrate, the number of nitrogen atoms is
a) one
b) two
c) three
d) four

Answer: b Key 1: A Section: 10

108. How many phosphorus atoms are in the formula for potassium dihydrogen phosphate?
a) 1
b) 2
c) 3
d) 4

Answer: a Key 1: A Section: 10

109. How many iron atoms are in the formula for iron(III) oxide?
a) 1
b) 2
c) 3
d) 4

Answer: b Key 1: A Section: 10

110. How many oxygen atoms are in the formula for iron(III) oxide?
a) 1
b) 2
c) 3
d) 4

Answer: c Key 1: A Section: 10

111. How many magnesium atoms are in the formula for magnesium nitride?
a) 1
b) 2
c) 3
d) 4

Answer: c Key 1: A Section: 10

112. How many nitrogen atoms are in the formula for magnesium nitride?
a) 1
b) 2
c) 3
d) 4

Answer: b Key 1: A Section: 10

SHORT ANSWER

113. The formula of sodium chromate is

Answer: Na_2CrO_4 Key 1: A Section: 10

MULTIPLE CHOICE

114. The formula of sodium chromate is
a) $NaCrO_4$
b) Na_2Cr
c) Na_2CrO_4
d) $Na_3(CrO_4)_2$

Answer: c Key 1: A Section: 10

115. What is the name of the compound with the formula CCl_4?
a) carbon chloride
b) carbon(IV) chloride
c) chlorine carbonide
d) carbon tetrachloride

Answer: d Key 1: A Section: 10

SHORT ANSWER

116. What is the name of the compound with the formula N_2O_4?

Answer: dinitrogen tetroxide Key 1: A Section: 10

MULTIPLE CHOICE

117. What is the name of the compound with the formula SO_3?
    a) sulfur(VI) oxide
    b) sulfur oxide(III)
    c) sulfur trioxide
    d) sulfur(I) oxide(III)

    Answer: c Key 1: A Section: 10

118. The common name of the compound with the formula NH_3 is
    a) ammonia
    b) vinegar
    c) methane
    d) alcohol

    Answer: a Key 1: A Section: 10

SHORT ANSWER

119. What is the formula of the compound with the name tetraphosphorus pentoxide?

    Answer: P_4O_5 Key 1: A Section: 10

MULTIPLE CHOICE

120. The compound dinitrogen trioxide would have the chemical formula
    a) NO_3
    b) N_3O_2
    c) N_2O_3
    d) N_2O_5

    Answer: c Section: 10

ESSAY

121. Use the line structure to draw the electron dot formula for carbon monoxide, CO.

    Answer: Key 1: A Section: 11

MULTIPLE CHOICE

122. The electron dot formula for carbon monoxide, CO, in which a line represents a pair of electrons is

   a) $|\overline{C} = \overline{O}|$
   b) $|\overline{C} - \overline{O}|$
   c) $|\overline{C} = \overline{O}|$
   d) $|C \equiv O|$

   Answer: d Key 1: A Section: 11

123. The electron dot formula for carbon dioxide, CO_2, in which a line represents a pair of electrons is
   a) $|\overline{O} = C = \overline{O}|$
   b) $|\overline{O} - \overline{C} - \overline{O}|$
   c) $|\overline{O} - \overline{C} - \overline{O}|$
   d) $|O \equiv C \equiv O|$

   Answer: a Key 1: A Section: 11

124. The structure of formaldehyde, CH_2O, has
   a) all ionic bonds
   b) all single covalent bonds
   c) a double covalent bond between carbon and oxygen
   d) a triple covalent bond between carbon and oxygen

   Answer: c Key 1: C Section: 11

ESSAY

125. Acetylene is used in high temperature metal cutting torches. The formula of acetylene is C_2H_2. Draw the electron dot structure for acetylene.

   Answer: Key 1: A Section: 11

MULTIPLE CHOICE

126. Acetylene is used in high temperature metal cutting torches. The formula of acetylene is CH_2. The structure of acetylene is
a) H-C-C-H
b) H-C=C-H
c) H-C≡C-H
d) C-H≡H-C

Answer: c Key 1: A Section: 11

127. When a silicon atom combines with hydrogen, how many bonds are formed?
a) 1
b) 2
c) 3
d) 4

Answer: d Key 1: A Section: 11

128. Atoms and molecules with odd numbers of electrons are called
a) ions
b) odd
c) covalent
d) free radicals

Answer: d Key 1: C Section: 12

129. Which one of the following is a free radical?
a) H_2O
b) NO
c) NH_3
d) CH_4

Answer: b Key 1: A Section: 12

130. Which one of the following compounds does not obey the "octet rule"?
a) H_2O
b) CH_4
c) NaCl
d) BF_3

Answer: d Key 1: A Section: 12

131. Which one of the following compounds does not obey the "octet rule"?
a) H_2O
b) CH_4
c) SF_6
d) NH_3

Answer: c Key 1: A Section: 12

132. The valence shell electron pair repulsion theory (VSEPR) is used to
  a) predict the bonding pattern in molecules
  b) predict the three dimensional structure of molecules
  c) predict the electronegativity of atoms
  d) predict the number of multiple bonds in a molecule

  Answer: b Key 1: C Section: 13

133. If a central atom has a total of two groups and/or lone pairs attached to it, the geometry about the central atom is
  a) linear
  b) triangular
  c) tetrahedral
  d) pyramidal

  Answer: a Key 1: A Section: 13

134. If a central atom has a total of three groups and/or lone pairs attached to it, the geometry about the central atom is
  a) linear
  b) triangular
  c) tetrahedral
  d) pyramidal

  Answer: b Key 1: A Section: 13

135. If a central atom has four groups and/or lone pairs attached to it, the geometry about the central atom is
  a) linear
  b) triangular
  c) tetrahedral
  d) pyramidal

  Answer: c Key 1: A Section: 13

136. The VSEPR theory is based on
  a) the neutralization of ionic charge in a molecule
  b) the minimization of repulsion among valence electron pairs
  c) the arrangement of core electrons in a molecule
  d) the loss and gain of electrons based on electronegativity

  Answer: b Key 1: C Section: 13

137. The shape of a water molecule is
  a) linear
  b) bent
  c) tetrahedral
  d) unknown

  Answer: b Key 1: A Section: 13

138. The shape of a methane molecule is best described as
a) linear
b) triangular
c) bent
d) tetrahedral

Answer: d Key 1: A Section: 14

139. The best description of the shape of an ammonia molecule is
a) linear
b) bent
c) pyramidal
d) tetrahedral

Answer: c Key 1: A Section: 14

140. The best description of the shape of a Boron trifluoride (BF_3) molecule is
a) pyramidal
b) triangular
c) tetrahedral
d) linear

Answer: a Key 1: A Section: 14

141. The shape of the carbon dioxide molecule is
a) pyramidal
b) triangular
c) tetrahedral
d) linear

Answer: d Key 1: A Section: 14

142. The shape of the Sulfur dioxide molecule, where sulfur is the central atom is
a) linear
b) bent
c) triangular
d) tetrahedral

Answer: b Key 1: A Section: 14

143. The theory used to explain the behavior of solids, liquids and gases is
a) the kinetic-molecular theory
b) the VSEPR theory
c) the molecular theory
d) the atomic theory

Answer: a Key 1: C Section: 15

144. Which state of matter is characterized by having molecules close together, but moving randomly?
a) gas
b) liquid
c) solid
d) all of these

Answer: b Key 1: C Section: 15

145. Which state of matter is characterized by having molecules far apart and moving randomly?
a) gas
b) liquid
c) solid
d) all of these

Answer: a Key 1: C Section: 15

146. Which state of matter is characterized by having molecules close together and confined in their movement?
a) gas
b) liquid
c) solid
d) all of these

Answer: c Key 1: C Section: 15

147. The temperature at which a solid becomes a liquid is called the
a) melting point
b) boiling point
c) condensation point
d) decomposition point

Answer: a Key 1: D Section: 15

148. The temperature at which a liquid becomes a gas is called the
a) melting point
b) boiling point
c) condensation point
d) decomposition point

Answer: b Key 1: D Section: 15

149. The process by which a liquid is converted to a gas is called
a) condensation
b) ionization
c) liquefaction
d) vaporization

Answer: d Key 1: D Section: 15

150. The process by which a gas is converted to a liquid is called
a) condensation
b) ionization
c) sublimation
d) vaporization

Answer: a Key 1: D Section: 15

151. The process by which a liquid is converted to a solid is called
a) condensation
b) freezing
c) liquefaction
d) vaporization

Answer: b Key 1: D Section: 15

152. In which one of the following is hydrogen bonding **NOT** a factor?
a) H_2O
b) NH_3
c) CH_4
d) CH_3OH

Answer: c Key 1: A Section: 15

153. Which physical state is most highly ordered?
a) gas
b) liquid
c) solid
d) all are the same

Answer: c Key 1: C Section: 15

154. Matter is more likely to exist in the __________ state as the temperature is lowered and/or the pressure is increased.
a) solid
b) liquid
c) gas
d) elemental

Answer: a Key 1: A Section: 15

155. The temperature at which a solid melts is the melting point of the solid. The melting point is an indication of the submicroscopic forces that hold the solid together. Water melts at 0° C. Table sugar (sucrose) melts at 285° C. Gallium, Ga, melts at 30° C. Which one of the following ranks the submicroscopic forces in these solids from the strongest to the weakest?
a) Ga > water > sucrose
b) sucrose > Ga > water
c) water > sucrose > Ga
d) Ga > sucrose > water

Answer: b Key 1: A Section: 15

156. The temperature at which a liquid boils is the boiling point of the liquid. The boiling point is an indication of the submicroscopic forces that hold the matter in the liquid state. Water, H_2O, boils at 100° C. Ethanol, C_2H_6O boils at 78° C. Ammonia, NH_3, boils at -33° C. Which one of the following ranks the submicroscopic forces in these liquids from the strongest to the weakest?
a) Water > Ammonia > Ethanol
b) Ammonia > Ethanol > Water
c) Ethanol > Water > Ammonia
d) Water > Ethanol > Ammonia

Answer: d Key 1: A Section: 15

157. The temperature at which a solid melts is the melting point of the solid. The melting point is an indication of the submicroscopic forces that holds a solid together. Aluminum melts at 660° C. Gold melts at 1064° C. Lead melts at 328° C. Which one of the following ranks the submicroscopic forces in these solid elements from the strongest to the weakest?
a) Au > Al > Pb
b) Al > Au > Pb
c) Pb > Au > Al
d) Au > Pb > Al

Answer: a Key 1: A Section: 15

158. The degree of order of matter is directly proportional to the cohesive forces that hold the matter together. In other words, the more organized the state of matter, the stronger the "glue" that holds it together. Which one of the following ranks these cohesive forces from the state with the strongest to that with the weakest cohesive forces?
a) gas > liquid > solid
b) liquid > solid > gas
c) solid > liquid > gas
d) solid = gas = liquid

Answer: c Key 1: C Section: 15

159. The degree of order of matter is directly proportional to the cohesive forces that hold the matter together. In other words, the more organized the state of matter, the stronger the "glue" that holds it together. Given the above which one of the states has the strongest cohesive forces?
a) gas
b) liquid
c) solid
d) all states must have the same cohesive forces

Answer: c Key 1: C Section: 15

160. Matter is more likely to exist in the __________ state as the temperature is raised and/or the pressure is reduced.
a) solid
b) liquid
c) gas
d) elemental

Answer: c Key 1: A Section: 15

161. Which of the following ranks the three states of matter from **most to least ordered**?
a) gas > liquid > solid
b) gas > solid > liquid
c) solid > gas > liquid
d) solid > liquid > gas

Answer: d Key 1: C Section: 15

162. Which physical state is most highly disordered?
a) gas
b) liquid
c) solid
d) all are the same

Answer: a Key 1: C Section: 15

163. What type of forces exist between oxygen molecules in liquid oxygen?
a) hydrogen bonding
b) dipole forces
c) dispersion forces
d) a mixture of all of these forces

Answer: c Key 1: A Section: 15

164. Liquid hydrogen is used as one part of the booster fuel in the space shuttle. What type of forces exist between hydrogen molecules in liquid hydrogen?
    a) hydrogen bonding
    b) dipole forces
    c) dispersion forces
    d) a mixture of all of these forces

    Answer: c Key 1: A Section: 15

165. Water is a liquid at room temperature while methane is a gas. Which statement compares the intermolecular forces in these molecules correctly?
    a) The intermolecular forces in methane are stronger than those in water.
    b) The intermolecular forces in water are stronger than those in methane.
    c) Both water and methane have the same intermolecular forces.
    d) There is not enough information to compare these forces.

    Answer: b Key 1: A Section: 15

166. What is the predominant force between IBr molecules in liquid IBr?
    a) covalent bonds
    b) dipole forces
    c) dispersion forces
    d) hydrogen bonds

    Answer: b Key 1: C Section: 15

167. Ionic compounds have strong forces between particles. This means that generally ionic compounds are ____________ at room temperature.
    a) solids
    b) liquids
    c) gases
    d) covalently bonded

    Answer: a Key 1: A Section: 15

168. If a substance is a liquid
    a) it has a definite volume and a definite shape.
    b) it has a definite shape but no definite volume.
    c) it has a definite volume but no definite shape.
    d) it is readily compressible.

    Answer: c Key 1: C Section: 15

Chapter 6: Chemical Accounting

SHORT ANSWER

1. What is the name of the compound with the formula, K_2S?

   Answer: potassium sulfide Key 1: A Section: 2

2. What is the formula of copper(I) sulfide?

   Answer: Cu_2S Key 1: A Section: 2

MULTIPLE CHOICE

3. Which one of the following reactions **IS NOT** balanced?
   a) $2\ CO + O_2 \rightarrow 2\ CO_2$
   b) $2\ SO_2 + O_2 \rightarrow 2SO_3$
   c) $2\ KNO_3 + 10\ K \rightarrow 5\ K_2O + N_2$
   d) $SF_4 + 3\ H_2O \rightarrow H_2SO_3 + 4\ HF$

   Answer: c Key 1: A Section: 1

ESSAY

4. Balance the equation:

   $$AlCl_3 + H_2SO_4 \rightarrow Al_2(SO_4)_3 + HCl$$

   Answer: Key 1: A Section: 1

MULTIPLE CHOICE

5. When the equation below is balanced, the coefficient of HCl is:

   $$AlCl_3 + H_2SO_4 \rightarrow Al_2(SO_4)_3 + HCl$$
   a) 2
   b) 3
   c) 6
   d) 12

   Answer: c Key 1: A Section: 1

ESSAY

6. Balance the equation: $C_8H_{18} + O_2 \rightarrow CO_2 + H_2O$

   Answer: Key 1: A Section: 1

MULTIPLE CHOICE

7. When the equation below is balanced, the coefficient of carbon dioxide is:

   $C_8H_{18} + O_2 \rightarrow CO_2 + H_2O$

   a) 2
   b) 8
   c) 16
   d) 25

   Answer: c Key 1: A Section: 1

ESSAY

8. Balance the equation: $C_3H_8 + O_2 \rightarrow CO_2 + H_2O$

   Answer: Key 1: A Section: 1

MULTIPLE CHOICE

9. When the equation below is balanced, the coefficient of carbon dioxide is:

   $C_3H_8 + O_2 \rightarrow CO_2 + H_2O$

   a) 1
   b) 3
   c) 6
   d) 12

   Answer: b Key 1: A Section: 1

ESSAY

10. Balance the equation: $Zn + CuSO_4 \rightarrow ZnSO_4 + Cu$

    Answer: Key 1: A Section: 1

MULTIPLE CHOICE

11. When the equation below is balanced, the coefficient of zinc is:

    $Zn + CuSO_4 \rightarrow ZnSO_4 + Cu$

    a) 0
    b) 1
    c) 2
    d) 3

    Answer: b Key 1: A Section: 1

12. When the equation below is balanced, the coefficient of silver is:

    $Cu + AgNO_3 \rightarrow Cu(NO_3)_2 + Ag$

    a) 0
    b) 1
    c) 2
    d) 3

    Answer: c Key 1: A Section: 1

13. When the equation below is balanced, the coefficient of copper(II) nitrate is:

    $Cu + AgNO_3 \rightarrow Cu(NO_3)_2 + Ag$

    a) 0
    b) 1
    c) 2
    d) 3

    Answer: b Key 1: A Section: 1

ESSAY

14. Balance the equation: $Cu + AgNO_3 \rightarrow Cu(NO_3)_2 + Ag$

    Answer: Key 1: A Section: 1

MULTIPLE CHOICE

15. When the equation below is balanced, the coefficient of silver(I) nitrate is:

    $Cu + AgNO_3 \rightarrow Cu(NO_3)_2 + Ag$

    a) 0
    b) 1
    c) 2
    d) 3

    Answer: c Key 1: A Section: 1

ESSAY

16. Balance the equation: $Fe + O_2 \rightarrow Fe_2O_3$

    Answer: Key 1: A Section: 1

MULTIPLE CHOICE

17. When the equation below is balanced, the coefficient of oxygen is:

    $Fe + O_2 \rightarrow Fe_2O_3$
    a) 0
    b) 1
    c) 2
    d) 3

    Answer: d Key 1: A Section: 1

18. When the equation below is balanced, the coefficient of the product is:

    $Fe + O_2 \rightarrow Fe_2O_3$
    a) 1
    b) 2
    c) 3
    d) 4

    Answer: b Key 1: A Section: 1

ESSAY

19. Balance the equation: $NaCN + H_2SO_4 \rightarrow Na_2SO_4 + HCN$

    Answer: Key 1: A Section: 1

MULTIPLE CHOICE

20. When the equation below is balanced, the coefficient of the hydrogen cyanide, HCN, is:

    $NaCN + H_2SO_4 \rightarrow Na_2SO_4 + HCN$
    a) 1
    b) 2
    c) 3
    d) 4

    Answer: b Key 1: A Section: 1

21. When the equation below is balanced, the coefficient of sodium cyanide is:
    $NaCN + H_2SO_4 \rightarrow Na_2SO_4 + HCN$
    a) 1
    b) 2
    c) 3
    d) 4

    Answer: b Key 1: A Section: 1

22. When the equation below is balanced, the coefficient of sulfuric acid, H_2SO_4 is:

$NaCN + H_2SO_4 \rightarrow Na_2SO_4 + HCN$

a) 1
b) 2
c) 3
d) 4

Answer: a Key 1: A Section: 1

23. The following reaction is important in the removal of sulfur dioxide, a major source of acid rain, from the smokestacks of coal burning power plants. When the equation below is balanced, the coefficient of calcium oxide (commonly called "lime") is:

$CaO + SO_2 + O_2 \rightarrow CaSO_4$

a) 1
b) 2
c) 3
d) 4

Answer: b Key 1: A Section: 1

24. The following reaction is important in the removal of sulfur dioxide, a major source of acid rain, from the smokestacks of coal burning power plants. When the equation below is balanced, the coefficient of calcium sulfate (commonly called "gypsum") is:

$CaO + SO_2 + O_2 \rightarrow CaSO_4$

a) 1
b) 2
c) 3
d) 4

Answer: b Key 1: A Section: 1

25. The following reaction is important in the removal of sulfur dioxide, a major source of acid rain, from the smokestacks of coal burning power plants. When the equation below is balanced, the coefficient of oxygen is:

$CaO + SO_2 + O_2 \rightarrow CaSO_4$

a) 1
b) 2
c) 3
d) 4

Answer: a Key 1: A Section: 1

26. Solid lithium hydride reacts with water to form aqueous lithium hydroxide and hydrogen gas. When this equation is written and balanced, the coefficient of lithium hydride is
 a) 1
 b) 2
 c) 3
 d) 4

 Answer: a Key 1: A Section: 1

ESSAY

27. Tin was among the the first metals used by humans. Elemental tin is produced by heating tin(IV) oxide, the principal ore of tin, with carbon. The products of this reaction are tin and carbon dioxide. Write and balance the equation.

 Answer: Key 1: A Section: 1

MULTIPLE CHOICE

28. Tin was among the the first metals used by humans. Elemental tin is produced by heating tin(IV) oxide, the principal ore of tin, with carbon. The products of this reaction are tin and carbon dioxide. When the equation is written and balanced, the coefficient of carbon is
 a) 1
 b) 2
 c) 3
 d) 4

 Answer: a Key 1: A Section: 1

29. Tin was among the the first metals used by humans. Elemental tin is produced by heating tin(IV) oxide, the principal ore of tin, with carbon. The products of this reaction are tin and carbon dioxide. When the equation is written and balanced, the coefficient of tin is
 a) 1
 b) 2
 c) 3
 d) 4

 Answer: a Key 1: A Section: 1

ESSAY

30. Ammonia can be prepared by the reaction of magnesium nitride with water. The products are ammonia and magnesium hydroxide. Write and balance the equation.

 Answer: Key 1: A Section: 1

MULTIPLE CHOICE

31. Ammonia can be prepared by the reaction of magnesium nitride with water. The products are ammonia and magnesium hydroxide. When the equation is written and balanced, the coefficient of magnesium nitride is
a) 1
b) 3
c) 6
d) 8

Answer: a Key 1: A Section: 1

32. Ammonia can be prepared by the reaction of magnesium nitride with water. The products are ammonia and magnesium hydroxide. When the equation is written and balanced, the coefficient of magnesium hydroxide is
a) 1
b) 3
c) 6
d) 8

Answer: b Key 1: A Section: 1

33. Ammonia can be prepared by the reaction of magnesium nitride with water. The products are ammonia and magnesium hydroxide. When the equation is written and balanced, the coefficient of ammonia is
a) 1
b) 2
c) 3
d) 6

Answer: b Key 1: A Section: 1

34. Ammonia can be prepared by the reaction of magnesium nitride with water. The products are ammonia and magnesium hydroxide. When the equation is written and balanced, the coefficient of water is
a) 1
b) 2
c) 3
d) 6

Answer: d Key 1: A Section: 1

ESSAY

35. When oxygen, O_2, is passed through an electrical spark (lightning is a good natural source of an electrical spark), ozone, O_3 is formed. Write and balance the equation.

Answer: Key 1: A Section: 1

MULTIPLE CHOICE

36. When oxygen, O_2, is passed through an electrical spark (lightning is a good natural source of an electrical spark), ozone, O_3 is formed. When the equation is balanced, the coefficient of ozone is
   a) 1
   b) 2
   c) 3
   d) 4

   Answer: b Key 1: A Section: 1

37. When oxygen, O_2, is passed through an electrical spark (lightning is a good natural source of an electrical spark), ozone, O_3 is formed. When the equation is balanced, the coefficient of oxygen is
   a) 1
   b) 2
   c) 3
   d) 4

   Answer: c Key 1: A Section: 1

38. The observations that gaseous reactants combine to form gaseous products in volume ratios that are simple whole numbers is most directly summarized by which of the following.
   a) The Law of Conservation of Mass
   b) The Law of Fixed Proportions
   c) The Law of Multiple Proportions
   d) The Law of Combining Volumes

   Answer: d Key 1: C Section: 2

39. When 2 liters of hydrogen gas and 1 liter of oxygen gas react to form water at a constant temperature and pressure, how many liters of water vapor (steam) will be formed?
   a) 1
   b) 2
   c) 3
   d) more information is required

   Answer: b Key 1: A Section: 2

40. When 1 liter of nitrogen gas reacts with 3 liters of hydrogen gas at constant temperature and pressure, how many liters of ammonia gas will be produced?
   a) 1
   b) 2
   c) 3
   d) 4

   Answer: b Key 1: A Section: 2

41. When 2 liters of nitrogen gas reacts with 3 liters of hydrogen gas at constant temperature and pressure, how many liters of ammonia gas will be produced?
    a) 2
    b) 3
    c) 4
    d) 5

    Answer: a Key 1: A Section: 2

42. The explanation of the observations leading to the law of combining volumes is often called "Avogadro's hypothesis." This explanation states that equal volumes of gases at the same temperature and pressure have
    a) the same number of molecules
    b) different numbers of molecules
    c) the same reactivity
    d) different energies

    Answer: a Key 1: C Section: 2

43. A liter of solid carbon and a liter of oxygen gas at the same temperature and pressure react to produce carbon dioxide. Using the law of combining volumes, how many liters of carbon dioxide will be produced?
    a) 1
    b) 2
    c) 3
    d) The law of combining volumes applies only to reactions involving all gases

    Answer: d Key 1: A Section: 2

44. Avogadro's number is
    a) 6.02×10^{23}
    b) 6.02×10^{-23}
    c) 3.02×10^{26}
    d) 2.06×10^{32}

    Answer: a Key 1: D Section: 3

45. Avogadro's number is big. If you had 6.02×10^{23} dollars, and could spend it at 1 billion (10^9) per second for your entire life ($\approx$75 years), what approximate percentage of your original money would you have left?
    a) 0%
    b) 10%
    c) 50%
    d) $\approx$100%

    Answer: d Key 1: A Section: 3

46. How many molecules are in 237 g (about a cup) of water?
    a) 13.1
    b) 4267
    c) 6.02×10^{23}
    d) 7.93×10^{24}

    Answer: d Key 1: A Section: 3

47. Which one of the following has the same number of **atoms** as 23 g of sodium?
    a) 23 g of potassium
    b) 19 g of potassium
    c) 24 g of magnesium
    d) 18 g of water

    Answer: c Key 1: A Section: 3

48. Which one of the following **does not** contain an Avogadro's number of particles?
    a) 1.0 mole of carbon
    b) 23 g of sodium
    c) 6.02×10^{23} atoms of silicon
    d) 12 g of water

    Answer: d Key 1: A Section: 3

49. The molar volume of a gas at STP is
    a) 12.4 liters
    b) 22.4 liters
    c) 12.4 gallons
    d) 6.02×10^{23} liters

    Answer: b Key 1: D Section: 4

50. At STP, 22.4 liters of nitrogen gas, N_2, will have a mass of
    a) 14.0 g
    b) 22.4 g
    c) 28.0 g
    d) 35.0 g

    Answer: c Key 1: C Section: 4

51. At STP, 22.4 liters of oxygen gas, O_2, will have a mass of
    a) 16.0 g
    b) 22.4 g
    c) 28.0 g
    d) 32.0 g

    Answer: d Key 1: A Section: 4

52. The density of He at STP is
    a) 0.179 g/L
    b) 0.500 g/L
    c) 1.00 g/L
    d) 5.60 g/L

    Answer: a Key 1: A Section: 4

53. Nitroglycerin has a formula $C_3H_5(NO_3)_3$. The molar mass of nitroglycerin is
    a) 65 g
    b) 227 g
    c) 309 g
    d) 398 g

    Answer: b Key 1: A Section: 4

54. Aspirin has a formula $C_9H_8O_4$. The molar mass of aspirin is
    a) 95 g
    b) 180 g
    c) 220 g
    d) 325 g

    Answer: b Key 1: A Section: 4

55. For a given amount of gas at a constant temperature, the volume of gas varies inversely with its pressure is a statement of ________ law.
    a) Charles's
    b) Avogadro's
    c) Boyle's
    d) Curie's

    Answer: c Key 1: C Section: 6

56. A gas is enclosed in a cylinder fitted with a piston. The volume of the gas is 2.00 L at 1.00 atm pressure. The piston is moved to increase the volume to 6.00 L. Which of the following is a reasonable value for the pressure of the gas at the greater volume?
    a) 3.00 atm
    b) 0.333 atm
    c) 6.00 atm
    d) 12.0 atm

    Answer: b Key 1: A Section: 6

57. A gas is enclosed in a 10.0 L tank at 1200 mm Hg pressure. Which of the following is a reasonable value for the pressure when the gas is pumped into a 5.00 L vessel?
a) 2400 mm Hg
b) 600 mm Hg
c) 24 mm Hg
d) .042 mm Hg

Answer: a Key 1: A Section: 6

58. The statement that the volume of a fixed amount of a gas at a constant pressure is directly proportional to its absolute temperature is known as ____ law.
a) Charles's
b) Boyle's
c) Gay-Lussac's
d) Avogadro's

Answer: a Key 1: C Section: 6

59. A balloon is inflated outdoors on a cold day in North Dakota at a temperature of -40 °C to a volume of 2.00 L. The pressure remains constant. What is the volume of the balloon indoors at a temperature of 25 °C?
a) 1.6 L
b) 2.6 L
c) 2.0 L
d) -3.2 L

Answer: b Key 1: A Section: 6

60. In the ideal gas law equation, PV=nRT, R is known as
a) the pressure
b) a radian
c) the universal gas constant
d) a revolution

Answer: c Key 1: C Section: 6

61. Use the ideal gas law to calculate the volume occupied by 0.200 mol of nitrogen gas at 1.00 atm pressure and at 27° C.
R = 0.0821 L* atm/(K*mol)
a) 0.44 L
b) 4.9 L
c) 22.4 L
d) 0.0821L

Answer: b Key 1: C Section: 6

62. In the reaction $CH_4 + 2\ O_2 \rightarrow CO_2 + 2\ H_2O$ how many moles of oxygen are required to burn 8.0 g of methane?
a) 0.5
b) 1.0
c) 2.0
d) 32

Answer: b Key 1: A Section: 5

63. In the reaction $CH_4 + 2\ O_2 \rightarrow CO_2 + 2\ H_2O$ how many moles of oxygen are required to burn 16.0 g of methane?
a) 0.50
b) 1.0
c) 2.0
d) 32

Answer: c Key 1: A Section: 5

64. Acetylene (C_2H_2) burns in pure oxygen with a very hot flame. The products of this reaction are carbon dioxide and water. How much oxygen is required to react with 52.0 g of acetylene?
a) 32.0
b) 52.0
c) 160.0
d) 240.0

Answer: c Key 1: A Section: 5

65. Calcium metal reacts with water to form calcium hydroxide and hydrogen gas. How many grams of hydrogen is formed when 0.50 g of calcium are added to water?
a) 0.025 g
b) 0.050 g
c) 0.10 g
d) 0.50 g

Answer: a Key 1: A Section: 5

66. Joseph Priestley discovered oxygen in 1774 by heating mercury(II) oxide. The compound decomposes into its elements. How much oxygen, O_2, is produced by the decomposition of 25 g of HgO?
a) 1.8
b) 3.7
c) 5.5
d) none of these

Answer: a Key 1: A Section: 5

67. A one molar solution is a solution that contains one mole of solute in:
    a) one mole of solvent
    b) one liter of solution
    c) one kilogram of solvent
    d) one kilogram of solution

    Answer: b Key 1: D Section: 7

68. A solution that is 1 molar contains:
    a) one mole of solute in one mole of solvent
    b) one mole of solute in one mole of solution
    c) one mole of solute in 100 g of solution
    d) one mole of solute in 1 liter of solution

    Answer: d Key 1: D Section: 7

69. Molarity is a measure of:
    a) the volume of a solution
    b) the mass of a substance
    c) the ability of a substance to ionize
    d) the concentration of a solute in a solution

    Answer: d Key 1: C Section: 7

70. The molarity of a solution is a measure of its:
    a) concentration
    b) surface tension
    c) temperature
    d) mass

    Answer: a Key 1: C Section: 7

71. Molarity is a useful measure of concentration because:
    a) it is based on the Bronsted-Lowry definition of an acid
    b) it allows measuring out quantities of chemical particles through the use of volumes of solutions
    c) equal volumes of solutions of the same molarity will contain equal weights of solutes
    d) it allows the conversion of percentage concentrations (by weight) into a form easily used in chemical calculations

    Answer: b Key 1: A Section: 7

72. Expressing concentrations in terms of molarity is especially convenient since it allows one to count chemical particles by measuring:
    a) the weights of solutes
    b) the weights of solutions
    c) the volumes of solvents
    d) the volumes of solutions

    Answer: d Key 1: C Section: 7

73. A one molar solution of NaOH in water contains:
    a) one mole of NaOH per liter of solution
    b) one g of NaOH per liter of solution
    c) one liter of NaOH per mole of solution
    d) one mole of NaOH per mole of solution

    Answer: a   Key 1: A   Section: 7

74. The molarity of a solution that contains 0.5 moles of NaOH in 200 milliliters of water is:
    a) 0.25
    b) 0.5
    c) 1.0
    d) 2.5

    Answer: d   Key 1: A   Section: 7

75. The molarity of a solution that contains 4.0 g of NaOH in a liter of solution is:
    a) 0.01
    b) 0.1
    c) 1
    d) 0.4

    Answer: b   Key 1: A   Section: 7

76. The number of moles of NaOH that are in 250 mL of a 3 molar solution is:
    a) 0.25
    b) 0.75
    c) 1.0
    d) 1.5

    Answer: b   Key 1: A   Section: 7

Chapter 7: Acids and Bases

MULTIPLE CHOICE

1. Which **IS NOT** a characteristic of acids?
   a) taste bitter
   b) turn litmus red
   c) react with bases to form salts
   d) react with active metals to form H_2 gas

   Answer: a Key 1: D Section: 1

2. Which **IS NOT** a characteristic of bases?
   a) taste bitter
   b) turn litmus red
   c) react with acids to form salts
   d) produce hydroxide ions when added to water

   Answer: b Key 1: D Section: 1

3. Lemon juice has a sour taste and turns litmus to red. Lemon juice is
   a) basic
   b) acidic
   c) neutral
   d) caustic

   Answer: b Key 1: A Section: 1

4. The four basic tastes are all related to acids and bases in some manner. The taste sensation with the least direct, least well understood, and probably most complex relationship between taste response and acid/base properties is
   a) bitter
   b) sour
   c) salt
   d) sweet

   Answer: d Key 1: C Section: 1

5. Many medicines have a bitter taste which manufacturers attempt to disguise. Many medicines are probably
   a) acids
   b) bases
   c) salts
   d) neutral

   Answer: b Key 1: A Section: 1

6. Which one of the following acids is responsible for the sour taste of yogurt?
   a) acetic
   b) citric
   c) lactic
   d) phosphoric

   Answer: c Key 1: A Section: 1

7. Foods that are acidic can be identified by their _____ taste.
   a) bitter
   b) sweet
   c) salty
   d) sour

   Answer: d Key 1: C Section: 1

8. Which of the following is/are characteristic(s) of acids?
   a) taste sour
   b) turn litmus red
   c) react with bases to form salts
   d) all are characteristics of adids

   Answer: d Key 1: C Section: 1

9. Which of the following is/are characteristic(s) of bases?
   a) taste bitter
   b) reacts with acids to form salts
   c) produce hydroxide ions when added to water
   d) all are characteristics of bases

   Answer: d Key 1: C Section: 1

10. H_3O^+ is called the
    a) hydrate ion
    b) hydrogen ion
    c) hydroxide ion
    d) hydronium ion

    Answer: d Key 1: C Section: 2

ESSAY

11. Why are acids sometimes referred to as "proton donors?"

    Answer: Key 1: C Section: 2

MULTIPLE CHOICE

12. An hydrogen ion, H^+, is the same as a(n)
    a) hydronium ion
    b) proton
    c) electron
    d) hydrate

    Answer: b Key 1: C Section: 2

13. Which one of the following is a correct definition of an acid that is not dependent upon the solvent?
    a) Acids produce hydronium ions
    b) Acids are proton donors
    c) Acids produce hydroxide ions
    d) Acids are proton acceptors

    Answer: b Key 1: C Section: 2

14. Which one of the following is an example of a nonmetal oxide?
    a) CO_2
    b) NaOH
    c) K_2O
    d) H_2SO_4

    Answer: a Key 1: A Section: 2

15. When added to water, which one of the following would produce an acid?
    a) Na
    b) MgO
    c) NH_3
    d) SO_3

    Answer: d Key 1: A Section: 3

16. When HCl is added to pure acetic acid (called glacial acetic acid), HCl molecules lose protons, while acetic acid molecules gain protons. In this reaction, HCl is a(n)
    a) acid
    b) base
    c) salt
    d) solvent

    Answer: a Key 1: A Section: 2

17. Sulfuric acid is the leading chemical produced and used industrially. What is the formula for sulfuric acid?
a) SO_4
b) HSO_4
c) $H_2(SO)_4$
d) H_2SO_4

Answer: d Key 1: D Section: 2

18. Phosphoric acid is added to many popular beverages to give them a tart flavor. The formula of phosphoric acid is
a) H_3PO_4
b) H_4PO_3
c) H_2PO_4
d) HPO_4

Answer: a Key 1: C Section: 2

19. All of the following are bases except
a) KOH
b) HNO_3
c) NH_3
d) $Mg(OH)_2$

Answer: b Key 1: A Section: 2

20. A useful broad view of reactions between acids and bases involves the
a) transfer of protons
b) transfer of electrons
c) conversion of protons into electrons
d) ionization of atoms

Answer: a Key 1: A Section: 2

21. When nonmetal oxides react with water the resulting solution is _____.
a) salty
b) acidic
c) neutral
d) basic

Answer: b Key 1: C Section: 3

22. When metal oxides react with water the resulting solution is generally ____.
a) salty
b) acidic
c) neutral
d) basic

Answer: d Key 1: C Section: 3

23. Which one of the following is a hydroxide ion?
    a) OH^-
    b) H^+
    c) H_3O^+
    d) H_2O^-

    Answer: a Key 1: C   Section: 2

24. Which one of the following is a correct definition of a base that is not dependent upon the solvent?
    a) Bases produce hydronium ions
    b) Bases are proton donors
    c) Bases produce hydroxide ions
    d) Bases are proton acceptors

    Answer: d Key 1: C   Section: 3

25. When added to water, which one of the following would produce a base?
    a) Na_2O
    b) CO_2
    c) Cl_2
    d) SO_3

    Answer: a Key 1: A   Section: 2

26. What base is formed by the addition of potassium oxide to water?
    a) KOH
    b) K_2OH
    c) KH
    d) KH_2

    Answer: a Key 1: A   Section: 3

ESSAY

27. Lime is used in farming to reduce the acidity of the soil. The chemical name for lime is calcium oxide. When water in the soil reacts with lime, what base is formed? Write the reaction.

    Answer: Key 1: A   Section: 3

MULTIPLE CHOICE

28. Lime is used in farming to reduce the acidity of the soil. The chemical name for lime is calcium oxide. When water in the soil reacts with lime, what base is formed?
    a) CaO
    b) $CaOH$
    c) Ca_2OH
    d) $Ca(OH)_2$

    Answer: d Key 1: A Section: 2

29. What is the formula for calcium hydroxide?
    a) $CaOH$
    b) Ca_2OH
    c) $Ca(OH)_2$
    d) $CaOH_2$

    Answer: c Key 1: A Section: 2

30. The compound CH_3NH_2 reacts with water to form $CH_3NH_3^+$ and OH-. In this reaction, CH_3NH_2 is acting as a(n)
    a) acid
    b) base
    c) salt
    d) catalyst

    Answer: b Key 1: A Section: 2

31. When added to water, which one of the following would produce an acid?
    a) Mg
    b) Na_2O
    c) NH_3
    d) CO_2

    Answer: d Key 1: A Section: 3

32. What acid is formed when SO_3 is added to water?
    a) hydrosulfuric
    b) hydrosulfurous
    c) sulfuric
    d) sulfurous

    Answer: c Key 1: A Section: 3

33. When added to water, which of the following would produce a base?
    a) MgO
    b) CaO
    c) BaO
    d) all would produce bases

    Answer: d Key 1: A Section: 3

34. When added to water, which of the following would produce a base?
    a) K_2O
    b) ClO_3
    c) P_4O_{10}
    d) CO_2

    Answer: a Key 1: A Section: 3

35. Which is a weak base in aqueous solution?
    a) NH_3
    b) HCN
    c) NaOH
    d) KOH

    Answer: a Key 1: C Section: 4

36. The same number of moles of acetic acid and hydrogen chloride are placed in beakers containing water. After this addition, the beaker with the HCl has more hydronium ions than the beaker with added acetic acid. HCl is classified as
    a) a weaker acid than acetic acid
    b) a stronger acid than acetic acid
    c) equal in acid strength to acetic acid
    d) a base

    Answer: b Key 1: A Section: 4

37. HCN is classified as a weak acid in water. This means that it produces
    a) no hydronium ions
    b) a relatively small fraction of the maximum number of possible hydronium ions
    c) a relatively large fraction of the maximum number of possible hydronium ions
    d) 100% of the maximum number of possible hydronium ions

    Answer: b Key 1: A Section: 4

38. Nitric acid, HNO_3, is classified as a strong acid in water. This means that it produces
    a) no hydronium ions
    b) a relatively small fraction of the maximum number of possible hydronium ions
    c) a relatively large fraction of the maximum number of possible hydronium ions
    d) 100% of the maximum number of possible hydronium ions

    Answer: d Key 1: A Section: 4

39. Ammonia is classified as a weak base in water. This means that it produces
    a) no hydroxide ions
    b) a relatively small fraction of the maximum number of hydroxide ions
    c) a relatively large fraction of the maximum number of hydroxide ions
    d) 100% of the maximum number of hydroxide ions

    Answer: b Key 1: A Section: 4

40. Sodium hydroxide is classified as a strong base in water. This means that it produces
    a) no hydroxide ions
    b) a relatively small fraction of the maximum number of hydroxide ions
    c) a relatively large fraction of the maximum number of hydroxide ions
    d) 100% of the maximum number of hydroxide ions

    Answer: d Key 1: A Section: 4

41. When an aqueous solution containing hydrochloric acid is just neutralized with an aqueous solution containing sodium hydroxide, the solution would taste
    a) sour
    b) bitter
    c) salty
    d) sweet

    Answer: c Key 1: C Section: 4

ESSAY

42. Write the balanced chemical reaction for the neutralization of calcium hydroxide with nitric acid.

    Answer: Key 1: A Section: 4

43. List three strong acids.

    Answer: Key 1: D Section: 4

MULTIPLE CHOICE

44. In the balanced chemical reaction for the neutralization of calcium hydroxide with nitric acid, HNO_3, the coefficient of nitric acid is
a) 1
b) 2
c) 3
d) 4

Answer: b Key 1: A Section: 4

45. In the balanced chemical reaction for the neutralization of sodium hydroxide with sulfuric acid, H_2SO_4, the coefficient of sulfuric acid is
a) 1
b) 2
c) 3
d) 4

Answer: b Key 1: A Section: 4

46. In the balanced chemical reaction for the neutralization of sodium hydroxide with sulfuric acid, H_2SO_4, the coefficient of sodium hydroxide is
a) 1
b) 2
c) 3
d) 4

Answer: b Key 1: A Section: 4

47. A ruptured tank in Anywhere, USA spilled hydrochloric acid. Officials were reported to be "concerned that the acid might mix with sodium hydroxide - caustic soda - in a neighboring tank and form a toxic gas." What toxic gas would be formed?
a) carbon dioxide
b) chlorine
c) chlorine dioxide
d) none

Answer: d Key 1: A Section: 4

48. All of the following are strong acids except
a) hydrochloric acid
b) sulfuric acid
c) nitric acid
d) acetic acid

Answer: d Key 1: A Section: 4

49. When citric acid is produced by the cells of an orange and dissolves in water, it produces a relatively small number of hydronium ions. Citric acid is best described as a
    a) dilute acid
    b) concentrated acid
    c) weak acid
    d) strong acid

    Answer: c Key 1: A Section: 4

50. An acid is strong if it
    a) is very concentrated.
    b) makes acid-base indicators change color.
    c) ionizes completely in water.
    d) causes metals to corrode.

    Answer: c Key 1: C Section: 4

51. A sample of rainwater has a pH of 3.5. What ion is sure to be present in relatively large concentration in this rain sample?
    a) H_3O^+
    b) SO_4^{2-}
    c) OH^-
    d) HSO_4^-

    Answer: a Key 1: A Section: 5

52. Nitrous acid, HNO_2, is classified as a weak acid in water. This means that it produces
    a) no hydronium ions
    b) a relatively small fraction of the maximum number of possible hydronium ions
    c) a relatively large fraction of the maximum number of possible hydronium ions
    d) 100% of the maximum number of possible hydronium ions

    Answer: b Key 1: C Section: 4

53. Which of the following is the correct balanced equation for the neutralization of barium hydroxide with hydrochloric acid?
    a) $Ba(OH)_2 + 2\ HCl \longrightarrow BaCl_2 + 2\ H_2O$
    b) $BaOH_2 + 2\ HCl \longrightarrow BaCl_2 + H_2O$
    c) $Ba(OH)_2 + HCl \longrightarrow BaCl_2 + H_2O$
    d) $BaOH + HCl \longrightarrow BaCl + H_2O$

    Answer: a Key 1: A Section: 4

54. Which of the following is the correct balanced equation for the neutralization of barium hydroxide with sulfuric acid?
a) $Ba(OH)_2 + H_2SO_4$ ------→ $BaSO_4 + 2H_2O$
b) $BaOH + H_2SO_4$ ------→ $BaSO_4 + 2H_2O$
c) $BaOH_2 + H_2SO_4$ ------→ $BaSO_4 + H_2O$
d) $Ba(OH)_2 + 2H_2SO_4$ ------→ $Ba(SO_4)_2 + 2H_2O$

Answer: a Key 1: A Section: 4

55. The pH of a sample of water from a river is 6.0. A sample of effluent from a food processing plant has a pH of 4.0. The concentration of hydronium ion in the effluent is
a) one and a half times (1.5x) larger than the river hydronium ion concentration
b) two times (2x) larger than the river hydronium ion concentration
c) four times (4x) larger than the river hydronium ion concentration
d) 100 times (100x) larger than the river hydronium ion concentration

Answer: d Key 1: A Section: 5

56. A solution with a pH of 10 has a hydronium ion concentration of
a) 10^{-10} mol/L
b) 10^{10} mol/L
c) 10 mol/L
d) -10 mol/L

Answer: a Key 1: A Section: 5

57. A solution of toilet bowl cleaner has a pH of 1.0 The solution is
a) strongly acidic
b) weakly acidic
c) strongly basic
d) weakly basic

Answer: a Key 1: A Section: 5

58. A window cleaner has a pH of 9. The cleaner would best be labelled
a) strongly acidic
b) weakly acidic
c) strongly basic
d) weakly basic

Answer: d Key 1: A Section: 5

59. An unknown substance is added to a solution and the pH decreases. The substance is best described as a(n)
a) acid
b) base
c) salt
d) solvent

Answer: a Key 1: A Section: 5

60. An unknown substance is added to a solution and the pH increases. The substance is best described as a(n)
a) acid
b) base
c) salt
d) solvent

Answer: b Key 1: A Section: 5

61. Which substance has the lowest pH?
a) blood
b) lemon juice
c) unpolluted rainwater
d) NaOH (4% solution)

Answer: b Key 1: A Section: 5

62. Which substance has the highest pH?
a) blood
b) lemon juice
c) unpolluted rainwater
d) NaOH (4% solution)

Answer: d Key 1: A Section: 5

63. If a solution has a pH of 13, it is
a) strongly acidic
b) strongly basic
c) weakly acidic
d) weakly basic

Answer: b Key 1: A Section: 5

64. If the concentration of a dilute solution of nitric acid is 0.0001 M, what is the pH of that solution?
a) 7
b) 14
c) 4
d) 5

Answer: c Key 1: A Section: 5

65. The pH of rain collected on a remote island in the Pacific is assumed to be unaffected by human pollution. The pH of the rainwater will be
a) less than 7
b) equal to 7
c) greater than 7
d) 0

Answer: a Key 1: C Section: 6

66. Hyperacidity means
a) too much acid
b) too little acid
c) too much antacid
d) too much base

Answer: a Key 1: C Section: 7

67. Sodium bicarbonate is an old standby antacid. It is not recommended for persons suffering from high blood pressure because
a) it is too strong an acid
b) it is too strong a base
c) of the presence of sodium ion
d) of the presence of bicarbonate ion

Answer: c Key 1: A Section: 7

68. Sodium bicarbonate is the common name for what compound?
a) sodium carbonate
b) sodium carbide
c) sodium hydrogen carbonate
d) sodium bismuth carbonate

Answer: c Key 1: C Section: 7

69. Sodium bicarbonate is commonly known as
a) baking soda
b) baking powder
c) washing soda
d) cherry soda

Answer: a Key 1: C Section: 7

70. All antacids are
a) acids
b) bases
c) neutral
d) salts

Answer: b Key 1: C Section: 7

71. Calcium carbonate is a common antacid. A problem with regular use of calcium carbonate based antacids is they cause
    a) constipation
    b) diarrhea
    c) high blood pressure
    d) destruction of the stomach lining

    Answer: a Key 1: A Section: 7

72. Which antacid also acts as an antidiarrheal agent?
    a) magnesium hydroxide
    b) aluminum hydroxide
    c) sodium bicarbonate
    d) calcium carbonate

    Answer: d Key 1: C Section: 7

73. Aluminum hydroxide is a popular antacid. The formula of aluminum hydroxide is
    a) $AlOH$
    b) $Al(OH)_2$
    c) $Al(OH)_3$
    d) Al_3OH

    Answer: c Key 1: A Section: 7

74. Hard water deposits (calcium carbonate) have built up around your bathroom sink. Which one of the following would be best to dissolve the deposit?
    a) ammonia
    b) bleach
    c) lye
    d) vinegar

    Answer: d Key 1: A Section: 7

75. When the pH of the blood is too high, the condition is called _____.
    a) acidosis
    b) alkalosis
    c) hyperacidity
    d) anemia

    Answer: b Key 1: C Section: 7

76. The acid in automobile batteries is
    a) hydrochloric acid
    b) nitric acid
    c) phosphoric acid
    d) sulfuric acid

    Answer: d Key 1: A Section: 8

77. A common name for hydrochloric acid is
    a) lye
    b) muriatic acid
    c) lime
    d) ammonia

    Answer: b Key 1: A Section: 8

FILL-IN-THE-BLANK

78. The leading chemical product in the US is ________________.

    Answer: Sulfuric acid Key 1: A Section: 8

MULTIPLE CHOICE

79. The cheapest and most widely used commercial base is _____.
    a) NH_3 (ammonia)
    b) Na_2O (sodium oxide)
    c) CaO (lime)
    d) NaOH (lye)

    Answer: c Key 1: A Section: 8

Chapter 8: Oxidation and Reduction

MULTIPLE CHOICE

1. With respect to energy content, reduced forms of matter are generally
   a) low in potential energy, and often make good fuels
   b) high in potential energy, and often make good fuels
   c) low in potential energy and are poor fuels
   d) high in potential energy, and are poor fuels

   Answer: b Key 1: C Section: 1

2. The corrosion of metals, such as the rusting of iron, is an example of
   a) reduction
   b) oxidation
   c) proton transfer
   d) transmutation

   Answer: b Key 1: C Section: 6

FILL-IN-THE-BLANK

3. The air that we breathe is composed of approximately ________% of oxygen by volume.

   Answer: 20% Key 1: D Section: 6

MULTIPLE CHOICE

4. The major element that composes the human body is
   a) oxygen
   b) carbon
   c) nitrogen
   d) water

   Answer: a Key 1: C Section: 6

FILL-IN-THE-BLANK

5. Over 20 billion kg of pure oxygen are produced industrially in the US each year. The source of this oxygen is ________________.

   Answer: air Key 1: D Section: 6

MULTIPLE CHOICE

6. With respect to volume, approximately what percentage of the air we breathe is composed of elemental oxygen, O_2?
   a) ≈10%
   b) ≈20%
   c) ≈50%
   d) ≈80%

   Answer: b Key 1: D Section: 6

ESSAY

7. When your car rusts, the major chemical reaction is that between the iron from the steel in the car body with the oxygen from the air to form iron(III) oxide. Write and balance the chemical equation.

   Answer: Key 1: A Section: 6

MULTIPLE CHOICE

8. When your car rusts, the major chemical reaction is that between the iron from the steel in the car body with the oxygen from the air to form iron(III) oxide. When the reaction is balanced, the coefficient of iron(III) oxide is
   a) 1
   b) 2
   c) 3
   d) 4

   Answer: b Key 1: A Section: 6

9. When metals react with oxygen they form
   a) new elements
   b) halides
   c) oxides
   d) metalloids

   Answer: c Key 1: D Section: 6

10. Magnesium burns brightly in the presence of oxygen. When magnesium reacts with oxygen, the product is
   a) MgO
   b) MgO_2
   c) Mg_2O
   d) $Mg + CO_2$

   Answer: a Key 1: A Section: 6

11. This substance is a powerful oxidizing agent and a harmful pollutant; yet a layer of it in the upper stratosphere serves as a shield from harmful ultraviolet radiation from the sun.
a) CO_2
b) O_2
c) SO_3
d) O_3 (ozone)

Answer: d Key 1: A Section: 6

12. Approximately what percentage of the Earth's crust is composed of oxygen?
a) ≈10%
b) ≈25%
c) ≈50%
d) ≈75%

Answer: c Key 1: C Section: 9

13. The composition of the sun is mostly ______.
a) oxygen
b) hydrogen
c) uranium
d) ozone

Answer: b Key 1: A Section: 9

TRUE/FALSE

14. Palladium metal can absorb up to 900 times its own volume of hydrogen.

Answer: True Key 1: A Section: 9

MULTIPLE CHOICE

15. A substance which lowers the activation energy of a chemical reaction is called a(n)
a) reducing agent
b) catalyst
c) oxidizing agent
d) carcinogen

Answer: b Key 1: A Section: 9

16. Which one of the following **IS NOT** one of the definitions of oxidation?
   a) Oxidation is the addition of oxygen to a substance
   b) Oxidation is the addition of hydrogen to a substance
   c) Oxidation is the loss of electrons from a substance
   d) Oxidation is the loss of hydrogen from a substance

   Answer: b Key 1: D Section: 3

17. Which one of the following **IS NOT** one of the definitions of reduction?
   a) Reduction is the loss of oxygen from a substance
   b) Reduction is the addition of hydrogen to a substance
   c) Reduction is the loss of electrons from a substance
   d) Reduction is the gain of electrons by a substance

   Answer: c Key 1: D Section: 1

18. When C_3H_8 is burned in oxygen, the products are
   a) $C + H_2$
   b) $CH_2 + H_2O$
   c) $CO_2 + H_2$
   d) $CO_2 + H_2O$

   Answer: d Key 1: A Section: 1

19. In which one of the following is the reactant undergoing oxidation? (Note: These reactions are not complete chemical equations.)
   a) Cl_2 ---> 2Cl-
   b) WO_3 ---> W
   c) $2H^+$ ---> H_2
   d) C ---> CO_2

   Answer: d Key 1: A Section: 1

20. Sodium bisulfite converts bromine (Br_2) to bromide (Br^-). Sodium bisulfite is a(n)
   a) acid
   b) base
   c) oxidizing agent
   d) reducing agent

   Answer: d Key 1: A Section: 1

21. In the following reaction: $C_2H_6O_2$ ----> $C_2H_4O_2 + H_2$ $C_2H_6O_2$ is
   a) oxidized
   b) reduced
   c) neutralized
   d) electrolyzed

   Answer: a Key 1: A Section: 1

22. In which one of the following is the reactant undergoing reduction? (Note: These reactions are not complete chemical equations.)
a) C_2H_4O ----> $C_2H_4O_2$
b) C_2H_4O ----> C_2H_6O
c) CO ----> CO_2
d) CH_4 ----> C

Answer: b Key 1: A Section: 1

23. In which one of the following partial reactions is the reactant undergoing reduction? (NOTE: the reactions are not complete)
a) PbO---->Pb
b) $KClO_2$---->$KClO_3$
c) SnO---->SnO_2
d) Cu_2O---->CuO

Answer: a Key 1: A Section: 1

24. In the reaction

$Cu^+ + Fe$ ----> $Cu + Fe^{2+}$

a) iron is reduced
b) copper is oxidized
c) copper(II) is the reducing agent
d) none of these

Answer: d Key 1: A Section: 1

25. In the reaction $Cu^+ + Fe$ -------> $Cu + Fe^{2+}$
a) Fe is the reducing agent
b) Cu is the reducing agent
c) Cu^+ is the reducing agent
d) Fe^{2+} is the reducing agent

Answer: a Key 1: A Section: 1

26. Every reduction reaction MUST be accompanied by:
a) an oxidation reaction
b) formation of covalent bonds
c) formation of ionic bonds
d) formation of water

Answer: a Key 1: C Section: 1

27. All redox reactions occur with the transfer of:
    a) protons
    b) electrons
    c) oxygen
    d) hydrogen

    Answer: b Key 1: C Section: 1

28. Which substance is an oxidizing agent?
    a) NaOH
    b) H_2O_2
    c) HCl
    d) NaCl

    Answer: b Key 1: A Section: 2

29. Hydrogen gas converts tungsten oxide to tungsten metal. Hydrogen (H_2) is a(n)
    a) acid
    b) base
    c) oxidizing agent
    d) reducing agent

    Answer: d Key 1: A Section: 2

30. Which substance is a reducing agent?
    a) C
    b) F_2
    c) H_2O_2
    d) CO_2

    Answer: a Key 1: A Section: 2

31. In a reaction, the substance undergoing reduction serves as the
    a) electron donor
    b) proton donor
    c) oxidizing agent
    d) reducing agent

    Answer: c Key 1: A Section: 2

32. In a reaction, the substance undergoing oxidation serves as the
    a) electron donor
    b) proton donor
    c) oxidizing agent
    d) reducing agent

    Answer: d Key 1: A Section: 2

33. In the reaction Fe_2O_3 + $3H_2$ ---> 2Fe + $3H_2O$ the reducing agent is
a) Fe_2O_3
b) H_2
c) Fe
d) H_2O

Answer: b Key 1: A Section: 2

34. Copper is plated on zinc by immersing a piece of zinc into a solution containing copper(II) ions. In the plating reaction, zinc
a) loses two electrons and is oxidized
b) loses two electrons and is reduced
c) gains two electrons and is oxidized
d) gains two electrons and is reduced

Answer: a Key 1: A Section: 3

35. Copper is plated on zinc by immersing a piece of zinc into a solution containing copper(II) ions. In the plating reaction, copper(II) ions
a) lose two electrons and are oxidized
b) lose two electrons and are reduced
c) gain two electrons and are oxidized
d) gain two electrons and are reduced

Answer: d Key 1: A Section: 3

36. Silver is plated on copper by immersing a piece of copper into a solution containing silver(I) ions. In the plating reaction, silver(I) ions
a) lose one electron and are oxidized
b) lose one electron and are reduced
c) gain one electron and are oxidized
d) gain one electron and are reduced

Answer: d Key 1: A Section: 3

37. Silver is plated on copper by immersing a piece of copper into a solution containing silver(I) ions. In the plating reaction, copper
a) is oxidized and is the oxidizing agent
b) is oxidized and is the reducing agent
c) is reduced and is the oxidizing agent
d) is reduced and is the reducing agent

Answer: b Key 1: A Section: 3

38. Silver is plated on copper by immersing a piece of copper into a solution containing silver(I) ions. In the plating reaction, silver(I)
a) is oxidized and is the oxidizing agent
b) is oxidized and is the reducing agent
c) is reduced and is the oxidizing agent
d) is reduced and is the reducing agent

Answer: c Key 1: A Section: 3

39. An electrochemical cell is a device that converts chemical energy into
a) electrical energy
b) chemical energy
c) nuclear energy
d) light energy

Answer: a Key 1: C Section: 3

40. A device that generates an electrical current by taking advantage of a difference in the spontaneous tendency of substances to lose and gain electrons is called a(n)
a) electrochemical cell
b) electrolysis cell
c) electroplating cell
d) electrolyte cell

Answer: a Key 1: C Section: 3

41. A battery is a device that converts chemical energy into
a) electrical energy
b) chemical energy
c) nuclear energy
d) light energy

Answer: a Key 1: C Section: 3

42. A major advantage of lead storage batteries is that they are
a) lightweight
b) rechargeable
c) disposable
d) all of the above

Answer: b Key 1: A Section: 3

43. The small button cells used in hearing aids and hand-calculators are being replaced by _______ cells.
a) Ni-Cad
b) fuel
c) zinc-air
d) lead-acid

Answer: c Key 1: A Section: 3

44. Which one of the following IS NOT one of the definitions of oxidation?
    a) Oxidation is the addition of oxygen to a substance
    b) Oxidation is the addition of electrons to a substance
    c) Oxidation is the loss of electrons from a substance
    d) Oxidation is the loss of hydrogen from a substance

    Answer: b Key 1: D Section: 3

45. A substance produced as a lead-acid storage battery generates an electric current is:
    a) Pb
    b) $PbSO_4$
    c) PbO_2
    d) H_2SO_4

    Answer: b Key 1: A Section: 3

46. A substance that is reduced as a lead-acid storage battery generates an electric current is:
    a) Pb
    b) $PbSO_4$
    c) PbO_2
    d) H_2SO_4

    Answer: c Key 1: A Section: 3

47. The approximate voltage generated in the reaction
    $Pb + PbO_2 + 2\ H_2SO_4 \text{ ---> } 2\ PbSO_4 + 2\ H_2O$ is:
    a) -0.4
    b) 1.33
    c) 1.69
    d) 2.04

    Answer: d Key 1: A Section: 3

48. The black, granular material that fills a common flashlight (between the carbon rod and the zinc shell) is manganese dioxide, MnO_2. The oxidation state of manganese in MnO_2 is:
    a) +2
    b) -2
    c) +4
    d) -4

    Answer: c Key 1: A Section: 3

49. Aluminum is more reactive than iron, yet it is used today for a variety of applications in which iron would corrode (cans, rain gutters, etc). The reason for the corrosion durability of aluminum is
a) aluminum does not react with oxygen
b) very unreactive aluminum oxide forms a thin layer on aluminum
c) aluminum does not undergo oxidation
d) all aluminum products are treated with a plastic coating

Answer: b Key 1: A Section: 4

50. The black tarnish on silver is
a) AgOH
b) Ag_2O
c) AgCl
d) Ag_2S

Answer: d Key 1: A Section: 4

51. The removal of silver tarnish from silverware using aluminum foil and a solution of electrolyte is an example of
a) oxidation of aluminum metal
b) reduction of silver ions
c) an example of an electrochemical cell
d) all of the above

Answer: d Key 1: A Section: 4

52. The strongest oxidizing agent among the following is:
a) lithium metal
b) liquid bromine
c) butane
d) chloride ion

Answer: b Key 1: A Section: 4

53. The strongest oxidizing agent among the following is:
a) oxygen
b) hydrogen
c) lithium
d) fluorine

Answer: d Key 1: A Section: 4

54. An oxidizing agent that is often used to oxidize black PbS to white $PbSO_4$ is
a) $Na_2Cr_2O_7$
b) O_2
c) H_2O_2
d) H_2

Answer: c Key 1: A Section: 5

55. Most chemical explosions are ______ reactions.
    a) nuclear fission
    b) oxidation-reduction
    c) neutralization
    d) precipitation

    Answer: b Key 1: A Section: 5

56. Which substance is a common oxidizing agent?
    a) C
    b) $Na_2Cr_2O_7$
    c) H_2
    d) Na

    Answer: b Key 1: A Section: 7

TRUE/FALSE

57. In Food Chemistry, reducing agents are sometimes referred to as antioxidants.

    Answer: True Key 1: A Section: 8

MULTIPLE CHOICE

58. In the reaction, $N_2 + 3H_2$ ---> $2NH_3$, hydrogen is
    a) a catalyst
    b) a product
    c) a reducing agent
    d) an oxidizing agent

    Answer: c Key 1: A Section: 9

59. Antiseptics are substances that
    a) are pain killers
    b) kill microorganisms
    c) relieve inflammation
    d) are the same as anesthetics

    Answer: b Key 1: A Section: 7

60. Given their mode of action, antiseptics are generally best classified as
    a) oxidizing agents
    b) reducing agents
    c) acids
    d) bases

    Answer: a Key 1: A Section: 7

61. Swimming pools are "chlorinated" in order to
    a) improve taste of the water
    b) disinfect the water
    c) clarify the water
    d) purify the water

    Answer: b Key 1: A Section: 7

62. Benzoyl peroxide, used in the treatment of acne, is
    a) an acid
    b) a base
    c) an oxidizing agent
    d) a reducing agent

    Answer: c Key 1: A Section: 7

63. Most household bleaches act as
    a) oxidizing agents
    b) reducing agents
    c) electron donors
    d) proton donors

    Answer: a Key 1: A Section: 7

64. The active ingredient in many laundry bleaches and bleaching powders is
    a) hydrogen peroxide, H_2O_2
    b) hypochlorite ion, ClO^-
    c) sodium dichromate, $Na_2Cr_2O_7$
    d) chlorine, Cl_2

    Answer: b Key 1: A Section: 7

65. Which substance is a common reducing agent used in the production of metals from ores?
    a) C
    b) $Na_2Cr_2O_7$
    c) H_2O
    d) NaCl

    Answer: a Key 1: A Section: 8

66. In a black and white photograph, the black area on the photographic negative represents
   a) the region where light fell and silver metal has been deposited during development
   b) the region where light fell and silver metal has been removed during development
   c) a region where light did not fall and silver metal has been deposited during development
   d) a region where light did not fall and silver metal has been removed during development

   Answer: a Key 1: A Section: 8

67. The chemical basis of converting light into a photographic silver image is based on the fact that
   a) Ag^+ exposed to light is easier to reduce to Ag than unexposed Ag^+
   b) Ag^+ exposed to light is more difficult to reduce to Ag than unexposed Ag^+
   c) Ag^+ exposed to light is easier to oxidize to Ag than unexposed Ag^+
   d) Ag^+ exposed to light is more difficult to oxidize to Ag than unexposed Ag^+

   Answer: a Key 1: A Section: 8

68. The "white" areas in a black & white "positive" print contain
   a) silver metal
   b) no silver metal
   c) fixer
   d) silver salts

   Answer: b Key 1: A Section: 8

69. The only natural process that produces oxygen is
   a) catalysis
   b) photosynthesis
   c) rainfall
   d) electrochemical cells

   Answer: b Key 1: A Section: 8

70. Human cells obtain energy by
   a) oxidizing carbohydrates
   b) reducing proteins
   c) reducing carbon dioxide
   d) absorbing sunlight

   Answer: a Key 1: C Section: 10

71. Photosynthesis involves the
    a) reduction of carbon dioxide
    b) oxidation of carbon dioxide
    c) reduction of carbohydrates
    d) oxidation of carbohydrates

    Answer: a Key 1: C Section: 10

72. In the photosynthesis reaction: $6CO_2 + 6H_2O \text{ ---> } C_6H_{12}O_6 + 6O_2$ carbon dioxide is
    a) oxidized
    b) reduced
    c) oxidized and reduced
    d) neither oxidized nor reduced

    Answer: b Key 1: A Section: 10

73. In the photosynthesis reaction: $6CO_2 + 6H_2O \text{ ---> } C_6H_{12}O_6 + 6O_2$ the substance that serves as the reducing agent is
    a) carbon dioxide
    b) water
    c) sunlight
    d) glucose, $C_6H_{12}O_6$

    Answer: b Key 1: A Section: 10

Chapter 9: Organic Chemistry

MULTIPLE CHOICE

1. Organic chemistry is most broadly defined as
   a) the chemistry of living systems
   b) the chemistry of substances produced by living systems
   c) the chemistry of the compounds of carbon
   d) the chemistry of the non-metallic compounds

   Answer: c Key 1: D Key 2: I

2. Approximately what percentage of known compounds are classified as organic compounds?
   a) ≈95%
   b) ≈70%
   c) ≈40%
   d) ≈20%

   Answer: a Key 1: C Key 2: I

SHORT ANSWER

3. What feature of carbon is probably most responsible for the fact that 95% of all compounds contain carbon? Discuss your answer briefly.

   Answer: catenation Key 1: C Section: 1

ESSAY

4. Comment on the following statement from *Chemistry for Changing Times*: "Carbon can form an almost infinite number of molecules of various shapes, sizes and compositions."

   Answer: Key 1: C Section: 1

MULTIPLE CHOICE

5. The most unique property of carbon is its ability to
   a) form four bonds
   b) bond to oxygen
   c) bond to nitrogen
   d) bond to carbon

   Answer: d Key 1: C Section: 1

6. The process by which carbon atoms bond to other carbon atoms to form long chains of carbon atoms is called
   a) catenation
   b) chaination
   c) chirality
   d) cationation

   Answer: a Key 1: D Section: 1

7. An organic compound is best defined as
   a) a compound containing carbon
   b) a compound of carbon and hydrogen
   c) a compound produced by a living organism
   d) a compound that is NOT produced in a laboratory

   Answer: a Key 1: D Section: 1

8. The first organic compound to be synthesized in a chemist's laboratory was
   a) cholesterol
   b) chlorophyll
   c) urea
   d) benzene

   Answer: c Key 1: A Section: 1

9. The first recorded synthesis of an organic compound in a scientific laboratory was by
   a) Isaac Newton in 1665
   b) Benjamin Franklin in 1788
   c) Friedrich Wholer in 1828
   d) Thomas Edison in 1888

   Answer: c Key 1: C Section: 1

10. Carbon is almost always
    a) monovalent
    b) divalent
    c) trivalent
    d) tetravalent

    Answer: d Key 1: C Section: 2

11. The unique aspect of a **saturated** hydrocarbon is that it must contain
    a) only carbon and hydrogen
    b) only single bonds
    c) single and double bonds
    d) single, double and triple bonds

    Answer: b Key 1: C Section: 2

12. The simplest alkane is
    a) monalkane
    b) ethane
    c) methane
    d) propane

    Answer: c Key 1: D Section: 2

FILL-IN-THE-BLANK

13. The formula of the three carbon alkane is ________________.

    Answer: C_3H_8 Key 1: A Section: 2

14. The name of the three carbon alkane is ________________.

    Answer: propane Key 1: A Section: 2

MULTIPLE CHOICE

15. Petroleum jelly is
    a) a mixture of low carbon number hydrocarbons
    b) a mixture of moderate carbon number hydrocarbons
    c) a mixture of higher carbon number hydrocarbons
    d) none of the above

    Answer: c Key 1: A Section: 2

FILL-IN-THE-BLANK

16. The formula for the two carbon alkane is ________________.

    Answer: C_2H_6 Key 1: A Section: 2

17. The name of the two carbon alkane is ________________.

    Answer: ethane Key 1: A Section: 2

MULTIPLE CHOICE

18. What is the name of the compound with a formula $CH_3CH_2CH_3$?
    a) methane
    b) ethane
    c) propane
    d) butane

    Answer: c Key 1: A Section: 2

19. A compound containing only carbon and hydrogen and which has no double bonds between atoms is classified as an
a) alkane
b) alkene
c) alkyne
d) aromatic

Answer: a Key 1: D Section: 2

20. What is the name of the compound with a formula CH_3CH_3?
a) methane
b) ethane
c) propane
d) butane

Answer: b Key 1: A Section: 2

21. What is the name of the compound with a formula $CH_3CH_2CH_2CH_3$?
a) methane
b) ethane
c) propane
d) butane

Answer: d Key 1: A Section: 2

22. How many different structural isomers are there for a hydrocarbon with the formula C_4H_{10}?
a) 1
b) 2
c) 3
d) 4

Answer: b Key 1: A Section: 2

23. How many different structural isomers are there for a hydrocarbon with the formula C_5H_{12}?
a) 1
b) 2
c) 3
d) 4

Answer: c Key 1: A Section: 2

24. How many different structural isomers are there for a hydrocarbon with the formula C_6H_{14}?
a) 1
b) 2
c) 3
d) >4

Answer: d Key 1: A Section: 2

25. Which of the following **IS NOT** a reason for the great variety of organic molecules?
    a) Catenation by carbon
    b) Carbon atoms can form more than four bonds
    c) Isomerism
    d) Carbon forms bonds with a variety of elements, such as H, O, N, Cl, Br,...

    Answer: b Key 1: C Section: 2

26. Alkanes are often called
    a) unsaturated hydrocarbons
    b) saturated hydrocarbons
    c) carbohydrates
    d) saturated fats

    Answer: b Key 1: C Section: 2

27. Compounds with the same number and kinds of atoms but with different structures are known as
    a) homologs
    b) isotopes
    c) isomers
    d) allotropes

    Answer: c Key 1: D Section: 2

28. The compounds CH_3CH_3 and $CH_3CH_2CH_3$ are
    a) isomers
    b) allotropes
    c) isotopes
    d) homologs

    Answer: d Key 1: D Section: 2

29. The condensed structural formula for the molecule below is

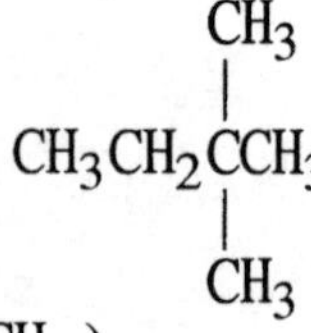

    a) $CH_3CH_2C(CH_3)_3$
    b) $CH_3CH_2CH_2(CH_3)_2CH_3$
    c) $CH_3CH_2CH_2CH_2CH_2CH_3$
    d) none of the above

    Answer: a Key 1: A Section: 2

30. The condensed structural formula for the molecule below is

$$\begin{array}{c} \quad\quad\quad\; CH_3 \\ \quad\quad\quad\; | \\ CH_3CH_2CH \\ \quad\quad\quad\; | \\ \quad\quad\quad\; CH_3 \end{array}$$

a) $CH_3CH_2C(CH_3)_2CH_3$
b) $CH_3CH_2CH(CH_3)CH_3$
c) $CH_3CH_2CH_2CH_2CH_2CH_3$
d) none of the above

Answer: b Key 1: A Section: 2

31. The formula for hexane is
a) C_6H_6
b) C_6H_{12}
c) C_6H_{14}
d) C_6H_{10}

Answer: c Key 1: A Section: 2

32. An emollient is a _____
a) skin softener
b) sun screen
c) laxative
d) detergent

Answer: a Key 1: A Section: 2

33. Which one of the following statements is NOT true of all alkanes?
a) All alkanes burn to produce carbon dioxide and water.
b) All alkanes consist of carbon and hydrogen.
c) All alkanes exist as two or more isomers.
d) All alkanes fit the general molecular formula C_nH_{2n+2}.

Answer: c Key 1: C Section: 2

34. The chemical formula of cyclopropane is
a) C_3H_3
b) C_3H_6
c) C_3H_7
d) C_3H_8

Answer: b Key 1: A Section: 3

35. The chemical formula of cyclohexane is
    a) C_6H_6
    b) C_6H_8
    c) C_6H_{10}
    d) C_6H_{12}

    Answer: d Key 1: A Section: 3

36. The chemical formula of cyclopentane is
    a) C_5H_6
    b) C_5H_8
    c) C_5H_{10}
    d) C_5H_{12}

    Answer: c Key 1: A Section: 3

37. Propane, benzene, acetylene, and 2-butene are all examples of
    a) alkenes
    b) alkanes
    c) aromatic compounds
    d) hydrocarbons

    Answer: d Key 1: A Section: 3

38. A molecular formula of an alkane is
    a) C_7H_{16}
    b) C_9H_{18}
    c) C_5H_8
    d) C_6H_6

    Answer: a Key 1: A Section: 3

39. The most important commercial organic compound is
    a) methane, CH_4
    b) ethane, CH_3CH_3
    c) ethylene, $CH_2{=}CH_2$
    d) propane, $CH_3CH_2CH_3$

    Answer: c Key 1: D Section: 4

40. Acetylene is
    a) CH_4
    b) C_2H_6
    c) C_2H_4
    d) C_2H_2

    Answer: d Key 1: A Section: 4

41. Acetylene is an
    a) alkane
    b) alkene
    c) alkyne
    d) aromatic compound

    Answer: c Key 1: A Section: 4

42. A hydrocarbon with six carbon atoms containing one ring and a double bond will have the formula
    a) C_6H_{16}
    b) C_6H_{14}
    c) C_6H_{12}
    d) C_6H_{10}

    Answer: d Key 1: A Section: 4

43. A hydrocarbon with seven carbon atoms containing a ring and two double bonds will have the formula
    a) C_7H_{16}
    b) C_7H_{14}
    c) C_7H_{12}
    d) C_7H_{10}

    Answer: d Key 1: C Section: 4

44. The formula for propyne is
    a) C_3H_6
    b) C_3H_4
    c) C_3H_8
    d) C_3H_3

    Answer: b Key 1: A Section: 4

45. The hydrocarbon that is used in torches along with oxygen to produce very hot flames for cutting and welding is
    a) ethylene
    b) methane
    c) propane
    d) acetylene

    Answer: d Key 1: A Section: 4

46. The hydrocarbon that is used by food distributors to ripen green fruits and vegetables is
    a) ethylene
    b) methane
    c) octane
    d) acetylene

    Answer: a Key 1: A Section: 4

47. Which of the following compounds is saturated?
    a) butene
    b) butane
    c) propyne
    d) butadiene

    Answer: b Key 1: C Section: 4

48. A molecular formula of an alkene is
    a) C_7H_{16}
    b) C_9H_{18}
    c) C_5H_8
    d) C_6H_6

    Answer: b Key 1: A Section: 4

49. A molecular formula of an alkyne is
    a) C_7H_{16}
    b) C_9H_{18}
    c) C_5H_8
    d) C_6H_6

    Answer: c Key 1: A Section: 4

50. The formula of benzene is
    a) C_2H_2
    b) C_4H_4
    c) C_6H_6
    d) C_6H_{12}

    Answer: c Key 1: D Section: 5

ESSAY

51. Although benzene is a cyclic hydrocarbon that appears to contain three double bonds, it does not act like a cyclic alkene. Discuss.

    Answer: Key 1: C Section: 5

52. Draw the structure of a compound that is an isomer of benzene.

    Answer: Key 1: C Section: 5

MULTIPLE CHOICE

53. Benzene is an unsaturated hydrocarbon. An interesting property of benzene is that
    a) it is a liquid at room temperature
    b) it does not undergo the same reactions as other unsaturated hydrocarbons
    c) it contains only carbon and hydrogen
    d) it has a ring of carbon atoms in its structure

    Answer: b Key 1: C Section: 5

54. The correct structure for benzene was proposed by _____ in 1865.
    a) Boyle
    b) Kekule
    c) Faraday
    d) Curie

    Answer: b Key 1: A Section: 5

55. Organic compounds that contain a benzene ring or possess certain properties similar to those of benzene are called ______ compounds.
    a) alkaloid
    b) acidic
    c) aromatic
    d) saturated

    Answer: c Key 1: A Section: 5

56. A molecular formula of an aromatic hydrocarbon is
    a) C_7H_{16}
    b) C_9H_{18}
    c) C_5H_8
    d) C_6H_6

    Answer: d Key 1: A Section: 5

57. Hydrocarbons that undergo substitution reactions as well as combustion reactions are
    a) alkanes and alkenes
    b) alkynes and alkenes
    c) alkanes and aromatics
    d) alkenes and aromatics

    Answer: c Key 1: C Section: 5

58. Chlorinated hydrocarbons, such as carbon tetrachloride CCl_4, make good dry cleaning solvents because
a) they dissolve in water
b) they dissolve water insoluble stains, like grease and oil
c) they are not liquids at room temperature
d) they cause no significant health problems

Answer: b Key 1: A Section: 6

59. The compound with the formula, $CHCl_3$, was used as an anesthetic in earlier times, but has been found to have some serious side effects. The compound is called
a) methyl chloride
b) methylene chloride
c) chloroform
d) carbon tetrachloride

Answer: c Key 1: A Section: 6

SHORT ANSWER

60. How is it that a class of compounds as chemically inert as the CFCs can pose an environmental problem like the destruction of the ozone layer?

Answer:
They are inert at the Earth's surface, but react in the high energy environment of the ozone layer.

Key 1: C Section: 6

61. Why do many chlorinated hydrocarbons, like DDT and PCBs, become concentrated in the tissues of animals?

Answer: Fat solubility Key 1: C Section: 6

MULTIPLE CHOICE

62. When carbon tetrachloride reacts with hot water it produces phosgene ($COCl_2$). Phosgene was used in poison-gas warfare in World War I. Based upon this chemistry, carbon tetrachloride is no longer used in
a) fire extinguishers
b) dry cleaning
c) chemical reactions
d) toilet bowl cleaners

Answer: a Key 1: A Section: 6

63. In general, CFCs are
    a) solids with high melting points
    b) solids with low melting points
    c) liquids with high boiling points
    d) gases, or liquids with low boiling points

    Answer: d Key 1: A Section: 6

64. CFCs are most likely to be found in
    a) refrigerators
    b) pesticides
    c) toasters
    d) gasoline

    Answer: a Key 1: A Section: 6

65. With respect to reactivity on the surface of the earth, chlorofluorocarbons are
    a) very reactive
    b) very unreactive
    c) moderately reactive
    d) variable depending upon the chlorofluorocarbon

    Answer: b Key 1: A Section: 6

66. Perfluorocarbons are
    a) hydrocarbons in which all hydrogen atoms have been replaced by fluorine
    b) hydrocarbons in which most hydrogen atoms have been replaced by fluorine
    c) hydrocarbons in which there is one fluorine per carbon atom
    d) none of the above

    Answer: a Key 1: D Section: 6

67. Perfluorocarbons have been used in which of the following?
    a) temporary blood substitutes
    b) nonstick cooking surfaces
    c) oxygen solvent and breathing liquid for mice
    d) all of the above

    Answer: d Key 1: A Section: 6

ESSAY

68. Explain what a functional group is and how it simplifies the study of organic chemistry.

    Answer: Key 1: C Section: 7

MULTIPLE CHOICE

69. In representing the general formula of various functional groups, the symbol **R** stands for
    a) a halogen atom
    b) a ring
    c) an aromatic group
    d) an alkyl group

    Answer: d Key 1: C Section: 7

70. Alcohols are characterized by which functional group?
    a) hydroxyl
    b) carboxyl
    c) halide
    d) ester

    Answer: a Key 1: C Section: 7

71. In organic chemistry, compounds are generally classified by
    a) state
    b) functional group
    c) color
    d) odor

    Answer: b Key 1: C Section: 7

72. The formula of methanol is
    a) COH
    b) CHOH
    c) CH_2OH
    d) CH_3OH

    Answer: d Key 1: A Section: 8

73. When wood is heated in the absence of air, the wood is destructively distilled and condensed to a liquid mixture. The primary component of this mixture is
    a) methanol
    b) ethanol
    c) rubbing alcohol
    d) gasoline

    Answer: a Key 1: A Section: 8

74. Methanol is an important solvent. It is also an important starting material for the synthesis of other molecules. Most methanol today is obtained from
    a) destructive distillation of wood
    b) hydrogenation of carbon monoxide
    c) fermentation of corn
    d) decomposition of animal waste

    Answer: b Key 1: A Section: 8

75. The intoxicating alcohol in "alcoholic" beverages is
    a) ethanol
    b) methanol
    c) propanol
    d) a mixture of the above

    Answer: a Key 1: D Section: 8

76. A bottle of rum is labelled as "80 proof." The percentage of ethanol by volume in this alcoholic beverage is
    a) 8%
    b) 40%
    c) 80%
    d) 160%

    Answer: b Key 1: A Section: 8

77. Distillation of fermented grain "beer" yields 95% ethanol. What is the proof of this "grain alcohol"?
    a) 47.5
    b) 95
    c) 190
    d) 200

    Answer: c Key 1: A Section: 8

78. Excessive ingestion of ethanol over a long period may cause which of the following?
    a) physiological addiction
    b) memory loss
    c) deterioration of the liver
    d) all of the above

    Answer: d Key 1: C Section: 8

79. Ethanol acts as a mild
    a) stimulant
    b) depressant
    c) hallucinogen
    d) narcotic

    Answer: b Key 1: A Section: 8

80. What is the percent alcohol by volume in a beverage that is 36 proof?
    a) 3.6%
    b) 18%
    c) 36%
    d) 72%

    Answer: b Key 1: A Section: 8

81. Which substance causes fetal alcohol syndrome?
    a) CH_3OH
    b) CH_3CH_2OH
    c) $CH_3CHOHCH_3$
    d) CH_3OCH_3

    Answer: b Key 1: D Section: 8

82. Citronellol, $C_{10}H_{19}OH$, is a constituent of rose and germanium oils. It is used in perfumery. Chemically, citronellol is an
    a) alcohol
    b) acid
    c) alkane
    d) amine

    Answer: a Key 1: C Section: 8

83. A homologous series of alcohols contains
    a) the same number of carbon atoms, but a different number of hydroxyl groups
    b) the same number of carbon atoms and the same number of hydroxyl groups
    c) a different number of carbon atoms, but the same number of hydroxyl groups
    d) only isomers

    Answer: c Key 1: C Section: 8

84. The main ingredient in most antifreezes is
    a) ethanol
    b) ethylene glycol
    c) glycerol
    d) gasoline

    Answer: b Key 1: A Section: 8

85. Glycerol is an alcohol with __________ hydroxyl groups
    a) one
    b) two
    c) three
    d) four

    Answer: c Key 1: C Section: 8

86. Compounds with a hydroxyl group attached directly to a benzene ring are called
    a) alcohols
    b) aromatic hydrocarbons
    c) ethers
    d) phenols

    Answer: d Key 1: A Section: 9

87. Compounds that have two alkyl groups attached to an oxygen atom are called
    a) alcohols
    b) phenols
    c) esters
    d) ethers

    Answer: d Key 1: A Section: 10

ESSAY

88. Give the structural formula of diethyl ether.

    Answer: Key 1: C Section: 10

SHORT ANSWER

89. Alcohols and ethers are similar functional groups, yet they have very different properties. Discuss the structural similarities and differences between ethers and alcohols.

    Answer: ROH vs ROR Key 1: C Section: 10

MULTIPLE CHOICE

90. Methyl tert-butyl ether (MTBE, $CH_3OC(CH_3)_3$) is an important additive in
    a) detergents
    b) foods
    c) gasoline
    d) plastics

    Answer: c Key 1: A Section: 10

91. Methyl tert-butyl ether (MTBE, $CH_3OC(CH_3)_3$) is an important gasoline additive. MTBE is an example of an ether with the general structure
a) ROR
b) ROH
c) ROR'
d) R'OH

Answer: c Key 1: A Section: 10

92. Diethyl ether is the most important of the ethers. It is an example of an ether with the general structure
a) ROR
b) ROH
c) ROR'
d) R'OH

Answer: a Key 1: A Section: 10

93. The abbreviation ROR' is used to represent the general formula of a(n)
a) ether
b) alcohol
c) ester
d) phenol

Answer: a Key 1: A Section: 10

94. Aldehydes and ketones share a common functional group. The group is the
a) hydroxyl group
b) phenol group
c) ether group
d) carbonyl group

Answer: d Key 1: C Section: 11

95. The compound below is a(n)

$$CH_3CH_2\overset{\overset{\displaystyle O}{\|}}{C}{-}H$$

a) carboxylic acid
b) aldehyde
c) ketone
d) alcohol

Answer: b Key 1: A Section: 11

96. The compound below is a(n)

$$CH_3CH_2\overset{\overset{\displaystyle O}{\|}}{C}CH_3$$

a) alcohol
b) aldehyde
c) carboxylic acid
d) ketone

Answer: d Key 1: A Section: 11

97. The compound below is a(n)

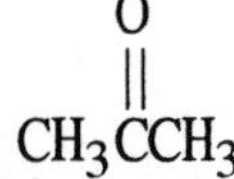

a) carboxylic acid
b) aldehyde
c) ketone
d) alcohol

Answer: c Key 1: A Section: 11

98. The compound below is a(n)

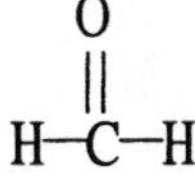

a) carboxylic acid
b) aldehyde
c) ketone
d) alcohol

Answer: b Key 1: A Section: 11

99. The general formula for a ketone is
a) ROR'
b) RCOOH
c) RCOR'
d) RCOOR'

Answer: c Key 1: C Section: 11

100. The compound below is commonly known as

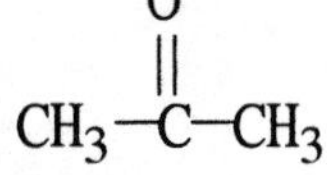

a) acetone
b) acetaldehyde
c) benzaldehyde
d) formaldehyde

Answer: a Key 1: A Section: 11

101. The compound below is commonly known as

$$CH_3-\overset{\overset{\displaystyle O}{||}}{C}-H$$

a) acetone
b) acetaldehyde
c) benzaldehyde
d) formaldehyde

Answer: b Key 1: A Section: 11

102. The simplest aldehyde is
a) acetaldehyde
b) formaldehyde
c) benzaldehyde
d) unaldehyde

Answer: b Key 1: A Section: 11

103. The functional group of the organic acids is the
a) hydroxyl group
b) amine group
c) carbonyl group
d) carboxyl group

Answer: d Key 1: C Section: 12

104. When a bee stings, one of the compounds it injects is
a) acetic acid
b) butyric acid
c) formic acid
d) hydrochloric acid

Answer: c Key 1: A Section: 12

105. One of the primary ingredients in vinegar is
a) acetic acid
b) butyric acid
c) formic acid
d) hydrochloric acid

Answer: a Key 1: A Section: 12

106. The -COOH group represents the
a) carboxyl group
b) carbonyl group
c) alcohol group
d) aldehyde group

Answer: a Key 1: C Section: 12

107. The simplest carboxylic acid is commonly known as
   a) acetic acid
   b) butyric acid
   c) formic acid
   d) propionic acid

   Answer: c Key 1: A Section: 12

108. One of the compounds that is present in rancid butter and body odor is
   a) acetic acid
   b) butyric acid
   c) benzaldehyde
   d) formaldehyde

   Answer: b Key 1: A Section: 12

109. The compound below is classified as a(n)

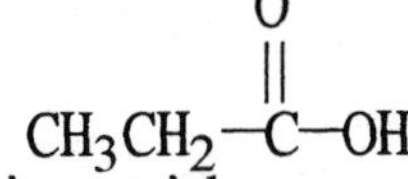

   a) carboxylic acid
   b) aldehyde
   c) ketone
   d) ester

   Answer: a Key 1: C Section: 12

110. The salts of carboxylic acids, such as sodium benzoate, are often used in foods as
   a) flavor enhancers
   b) colorings
   c) sweeteners
   d) preservatives

   Answer: d Key 1: A Section: 12

111. The general formula for a carboxylic acid is
   a) ROR'
   b) RCOOH
   c) RCOR'
   d) RCOOR'

   Answer: b Key 1: C Section: 12

ESSAY

112. Structurally, aldehydes are to ketones as carboxylic acids are to esters. Use the general formulas of these compounds to make sense of this comparison.

   Answer: Key 1: C Section: 13

MULTIPLE CHOICE

113. This compound is named

$$CH_3CH_2CH_2\overset{\overset{\displaystyle O}{\|}}{C}{-}OCH_2CH_3$$

a) hexanone
b) ethyl butyl ether
c) butyl ethylate
d) ethyl butyrate

Answer: d Key 1: A Section: 13

114. The compound below is classified as a(n)

$$CH_3CH_2CH_2\overset{\overset{\displaystyle O}{\|}}{C}{-}OCH_2CH_3$$

a) aldehyde
b) carboxylic acid
c) ester
d) ketone

Answer: c Key 1: C Section: 13

115. The general formula for an ester is
a) ROR'
b) RCOOH
c) RCOR'
d) RCOOR'

Answer: d Key 1: A Section: 13

SHORT ANSWER

116. Name and draw the structure of the compound formed by the reaction of ethanol with formic acid.

Answer: ethyl formate Key 1: A Section: 13

117. Name and draw the structure of the compound formed by the reaction of ethanol with acetic acid.

Answer: ethyl acetate Key 1: A Section: 13

MULTIPLE CHOICE

118. The compound formed by the reaction of a carboxylic acid with an alcohol is a(n)
    a) aldehyde
    b) ester
    c) ether
    d) ketone

    Answer: b Key 1: C Section: 13

119. Many of the flavors isolated from foods are
    a) carboxylic acids
    b) esters
    c) alcohols
    d) ketones

    Answer: b Key 1: A Section: 13

120. An analgesic is a substance known as a(n)
    a) fever reducer
    b) disinfectant
    c) anesthetic
    d) pain reliever

    Answer: d Key 1: A Section: 13

121. This substance used as an analgesic was first isolated from willow bark.
    a) benzene
    b) acetic acid
    c) salicylic acid
    d) ethanol

    Answer: c Key 1: A Section: 13

122. This substance is an ester of the phenol group of salicylic acid with acetic acid and is commonly called
    a) aspirin
    b) Maalox
    c) Milk of Magnesia
    d) Tylenol

    Answer: a Key 1: A Section: 13

ESSAY

123. Aldehydes and ketones are similar functional groups. What is the difference between an aldehyde and a ketone? Use acetaldehyde and acetone as examples.

     Answer: Key 1: C Section: 14

MULTIPLE CHOICE

124. Amines are derivatives of
     a) ammonia
     b) methane
     c) water
     d) amino acids

     Answer: a Key 1: C Section: 14

125. The compound CH_3NH_2 is called
     a) methylamine
     b) dimethylamine
     c) trimethylamine
     d) methyl ammonia

     Answer: a Key 1: A Section: 14

126. The compound $(CH_3)_3N$ is called
     a) methylamine
     b) dimethylamine
     c) trimethylamine
     d) methyl ammonia

     Answer: c Key 1: A Section: 14

ESSAY

127. There are two amines with the formula C_2H_7N. Draw and name the two isomers.

     Answer: Key 1: A Section: 14

128. There are four isomeric amines with the formula C_3H_9N. Draw three different isomers for this formula.

     Answer: Key 1: A Section: 14

129. There are many isomeric amines with the formula C_4H_7N. Draw and name three isomers.

     Answer: Key 1: A Section: 14

MULTIPLE CHOICE

130. When an amine dissolves in water the pH of the solution will be
   a) < 7
   b) = 7
   c) > 7
   d) more information is needed to predict pH

   Answer: c Key 1: A Section: 14

131. Amines are
   a) acidic
   b) basic
   c) neutral
   d) variable with respect to acid/base behavior

   Answer: b Key 1: C Section: 14

132. The **simplest** aromatic amine is called
   a) aniline
   b) acetaldehydemino group
   c) aromatic ammonia
   d) acetamide

   Answer: a Key 1: A Section: 14

133. The reaction between a carboxylic acid and an amine yields a(n)
   a) aldehyde
   b) amide
   c) ester
   d) ketone

   Answer: b Key 1: C Section: 14

134. The compound below is a(n)

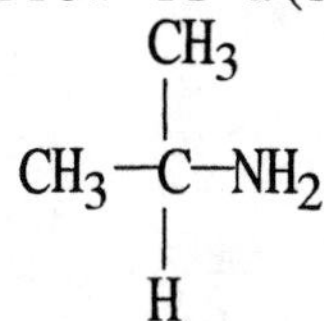

   a) acid
   b) amine
   c) amide
   d) ester

   Answer: b Key 1: C Section: 14

135. Amino acids are multifunctional compounds that contain
a) carboxyl and amine groups
b) carboxyl and amide groups
c) ester and amine groups
d) aldehyde and amide groups

Answer: a Key 1: C Section: 14

136. Amino acids are the "building blocks" of
a) carbohydrates
b) fats
c) proteins
d) vitamins

Answer: c Key 1: C Section: 14

137. The following multifunctional compound is a(n)

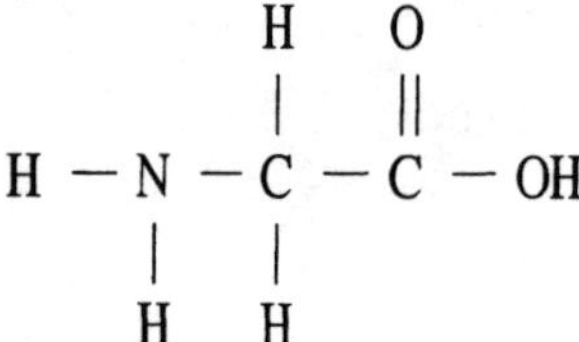

a) amino acid
b) ester
c) nucleic acid
d) protein

Answer: a Key 1: C Section: 14

138. Organic compounds with rings that contain atoms other than carbon are called
a) aromatic compounds
b) heterocyclic compounds
c) heterogeneous compounds
d) perfluoro compounds

Answer: b Key 1: C Section: 15

139. The non-carbon atom(s) generally found in heterocyclic compounds are
a) sulfur
b) sulfur and nitrogen
c) sulfur, nitrogen and oxygen
d) halogens

Answer: c Key 1: C Section: 15

140. Alkaloids, like morphine, caffiene, nicotine and cocaine, are heterocyclic
    a) amines
    b) amides
    c) ethers
    d) esters

    Answer: a Key 1: A Section: 15

141. Compounds related to the heterocyclics pyrimidine and purine are constituents of ________.
    a) amino acids
    b) nucleic acids
    c) proteins
    d) plastics

    Answer: b Key 1: A Section: 15

Chapter 10: Polymers

MULTIPLE CHOICE

1. Monomers are
   a) small building blocks of polymers
   b) small polymers
   c) ethylene
   d) all of the above

   Answer: a Key 1: D Section: 1

2. The word polymer means many
   a) parts
   b) sides
   c) rings
   d) carbons

   Answer: a Key 1: D Section: 1

SHORT ANSWER

3. What is polymerization?

   Answer: the process of building polymers from monomers Key 1: D

   Section: 1

4. What is a macromolecule?

   Answer:
   a relatively huge molecule composed of a repeating pattern of smaller units
   Key 1: D Section: 1

MULTIPLE CHOICE

5. Which statement relating monomers and polymers is correct?
   a) They have the same chemical and physical properties.
   b) They have different chemical and physical properties.
   c) The monomer is usually a solid, while the polymer is usually a liquid or gas.
   d) They have the same chemical formula.

   Answer: b Key 1: C Section: 1

6. Which of the following natural polymers is a polyamide?
   a) Cotton fibers
   b) wood fibers
   c) silk
   d) starch

   Answer: c Key 1: D Section: 1

7. Which of the following natural polymers are in the same classification as nylons?
   a) Human hair
   b) alligator skin
   c) sheep's wool
   d) all are in this classification

   Answer: d Key 1: C Section: 1

8. Which one is **not** a natural polymer?
   a) cotton
   b) wool
   c) starch
   d) celluloid

   Answer: d Key 1: A Section: 2

9. Natural polymers which carry the coded genetic information that makes each individual unique are
   a) proteins
   b) carboxylic acids
   c) esters
   d) nucleic acids

   Answer: d Key 1: A Section: 2

10. Celluloid is a chemical modification of which natural product?
    a) cellulose
    b) cells
    c) ivory
    d) cellophane

    Answer: a Key 1: A Section: 3

11. The first "practical" application of celluloid was
    a) billiard balls
    b) movie film
    c) stiff collars
    d) airplane wings

    Answer: a Key 1: C Section: 3

12. Which of the following is the simplest synthetic polymer?
    a) polymethane
    b) polyethylene
    c) polyvinyl chloride
    d) polystyrene

    Answer: b Key 1: A Section: 4

13. Polyethylene is
    a) tough
    b) flexible
    c) thermoplastic
    d) all of these

    Answer: d Key 1: A Section: 4

SHORT ANSWER

14. What is the connection between polyethylene and the "Battle of Britain" in the second World War?

    Answer: PE as insulation for radar Key 1: C Section: 4

MULTIPLE CHOICE

15. One of the first applications of polyethylene was
    a) billiard balls
    b) garbage bags
    c) electrical insulation
    d) parachutes

    Answer: c Key 1: A Section: 4

16. High-density polyethylene is composed of
    a) primarily linear, unbranched chains of polyethylene in a close packing arrangement
    b) primarily highly branched, non-linear chains of polyethylene in a diffuse packing arrangement
    c) a mixture of polyethylene and polystyrene
    d) polyethylene with high density plastizers added to increase density

    Answer: a Key 1: A Section: 4

17. Low-density polyethylene is composed of
    a) primarily linear, unbranched chains of polyethylene in a close packing arrangement
    b) primarily highly branched, non-linear chains of polyethylene in a diffuse packing arrangement
    c) a mixture of polyethylene and polystyrene
    d) polyethylene with low density plastizers added to increase density

    Answer: b Key 1: C Section: 4

18. HDPE finds applications in
    a) food wrap
    b) rigid containers
    c) squeeze bottles
    d) garbage bags

    Answer: b Key 1: A Section: 4

19. LDPE finds applications as
    a) food wrap
    b) rigid containers
    c) drain pipes
    d) television cabinets

    Answer: a Key 1: A Section: 4

20. LDPE stands for
    a) linearly dense polyethylene
    b) light diffuse polyethylene
    c) low-density polyethylene
    d) lightly doped polyethylene

    Answer: c Key 1: C Section: 4

21. HDPE stands for
    a) high-density polyethylene
    b) hot-dipped polyethylene
    c) high-dose polyethylene
    d) highly-diffuse polyethylene

    Answer: a Key 1: C Section: 4

SHORT ANSWER

22. What is LLDPE?

    Answer: linear low density polyethylene Key 1: C Section: 4

ESSAY

23. Compare and contrast the molecular structure and performance characteristics of LDPE and HDPE.

    Answer: Key 1: C Section: 4

MULTIPLE CHOICE

24. Thermoplastic polymers may be
    a) heated and reformed
    b) heated, but not reformed
    c) decomposed by heating
    d) changed in color by heating

    Answer: a Key 1: A Section: 4

25. The most widely used synthetic polymer is
    a) polyethylene
    b) polyvinyl chloride
    c) polystyrene
    d) polytetrafluoroethylene (Teflon)

    Answer: a Key 1: A Section: 4

26. The polymer segment...$CH_2CH_2CH_2CH_2CH_2CH_2CH_2$ ...represents
    a) polyethylene
    b) polypropylene
    c) polystyrene
    d) polyvinyl chloride

    Answer: a Key 1: C Section: 4

ESSAY

27. Compare thermoplastic and thermosetting polymers.

    Answer: Key 1: C Section: 4

MULTIPLE CHOICE

28. The monomer of polypropylene is
    a) $CH_2{=}CH_2$
    b) $CH_2{=}CH\text{-}CH_3$
    c) CH_3CH_3
    d) $CH_3CH_2CH_3$

    Answer: b Key 1: C Section: 5

29. The monomer of PVC differs from the monomer of PE by
    a) one atom
    b) two atoms
    c) three atoms
    d) four atoms

    Answer: a Key 1: A Section: 5

ESSAY

30. Polyvinyl chloride is used for drain pipe in plumbing applications. It has replaced traditional cast iron pipe for this purpose. List the advantages of PVC for plumbers, the plumbing industry and homeowners.

    Answer: Key 1: A Section: 5

MULTIPLE CHOICE

31. Polyvinyl chloride is used for drain pipe in plumbing applications. It has replaced traditional cast iron pipe for this purpose. The major advantage of PVC in replacing cast iron for this application (particularly if you are a plumber or homeowner) is
    a) lighter weight
    b) easier to handle and cut
    c) more resistant to corrosion
    d) all of the above

    Answer: d Key 1: A Section: 5

32. Another name for Teflon is
    a) LDPE
    b) PVC
    c) PTFE
    d) HDPE

    Answer: c Key 1: A Section: 5

33. The monomer used to make Teflon is
    a) $H_2C{=}CH_2$
    b) $Cl_2C{=}CH_2$
    c) $H_2C{=}CHCl$
    d) $F_2C{=}CF_2$

    Answer: d Key 1: A Section: 5

34. The monomer used to make PVC is
    a) $H_2C{=}CH_2$
    b) $Cl_2C{=}CH_2$
    c) $H_2C{=}CHCl$
    d) $F_2C{=}CF_2$

    Answer: c Key 1: A Section: 5

35. One of the problems in the production of PVC is
    a) vinyl chloride is explosive
    b) vinyl chloride is carcinogenic
    c) vinyl chloride is toxic
    d) vinyl chloride is a solid at room temperature

    Answer: b Key 1: A Section: 5

36. A polymer that conducts electricity is
    a) polyacetylene
    b) polyethylene
    c) polyvinyl chloride
    d) polystyrene

    Answer: a Key 1: A Section: 5

ESSAY

37. Draw part of the repeating structure of polystyrene.

    Answer: Key 1: C Section: 5

38. Draw part of the repeating structure of polyacetylene.

    Answer: Key 1: C Section: 5

MULTIPLE CHOICE

39. The plastic material used to make transparent "throw-away" drinking cups and disposable coffee cups is
    a) polyvinyl chloride
    b) polystyrene
    c) polyethylene
    d) bakelite plastic

    Answer: b Key 1: A Section: 5

40. This formula in which n can be a very large number represents which of the following polymers?

```
   H H
   | |
-(-C-C-)n-
   | |
   H H
```

a) polyethylene
b) polyvinyl chloride
c) polypropylene
d) teflon

Answer: a Key 1: C Section: 5

41. This formula in which n can be a very large number represents which of the following polymers?

```
   H H
   | |
-(-C-C-)n-
   | |
   HCH3
```

a) polyethylene
b) polyvinyl chloride
c) polypropylene
d) teflon

Answer: c Key 1: C Section: 5

42. This formula in which n can be a very large number represents which of the following polymers?

```
   H H
   | |
-(-C-C-)n-
   | |
   H Cl
```

a) polyethylene
b) polyvinyl chloride
c) polypropylene
d) teflon

Answer: b Key 1: C Section: 5

43. This formula in which n can be a very large number represents which of the following polymers?

```
   F F
   | |
-(-C-C-)n-
   | |
   F F
```

a) polyethylene
b) polyvinyl chloride
c) polypropylene
d) teflon

Answer: d Key 1: C Section: 5

44. This formula in which n can be a very large number represents which of the following polymers?

```
   H H
   | |
-(-C-C-)n-
   | |
   H C6H5
```

a) polyethylene
b) polyvinyl chloride
c) polypropylene
d) polystyrene

Answer: d Key 1: C Section: 5

45. Natural rubber can be made from the monomer
a) ethylene
b) propylene
c) butadiene
d) isoprene

Answer: d Key 1: C Section: 6

46. Vulcanization of rubber was discovered by
a) Charles Goodrich
b) Charles Goodyear
c) Charles Firestone
d) Charles Vulcan

Answer: b Key 1: A Section: 6

47. Vulcanization makes rubber
a) hard
b) sticky
c) soft
d) less elastic

Answer: a Key 1: A Section: 6

ESSAY

48. Sulfur acts as a cross-linker when rubber is vulcanized. Explain why this cross-linking improves the performance of rubber.

    Answer: Key 1: C Section: 6

MULTIPLE CHOICE

49. In the vulcanization of rubber, sulfur
    a) is inserted into the carbon chain
    b) breaks long carbon chains into smaller chains
    c) forms links between polymer chains
    d) links all chains into one long chain

    Answer: c Key 1: C Section: 6

50. Elastomers are synthetic polymers that mimic the properties of
    a) vulcanized rubber
    b) polyethylene
    c) celluloid
    d) PVC

    Answer: a Key 1: D Section: 6

ESSAY

51. Distinguish between a polymer like polyethylene and a copolymer like styrene-butadiene rubber (SBR).

    Answer: Key 1: C Section: 6

MULTIPLE CHOICE

52. A copolymer is composed of
    a) two or more different monomers
    b) different polymers linked end to end
    c) different polymers cross-linked
    d) none of the above

    Answer: a Key 1: C Section: 6

53. Styrene-butadiene rubber (SBR) is a
    a) condensation polymer
    b) vulcanized rubber
    c) copolymer
    d) all of the above

    Answer: c Key 1: A Section: 6

TRUE/FALSE

54. Neoprene is an elastomer that shows better resistance to oil and gasoline than other elastomers.

Answer: True Key 1: A Section: 6

MULTIPLE CHOICE

55. The plastic that is used in light weight, rustproof plumbing pipes is
a) teflon
b) polyethylene
c) PVC
d) Bakelite

Answer: c Key 1: A Section: 6

56. The main use of elastomers is making
a) tires
b) synthetic body parts
c) plastic bottles
d) film

Answer: a Key 1: A Section: 6

57. One of the disadvantages of polybutadiene rubber for automobile tires is
a) poor resistance to gasoline and oils
b) its color
c) density
d) expense

Answer: a Key 1: A Section: 6

58. The substance in paints that hardens to form a continous surface coating is called a
a) pigment
b) binder
c) solvent
d) thinner

Answer: b Key 1: A Section: 6

59. In order for a synthetic polymer to be used as a binder in water-base latex paints, it must have ________ properties.
a) reactive
b) inert
c) rubberlike
d) aromatic

Answer: c Key 1: A Section: 6

60. The molecule most commonly split out between monomers to make a condensation polymer is
    a) H_2O
    b) NH_3
    c) HCl
    d) H_2S

    Answer: a Key 1: C Section: 6

61. Nylon is a
    a) polyethylene
    b) polyamide
    c) polyester
    d) polyacrylonitrile

    Answer: b Key 1: A Section: 7

ESSAY

62. Explain how an addition polymer differs from a condensation polymer.

    Answer: Key 1: A Section: 7

MULTIPLE CHOICE

63. A condensation polymer is
    a) polyethylene
    b) nylon
    c) Teflon
    d) polystyrene

    Answer: b Key 1: A Section: 7

64. When polyester is formed as a film as opposed to a fiber, it is used as
    a) audio/video tape
    b) floor tile
    c) bulletproof vests
    d) artificial limbs

    Answer: a Key 1: A Section: 7

65. The segment of a polymer shown below represents a

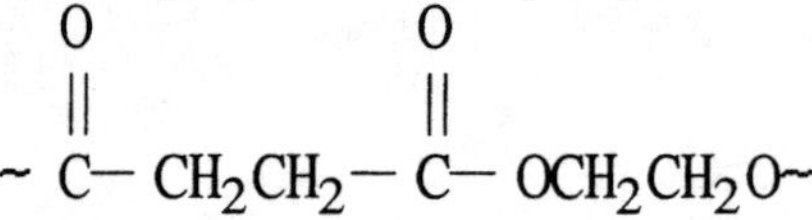

a) polyamide
b) polyester
c) polyethylene
d) polystyrene

Answer: b Key 1: A Section: 7

66. The segment of a polymer shown below represents a

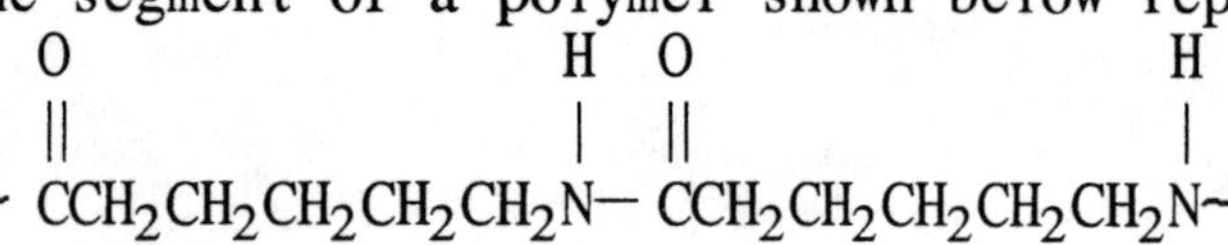

a) polyamide
b) polyester
c) polyethylene
d) polystyrene

Answer: a Key 1: A Section: 7

ESSAY

67. What are composite materials? What are their advantages? Give two examples of products that use composite materials.

Answer: Key 1: A Section: 7

SHORT ANSWER

68. What type of polymer is used for synthetic body parts?

Answer: silicones Key 1: A Section: 7

MULTIPLE CHOICE

69. Nylons are named according to the number of _______ atoms in each monomer unit.
a) hydrogen
b) nitrogen
c) oxygen
d) carbon

Answer: d Key 1: A Section: 7

70. The first synthetic polymer produced in 1909 is known as
    a) polyethylene
    b) celluloid
    c) bakelite
    d) plexiglass

    Answer: c Key 1: A Section: 7

71. Which of the following is/are condensation polymers?
    a) polyamide
    b) polyurethane
    c) polyester
    d) all are condensation polymers

    Answer: d Key 1: D Section: 7

SHORT ANSWER

72. Name three advantages of acrylic fiber yarns over wool.

    Answer:
    don't shrink in water, are not attacked by moths, and are non-allergenic.

    Key 1: A Section: 8

MULTIPLE CHOICE

73. The temperature inside the mouth is about 37° C. Polyvinyl acetate, a polymer used in chewing gum, has a T_g
    a) above 37° C
    b) below 37° C
    c) exactly 37° C
    d) above 100° C

    Answer: b Key 1: C Section: 8

74. Amorphous polymers are composed of
    a) randomly organized polymer chains
    b) highly organized polymer chains
    c) a mixture of random and highly organized polymer chains
    d) none of the above

    Answer: a Key 1: C Section: 8

75. Crystalline polymers are composed of
    a) randomly organized polymer chains
    b) highly organized polymer chains
    c) a mixture of random and highly organized polymer chains
    d) none of the above

    Answer: b Key 1: C Section: 8

76. Lycra bicycle shorts and exercise clothing contain fibers that have great strength and rigidity as well as the ability to stretch. These fibers are probably composed of
    a) natural rubber
    b) amorphous polymers
    c) crystalline polymers
    d) a creative combination of amorphous and crystalline polymers

    Answer: d Key 1: A Section: 8

77. What is Kevlar used for?
    a) film
    b) non-stick cook ware
    c) bullet-proof vests
    d) garbage bags

    Answer: c Key 1: A Section: 8

78. Plexiglas is a polymethyl methacrylate polymer that is used as a glass substitute. The T_g of Plexiglas is
    a) low
    b) high
    c) moderate
    d) not important

    Answer: b Key 1: A Section: 8

79. The temperature in many parts of the world can range between 40 EC and 0EC, therefore we want the T_g of car tires to be
    a) greater than 40
    b) less than 40 but greater than 0
    c) exactly 0
    d) less than 0

    Answer: d Key 1: A Section: 8

80. The temperature in many parts of the world can range between 40 EC and 0EC, therefore we want the T_g of PVC used as seat covers in cars to be
 a) greater than 40
 b) less than 40 but greater than 0
 c) exactly 0
 d) less than 0

 Answer: d Key 1: A Section: 8

81. One of the advantages of incineration of plastics is
 a) high fuel value
 b) no air pollution
 c) all polymers burn efficiently
 d) all of the above

 Answer: a Key 1: C Section: 9

82. Toxic hydrogen cyanide (HCN) is generated by burning
 a) polyacrylonitrile (acrylics)
 b) styrofoam
 c) polyvinyl chloride (vinyl plastics)
 d) polyethylene

 Answer: a Key 1: A Section: 10

83. The greatest hazard in using plastics in home building materials and furnishings is that some
 a) poison children who eat them
 b) cause cancer
 c) are slippery
 d) form poisonous gases when burned

 Answer: d Key 1: A Section: 10

84. Production of PCBs was discontinued in 1977, yet PCBs are still found in the environment. The reason for this is
 a) PCBs are formed naturally by plants and animals
 b) PCBs are very stable molecules
 c) PCBs are very reactive molecules
 d) PCBs are imported from other countries where their production is not banned

 Answer: b Key 1: C Section: 11

ESSAY

85. How are polymers linked to the earth's petroleum reserves?

 Answer: Key 1: C Section: 12

MULTIPLE CHOICE

86. The source of starting materials for synthetic polymers is primarily
    a) plants
    b) coal and petroleum
    c) recycled plastics
    d) animals

    Answer: b Key 1: C Section: 12

Chapter 11: Chemistry of the Earth

MULTIPLE CHOICE

1. The three major structural parts of the Earth are
   a) core, mantle and crust
   b) lithosphere, atmosphere and crust
   c) mantle, crust and atmosphere
   d) lithosphere, hydrosphere and atmosphere

   Answer: a Key 1: D Key 2: I

2. The Earth's crust is subdivided into
   a) core, mantle and atmosphere
   b) lithosphere, hydrosphere and atmosphere
   c) troposphere, stratosphere and ionosphere
   d) hydrosphere, geosphere and stratosphere

   Answer: b Key 1: D Key 2: I

3. As a source of raw materials, the Earth's mantle is
   a) readily accessible today
   b) readily accessible today, but of little practical use
   c) possibly accessible in the future, but probably not very useful
   d) possibly accessible in the future, and probably very useful

   Answer: c Key 1: A Section: 1

4. The second most abundant element in the Earth's crust is
   a) carbon
   b) hydrogen
   c) oxygen
   d) silicon

   Answer: d Key 1: C Section: 1

5. In terms of composition, nine elements compose approximately what percentage of the Earth's crust?
   a) $\approx 50\%$
   b) $\approx 75\%$
   c) $\approx 90\%$
   d) $>95\%$

   Answer: d Key 1: A Section: 1

6. The lithosphere is the __________ part of the Earth's crust.
   a) gaseous
   b) liquid
   c) solid
   d) water

   Answer: c Key 1: C Section: 1

7. The majority of metals and minerals come from the
   a) lithosphere
   b) hydrosphere
   c) mantle
   d) atmosphere

   Answer: a Key 1: C Section: 2

8. The inorganic portion of the lithosphere is made up of silicon, and non-metals like oxygen, sulfur and carbon chemically combined with
   a) metals
   b) non-metals
   c) carbon
   d) water

   Answer: a Key 1: C Section: 2

9. The common element of the organic portion of the lithosphere is
   a) carbon
   b) hydrogen
   c) oxygen
   d) silicon

   Answer: a Key 1: C Section: 2

10. Which one of the following correctly summarizes the relative composition of the lithosphere with respect to inorganic and organic material?
    a) inorganic >> organic
    b) inorganic = organic
    c) inorganic << organic
    d) there is no organic matter in the lithosphere

    Answer: a Key 1: C Section: 2

11. Carbonates are composed of
    a) carbon and oxygen
    b) carbon, oxygen and metals
    c) carbon, sulfur and metals
    d) carbohydrates and metals

    Answer: b Key 1: D Section: 3

TRUE/FALSE

12. One of the more common rocks on earth is limestone.

    Answer: True Key 1: A Section: 3

MULTIPLE CHOICE

13. Which one of the following is not $CaCO_3$?
    a) seashells
    b) eggshells
    c) granite
    d) chalk

    Answer: c Key 1: A Section: 3

14. Silicates are compounds composed of
    a) silicon only
    b) silicon and metals
    c) silicon, oxygen and metals
    d) silicon, sulfur and metals

    Answer: c Key 1: C Section: 4

15. Pure quartz is composed of
    a) silicon and oxygen
    b) silicon, oxygen and metals
    c) silicon, sulfur and metals
    d) calcium, oxygen and metals

    Answer: a Key 1: C Section: 4

16. The basic unit of silicates is
    a) SiO
    b) SiO_2
    c) SiO_3
    d) SiO_4

    Answer: d Key 1: C Section: 4

17. The risk of lung cancer due to asbestos exposures is increased by the synergistic effect of
    a) aerobic exericse
    b) sugar consumption
    c) selenium in the diet
    d) exposure to cigarette smoke

    Answer: b Key 1: A Section: 4

ESSAY

18. What is a synergistic effect? Use asbestos and cigarette smoking as an example.

    Answer: Key 1: C Section: 4

MULTIPLE CHOICE

19. Which material is characterized by a well-ordered, three dimensional structure of SiO_4 tetrahedra?
a) asbestos
b) mica
c) glass
d) quartz

Answer: d Key 1: A Section: 4

20. Which material is characterized by a two dimensional sheetlike arrangement of SiO_4 tetrahedra?
a) asbestos
b) mica
c) glass
d) quartz

Answer: b Key 1: C Section: 4

21. Which material is characterized by a chain arrangement of SiO_4 tetrahedra?
a) asbestos
b) mica
c) glass
d) quartz

Answer: a Key 1: C Section: 4

22. The desirability quotient (DQ) for the removal of asbestos from schools and other buildings is
a) high
b) moderate
c) low
d) uncertain

Answer: d Key 1: A Section: 4

23. The color of quartz crystals is due to
a) the arrangement of silicon and oxygen atoms
b) inorganic impurities
c) magnesium
d) organic substances

Answer: b Key 1: A Section: 4

24. Which of the following is not a kind of quartz?
    a) calcite
    b) agate
    c) jasper
    d) onyx

    Answer: a Key 1: A Section: 4

25. Great quantities of _______ have been used to insulate furnaces, heating ducts, and steam pipes.
    a) asbestos
    b) mica
    c) agate
    d) cotton

    Answer: a Key 1: A Section: 4

26. Cigarette smoke and asbestos fibers act in such a way that each enhances the action of the other. This is known as a/an _______ effect.
    a) isotope
    b) synergistic
    c) dilution
    d) concentration

    Answer: b Key 1: A Section: 4

TRUE/FALSE

27. The harmful effects of asbestos are due mainly to a relatively rare form called crocidolite.

    Answer: True Key 1: A Section: 5

MULTIPLE CHOICE

28. Pottery is made nonporous by
    a) heating
    b) firing
    c) glazing
    d) painting

    Answer: c Key 1: A Section: 5

29. Which one of the following materials is longest lasting?
    a) ceramics
    b) concrete
    c) glass
    d) plastic

    Answer: c Key 1: A Section: 5

30. As opposed to most solids, when glass is heated, it
    a) melts rapidly to a liquid over a narrow temperature range
    b) goes directly into the gas phase; a process known as sublimation
    c) separates into its individual components
    d) gradually softens over a wide temperature range

    Answer: d Key 1: A Section: 5

31. The properties of glass are modified by which approach?
    a) firing at higher temperatures
    b) glazing at low temperatures
    c) addition of various metal oxides
    d) substituting carbon dioxide for silicon dioxide

    Answer: c Key 1: A Section: 5

32. One of the major problems associated with the production of glass is
    a) the amount of energy required.
    b) the amount of sand required.
    c) the amount of limestone required.
    d) the amount of sodium carbonate.

    Answer: a Key 1: A Section: 5

33. Which one of the following containers probably has the longest lifetime in a landfill?
    a) aluminum can
    b) styrofoam cup
    c) steel can
    d) glass jar

    Answer: d Key 1: C Section: 5

34. The two major components in cement are
    a) clay and limestone
    b) sand and limestone
    c) calcium carbonate and limestone
    d) quartz and limestone

    Answer: a Key 1: A Section: 5

ESSAY

35. Although cement and concrete themselves are relatively non-polluting, their production and use are a source of several potential environmental problems. Describe two examples.

    Answer: Key 1: A Section: 5

MULTIPLE CHOICE

36. Cement and concrete have been used as structural materials for approximately
    a) 50 years
    b) 300 years
    c) 1000 years
    d) 2000 years

    Answer: d Key 1: C Section: 5

37. The chemistry of cement is
    a) completely understood
    b) somewhat understood
    c) not at all understood
    d) not an area of study

    Answer: b Key 1: C Section: 5

38. Cement is made from limestone and
    a) clay
    b) sand
    c) coal
    d) iron ore

    Answer: a Key 1: A Section: 5

39. The amount of iron on the Earth today as compared to the amount of iron 120 years ago (approximately the beginnings of the Industrial Revolution) is
    a) less
    b) essentially the same
    c) more
    d) can not be estimated or predicted

    Answer: b Key 1: C Section: 6

40. Bronze is a(n)
    a) alloy
    b) compound
    c) element
    d) pure substance

    Answer: a Key 1: A Section: 6

41. Probably the first metal to be freed from its ore by smelting was
    a) aluminum
    b) copper
    c) lead
    d) iron

    Answer: b Key 1: A Section: 6

42. The principal raw materials for making iron are iron ore, limestone and
    a) sand
    b) coal
    c) oil
    d) chromium

    Answer: b Key 1: A Section: 6

43. In the production of iron, "coke" is used. Coke is
    a) previously heated limestone
    b) previously heated coal
    c) black water formed from mixing coal and water
    d) a mineral containing a variety of metals

    Answer: b Key 1: A Section: 6

44. Limestone is added to the iron producing mixture in a furnace to
    a) add carbon to the mixture
    b) provide an additional reducing agent to extract all of the iron from the ore
    c) combine with silicates to remove impurities in the form of a slag
    d) produce a more corrosion resistant iron

    Answer: c Key 1: A Section: 6

45. Steel is formed from a mixture of
    a) heating iron at high temperature for a long time
    b) iron, carbon and transition metals such as chromium and nickel
    c) oxidizing some of the iron to iron oxides
    d) adding sand and heating to a high temperature

    Answer: b Key 1: A Section: 6

46. The feature that makes iron a useful material is
    a) resistance to corrosion
    b) low weight to strength ratio
    c) high weight to strength ratio
    d) ability to form a variety of alloys with a variety of metals

    Answer: d Key 1: C Section: 6

ESSAY

47. The "coking" process in steel making is a significant source of pollution. Why? What are some alternatives to "coke?"

Answer: Key 1: C Section: 6

MULTIPLE CHOICE

48. The name of the ore from which most aluminum is produced is
a) alumicite
b) bauxite
c) malachite
d) taconite

Answer: b Key 1: D Section: 6

49. The extraction of aluminum from its ore requires a great deal of
a) heat
b) electricity
c) water
d) sunlight

Answer: b Key 1: C Section: 6

50. In comparing the actual relative costs of aluminum and steel, which of the following should be considered?
a) cost of mining and transporting the ore
b) cost of environmental maintenance
c) cost of extracting the metal
d) all of the above must be considered

Answer: d Key 1: A Section: 6

ESSAY

51. List two additional important metals, not including Fe, Cu and Al, and their uses.

Answer: Key 1: A Section: 6

MULTIPLE CHOICE

52. Tin cans are made of ______ with a tin coating.
a) iron
b) aluminum
c) steel
d) cobalt

Answer: c Key 1: A Section: 6

ESSAY

53. Discuss energy advantages of using more aluminum and less steel in the construction of a car.

    Answer: Key 1: C Section: 6

MULTIPLE CHOICE

54. Steel, in all of its variations, is a(n)
    a) alloy
    b) compound
    c) element
    d) pure substance

    Answer: a Key 1: A Section: 6

TRUE/FALSE

55. Low-grade ores are undesirable because extracting the metals requires more energy per pound than high-grade ores.

    Answer: True Key 1: A Section: 7

56. In the United States there are adequate reserves of high-grade ores of iron and copper.

    Answer: False Key 1: A Section: 7

MULTIPLE CHOICE

57. Nodules rich in _____ cover vast areas of the ocean floor.
    a) iron
    b) gold
    c) silver
    d) manganese

    Answer: d Key 1: A Section: 7

58. If we should "run out" of aluminum someday, it would be because we had
    a) converted too much aluminum to another metal
    b) destroyed too much aluminum
    c) used too much aluminum
    d) scattered aluminum too widely in the environment for efficient recovery

    Answer: d Key 1: C Section: 7

59. The chemical law that is the heart of recycling metallic waste is
    a) law of conservation of matter
    b) law of definite proportions
    c) law of multiple proportions
    d) law of conservation of energy

    Answer: a Key 1: C Section: 7

60. The largest percentage by mass of solid waste is
    a) plastic
    b) paper
    c) food
    d) yard wastes

    Answer: b Key 1: A Section: 8

61. The number of sanitary landfills in the future will
    a) remain constant
    b) increase
    c) decrease
    d) can not be reliably predicted

    Answer: c Key 1: A Section: 8

62. An advantage of incineration of garbage is
    a) dramatic decrease in the volume of solid waste
    b) heat produced may be used as an energy source
    c) non-combustibles, like glass and metals, may be recycled
    d) all of the above appear to be advantages

    Answer: d Key 1: A Section: 8

63. A disadvantage of incineration is
    a) production of a variety of gases
    b) potential raw materials are converted to a less useful state
    c) some prior separation of materials from garbage is required before burning
    d) all of the above are potential disadvantages of incineration

    Answer: d Key 1: A Section: 8

64. The best way to handle solid waste is to
    a) incinerate it
    b) dump it
    c) bury it
    d) reduce it, reuse it and recycle it

    Answer: d Key 1: C Section: 8

65. The best way to deal with the mounting problem of solid waste is
    a) by reducing the amount throw-away material produced
    b) reusing articles and containers repeatedly
    c) recycle the raw material from which articles are made
    d) burning solid wastes for fuel

    Answer: a   Key 1: C   Section: 9

TRUE/FALSE

66. It takes more energy to manufacture a nonreturnable half-liter bottle than it does to make a half-liter reusable glass bottle.

    Answer: False   Key 1: C   Section: 9

67. Over the lifetime of a reusable glass bottle there is an energy advantage over using a nonreturnable bottle.

    Answer: True   Key 1: C   Section: 9

MULTIPLE CHOICE

68. Over the lifetime of a reusable glass bottle there is an energy advantage over the nonreturnable bottle
    a) because the energy per use is only 10% of the energy of production of the nonreturnable
    b) because the reusable bottle is better constructed
    c) because it is easier to prevent germs by washing the reusable bottle
    d) because it takes less energy to melt and recycle a returnable bottle than it does a nonreturnable bottle

    Answer: a   Key 1: C   Section: 9

69. For which of the following materials is there no net gain in energy conservation by recycling?
    a) aluminum
    b) iron
    c) copper
    d) glass

    Answer: d   Key 1: A   Section: 9

70. When scrap (recycling) to make new iron and steel products there is also a reduction in
    a) energy consumption
    b) water pollution
    c) air pollution
    d) all of these

    Answer: d   Key 1: C   Section: 9

71. The approximate human population of Earth is
    a) 1 billion
    b) 2.5 billion
    c) 5.5 billion
    d) 10 billion

    Answer: c Key 1: C Section: 10

ESSAY

72. What is meant by exponential growth? Use world human population as an example.

    Answer: Key 1: C Section: 10

MULTIPLE CHOICE

73. At the present rate of growth, world population will be approximately _______ billion by 2025.
    a) 1
    b) 8
    c) 10
    d) 25

    Answer: c Key 1: A Section: 10

Chapter 12: Air

ESSAY

1. Sketch a diagram that illustrates the major parts of the atmosphere.

   Answer: Key 1: A Section: 1

TRUE/FALSE

2. The layer of the atmosphere in which we interact is called the stratosphere.

   Answer: False Key 1: D Section: 1

MULTIPLE CHOICE

3. The layer of the atmosphere in which the ozone layer is found is called the
   a) biosphere
   b) stratosphere
   c) troposphere
   d) ionosphere

   Answer: b Key 1: D Section: 1

4. The most abundant component of dry air is
   a) argon
   b) carbon dioxide
   c) nitrogen
   d) oxygen

   Answer: c Key 1: D Section: 1

5. The second most abundant component of dry air is
   a) argon
   b) carbon dioxide
   c) nitrogen
   d) oxygen

   Answer: d Key 1: D Section: 1

6. The most important of the minor components of dry air is
   a) argon
   b) carbon dioxide
   c) helium
   d) neon

   Answer: b Key 1: A Section: 1

7. The concentration of which component of the atmosphere has increased dramatically since 1900?
   a) argon
   b) carbon dioxide
   c) oxygen
   d) nitrogen

   Answer: b Key 1: C Section: 1

8. Which component of the atmosphere is predicted to continue to rise in the foreseeable future?
   a) argon
   b) carbon dioxide
   c) nitrogen
   d) oxygen

   Answer: b Key 1: C Section: 1

9. With respect to reactivity at normal temperatures, nitrogen is best classified as
   a) highly reactive
   b) somewhat reactive
   c) relatively unreactive
   d) comparable to helium in its reactivity

   Answer: c Key 1: C Section: 2

10. In order for nitrogen to be used by most plants and all animals, it must be
   a) separated
   b) purified
   c) liquefied
   d) fixed

   Answer: d Key 1: C Section: 2

ESSAY

11. Describe the nitrogen cycle. Use specific examples to illustrate the cycle.

   Answer: Key 1: C Section: 2

MULTIPLE CHOICE

12. The industrial fixation of nitrogen to produce nitrogen fertilizers has drastically increased food supply primarily because
    a) plants need nitrogen
    b) plants fix nitrogen slowly
    c) fixed nitrogen is often a limiting factor in plant growth
    d) nitrogen in the atmosphere has decreased over the past two centuries

    Answer: c Key 1: C Section: 2

TRUE/FALSE

13. One of the steps in the nitrogen cycle produces nitric acid.

    Answer: True Key 1: A Section: 2

MULTIPLE CHOICE

14. Which of the following is a form of nitrogen fixation?
    a) N_2 + O_2 + energy(lightning) ! 2 NO
    b) N_2 + O_2 + energy(spark plug) ! 2 NO
    c) N_2 + bacteria ! nitrates
    d) all are forms of nitrogen fixation

    Answer: d Key 1: A Section: 2

15. Nitrogen is converted to nitrates by which of the following reactions?
    a) N_2 + O_2 + energy(lightning) ! 2 NO
    b) 2 NO + O_2 ! 2 NO_2
    c) 3 NO_2 + H_2O ! 2 HNO_3 + NO
    d) 3 H_2 + N_2 ! 2 NH_3

    Answer: d Key 1: A Section: 2

16. The major source of oxygen on Earth is
    a) land plants
    b) ocean based phytoplankton
    c) animals
    d) decomposition of water in the oceans

    Answer: b Key 1: C Section: 3

17. With respect to reactivity, oxygen is best classified as
    a) highly reactive
    b) somewhat reactive
    c) relatively unreactive
    d) comparable to helium in its reactivity

    Answer: a Key 1: C Section: 3

18. In the stratosphere, oxygen (O_2) is converted to ozone (O_3) by high energy ultraviolet light. When the equation is written and balanced using whole number coefficients, the coefficient of oxygen is
    a) 1
    b) 2
    c) 3
    d) 4

    Answer: c Key 1: A Section: 3

ESSAY

19. Describe the oxygen cycle. Use specific examples to illustrate the cyclic nature of the cycle.

    Answer: Key 1: A Section: 3

20. Explain how ozone can be both an air pollutant and necessary component in the Earth's atmosphere.

    Answer: Key 1: A Section: 3

MULTIPLE CHOICE

21. This reaction, $6\ CO_2 + 6\ H_2O$! $C_6H_{12}O_6 + 6\ O_2$, is part of the oxygen cycle and is called
    a) respiration
    b) photosynthesis
    c) transpiration
    d) all of these

    Answer: b Key 1: C Section: 3

22. This reaction, $6\ CO_2 + 6\ H_2O$! $C_6H_{12}O_6 + 6\ O_2$, is part of the oxygen cycle and takes place in
    a) animals
    b) rocks
    c) soil
    d) green plants and phytoplankton

    Answer: d Key 1: C Section: 3

23. An atmospheric inversion is a phenomenon that may have disasterous effects with respect to air pollution. An atmospheric inversion is when a
    a) lower layer of cool air is trapped by an upper layer of warmer air
    b) lower layer of warm air is trapped by an upper layer of cooler air
    c) lower layer of oxygen rich air is trapped by an upper layer of oxygen deficient air
    d) lower layer of oxygen deficient air is trapped by an upper layer of oxygen rich air

    Answer: a Key 1: A Section: 4

ESSAY

24. List three natural sources of air pollution.

    Answer: Key 1: A Section: 5

MULTIPLE CHOICE

25. Volcanoes release large amounts of the pollutant, _______.
    a) HCN
    b) NO_2
    c) SO_2
    d) NH_3

    Answer: c Key 1: A Section: 5

26. The eruption of Mt. Pinatubo in the Philippines in 1991 is estimated to have dumped 20 million tons of sulfur dioxide into the atmosphere. This is an example of
    a) impact of natural processes on the Earth's environment
    b) air pollution from a natural source
    c) the magnitude of the chemistry associated with the environment
    d) all of the above

    Answer: d Key 1: A Section: 5

TRUE/FALSE

27. Air pollution was never a problem prior to 1800 AD.

    Answer: False Key 1: A Section: 6

MULTIPLE CHOICE

28. One of the earliest recorded records of polluted air was written by the Roman, _______, in 61 A.D.
    a) Caesar Augustus
    b) Seneca
    c) Cato the Elder
    d) Pliny

    Answer: b Key 1: C Section: 6

29. Which of the following human activities contributed to the pollution of our ancestral air?
    a) discovery, making, and using tools
    b) discovery and use of fire
    c) the development of crop farming
    d) all of these contributed

    Answer: d Key 1: C Section: 6

30. A definition of a pollutant is a chemical
    a) in the wrong place but at the right concentration
    b) in the wrong place and at the wrong concentration
    c) in the right place but at the wrong concentration
    d) in the right place and at the right concentration

    Answer: b Key 1: C Section: 7

TRUE/FALSE

31. The smog in the Los Angeles basin has no effect on vegetation 100 miles away.

    Answer: False Key 1: A Section: 7

32. Air pollution is a world-wide problem today.

    Answer: True Key 1: A Section: 7

MULTIPLE CHOICE

33. The worst example of people mistreating their environment can be seen in
    a) America
    b) Brazil
    c) the former Soviet Union
    d) Mexico

    Answer: c Key 1: A Section: 7

34. The main difference between air pollution problems today and problems in the past is
    a) global warming
    b) less polar ice
    c) a worldwide problem
    d) less rainfall

    Answer: c Key 1: A Section: 7

35. The word smog is believed to have originated in
    a) London
    b) Los Angeles
    c) Mexico City
    d) Buenos Aires

    Answer: a Key 1: C Section: 8

36. In December, 1952 in London, a four day long atmospheric inversion created the worst smog in history. The death toll attributed to the smog was estimated at
    a) 10
    b) 100
    c) 2000
    d) 8000

    Answer: d Key 1: A Section: 8

37. London smog is attributed primarily to
    a) the burning of coal
    b) automobile exhaust
    c) sunlight and nitrogen oxides
    d) ozone

    Answer: a Key 1: A Section: 8

38. Unburned carbon produced during the inefficient burning of coal is called
    a) ash
    b) soot
    c) carbon dioxide
    d) clinkers

    Answer: b Key 1: A Section: 8

39. Sulfur dioxide reacts with oxygen to form
    a) SO_3
    b) S_2O_3
    c) S_3O_5
    d) H_2SO_4

    Answer: a Key 1: C Section: 8

40. Sulfur trioxide reacts with water to form
    a) sulfur dioxide
    b) sulfur monoxide
    c) sulfurous acid
    d) sulfuric acid

    Answer: d Key 1: A Section: 8

41. Sulfur dioxide is readily absorbed in the respiratory system where it is
    a) soothing
    b) a powerful irritant
    c) mildly irritating
    d) unreactive

    Answer: b Key 1: A Section: 8

42. According to the World Health Organization (WHO), air pollution killed approximately ________ people worldwide in 1990.
    a) 25,000
    b) 100,000
    c) 600,000
    d) 1,000,000

    Answer: c Key 1: A Section: 8

43. Alveoli are found in
    a) the air
    b) swamp water
    c) the lungs
    d) the ocean

    Answer: c Key 1: A Section: 8

ESSAY

44. Describe one method for the removal of particulates from smokestack gases.

    Answer: Key 1: A Section: 8

MULTIPLE CHOICE

45. Removal of particulates from smokestack gases
    a) decreases the plant's energy efficiency
    b) creates a solid waste disposal problem
    c) increases the costs of producing energy
    d) causes all of the above

    Answer: d Key 1: A Section: 8

46. The reaction: 2 CaO(s) + 2 SO_2(g) + O_2(g) ----> $CaSO_4$(s) is the basis of
    a) electrostatic precipitators
    b) chemical SO_2 scrubbers
    c) particulate removal
    d) all of the above

    Answer: b Key 1: A Section: 8

47. An electrostatic precipitator is a device used
    a) in the laboratory study of pollution
    b) to precipitate ions in water
    c) to remove particles from smokestack gases
    d) to remove CO_2 from the atmosphere

    Answer: c Key 1: A Section: 8

ESSAY

48. Compare and contrast London smog and Los Angeles smog.

    Answer: Key 1: A Section: 9

FILL-IN-THE-BLANK

49. Los Angeles smog is more commonly referred to as ____________ smog.

    Answer: photochemical Key 1: A Section: 9

MULTIPLE CHOICE

50. Which one of the following is not one of the prinicipal components required for photochemical smog?
    a) nitrogen oxides
    b) hydrocarbons
    c) sulfur dioxide
    d) sunshine

    Answer: c Key 1: C Section: 9

51. The major source of photochemical smog is
    a) automobile emissions
    b) industrial emissions
    c) fossil fuel power plant emissions
    d) nuclear power plant emissions

    Answer: a Key 1: C Section: 9

52. Which one of the following IS NOT a property of carbon monoxide?
    a) odorless
    b) tasteless
    c) colorless
    d) undetectable

    Answer: d Key 1: A Section: 9

FILL-IN-THE-BLANK

53. Carbon monoxide blocks the ability of ________________ to bind and transport __________________.

    Answer: hemoglobin, oxygen Key 1: A Section: 9

54. The only symptom of carbon monoxide poisoning is usually _______________.

    Answer: drowsiness Key 1: A Section: 9

TRUE/FALSE

55. All except the most severe cases of CO poisoning are reversible.

    Answer: True Key 1: C Section: 9

56. Low level carbon monoxide exposure over a long period of time places stress on the heart.

    Answer: True Key 1: C Section: 9

MULTIPLE CHOICE

57. Usually the symptom of carbon monoxide poisoning is
    a) shortness of breath
    b) uncontrollable shaking
    c) drowsiness
    d) yellowing of the eyes and skin

    Answer: c Key 1: A Section: 9

58. Carbon monoxide pollution is best described as a(n)
    a) rural problem
    b) urban problem
    c) global problem
    d) none of the above

    Answer: b Key 1: C Section: 9

59. Hemoglobin is the blood protein responsible for the transport of oxygen. Carbon monoxide disturbs oxygen transport by
a) destroying hemoglobin
b) destroying oxygen in the lung
c) binding more strongly to hemoglobin than oxygen
d) destroying lung aveoli

Answer: c Key 1: C Section: 9

60. The number of hydrocarbons that make up the mixture called gasoline number
a) less than 100
b) less than 1000
c) more than 1000
d) more than 1,000,000

Answer: b Key 1: A Section: 9

61. At the high temperature in an internal combustion engine, a fraction of the nitrogen in air is converted to
a) carbon monoxide
b) carbon dioxide
c) ammonia
d) nitrogen oxides

Answer: d Key 1: C Section: 9

62. The presence of nitrogen dioxide in smog is most easily recognized by
a) color
b) smell
c) taste
d) chemical analysis

Answer: a Key 1: C Section: 9

63. The primary reaction in the formation of photochemical smog is
a) $2\ NO + O_2$ ----> $2\ NO_2$
b) NO_2 + sunlight ----> $NO + O$
c) $O + O_2$ ----> O_3
d) O_3 + hydrocarbons ----> aldehydes

Answer: b Key 1: C Section: 9

64. The day starts out bright and sunny. Later, a brown haze develops. This indicates the presence of
a) nitrogen dioxide
b) ozone
c) carbon dioxide
d) carbon monoxide

Answer: a Key 1: C Section: 9

65. A secondary reaction in the formation of photochemical smog is
    a) 2 NO + O_2 ----> 2 NO_2
    b) NO_2 + sunlight ----> NO + O
    c) O + O_2 ----> O_3
    d) O_3 + hydrocarbons ----> aldehydes

    Answer: c Key 1: C Section: 9

TRUE/FALSE

66. Sunlight breaks down nitrogen dioxide into nitric oxide and oxygen atoms.

    Answer: True Key 1: C Section: 9

ESSAY

67. Discuss how oxygen atoms promote the formation of a variety of substances in smog.

    Answer: Key 1: C Section: 9

68. What crucial role does sunlight play in photochemical smog?

    Answer: Key 1: C Section: 9

MULTIPLE CHOICE

69. A tertiary reaction in the formation of photochemical smog is
    a) O + hydrocarbons ----> aldehydes
    b) NO_2 + sunlight ----> NO + O
    c) N_2 + O_2 ----> 2 NO
    d) O_3 + hydrocarbons ----> aldehydes

    Answer: d Key 1: C Section: 9

70. Tetraethyllead was a(n) additive used in ________ that produced toxic air pollution.
    a) gasoline
    b) fertilizers
    c) paints
    d) oil refineries

    Answer: a Key 1: A Section: 10

71. The banning of tetraethyllead from gasolines in 1974 has reduced lead air pollution by
    a) 30%
    b) 45%
    c) 60%
    d) 90%

    Answer: d Key 1: A Section: 10

72. In terms of reactivity, ozone is best classified as
    a) very reactive
    b) somewhat reactive
    c) unreactive
    d) similar to He

    Answer: a Key 1: C Section: 11

73. Ozone (O_3) and oxygen (O_2) are
    a) allotropes
    b) isoelectronic
    c) isomers
    d) isotopes

    Answer: a Key 1: D Section: 11

74. Ozone is a very strong
    a) acid
    b) base
    c) oxidizing agent
    d) reducing agent

    Answer: c Key 1: D Section: 11

75. One of the results of ozone pollution in an urban environment is
    a) destruction of glass windows
    b) decomposition of granite buildings
    c) cracking of sidewalks
    d) shortens the life of automobile tires

    Answer: d Key 1: A Section: 11

76. In the troposphere, the reactivity of CFCs is
    a) low
    b) moderate
    c) high
    d) comparable to neon

    Answer: a Key 1: C Section: 11

TRUE/FALSE

77. CFCs are inert in the troposphere and reactive in the stratosphere.

Answer: True Key 1: C Section: 11

MULTIPLE CHOICE

78. In the stratosphere, the reactivity of CFCs is
a) low
b) moderate
c) high
d) comparable to neon

Answer: c Key 1: C Section: 11

79. The impact of CFCs on the ozone layer is amplified by the fact that
a) CFCs replicate in the stratosphere
b) CFCs decompose before reaching the stratosphere
c) CFCs react with oxygen to produce many reactive intermediates
d) one CFC molecule will lead to the decomposition of many ozone molecules

Answer: d Key 1: C Section: 11

80. Even if all CFC production could be stopped today, the ozone depletion problem in the stratosphere would continue for many years because
a) some nations would not follow the ban
b) CFCs are produced naturally in the troposphere
c) CFCs are widespread and very stable in the troposphere
d) ozone is naturally depleted by sunlight

Answer: c Key 1: C Section: 11

81. Which of the following are true about O_2 and O_3?
a) they are elemental forms of oxygen
b) they are molecules of oxygen
c) they are called allotropes
d) all of the above are true

Answer: d Key 1: C Section: 11

82. A term that describes the relationship between O_2 and O_3 is
a) allotropes
b) isomers
c) conformers
d) transformers

Answer: a Key 1: C Section: 12

83. Most hydrocarbons in the urban areas arise from
    a) automobile exhaust
    b) processing and use of gasoline
    c) industrial emissions
    d) natural sources

    Answer: c Key 1: A Section: 16

84. Most hydrocarbons in the atmosphere arise from
    a) automobile exhaust
    b) evaporation of gasoline
    c) industrial emissions
    d) natural sources

    Answer: d Key 1: A Section: 16

85. Catalytic converters on automobiles are designed to reduce the emission of
    a) nitrogen oxides
    b) carbon monoxide
    c) carbon dioxide
    d) sulfur oxides

    Answer: b Key 1: A Section: 9

ESSAY

86. Lowering the temperature of an automobile engine or using a richer fuel mixture reduces the amount of nitrogen oxides in the exhaust. What are the tradeoffs of this approach to reduction of nitrogen oxides?

    Answer: Key 1: A Section: 9

MULTIPLE CHOICE

87. The metal catalyst in catalytic converters is often
    a) iron
    b) gold
    c) platinum
    d) zinc

    Answer: c Key 1: C Section: 9

ESSAY

88. Is an electric car really a "zero-emission" vehicle? Justify your response.

    Answer: Key 1: A Section: 9

TRUE/FALSE

89. By the year 1998, 2% of all cars sold in California must be zero-emission electric vehicles.

    Answer: True Key 1: A Section: 9

MULTIPLE CHOICE

90. Running an engine with a richer (more fuel, less air) combustion mixture lowers nitrogen oxide emissions from automobiles. The problem is that
    a) hydrocarbon emission increases
    b) carbon monoxide emission increases
    c) fuel efficiency decreases
    d) all of the above occur

    Answer: d Key 1: A Section: 9

91. Acid rain is precipitation with a pH
    a) above 10
    b) above 7
    c) below 5.6
    d) below 2

    Answer: c Key 1: D Section: 12

92. "Pure" rainfall (rainfall undisturbed by human influences) has a pH of approximately 5.6. The pH of rain in some areas has been measured at 2.6. The acidity of this rain is
    a) three times that of normal rain
    b) 10 times that of normal rain
    c) 100 times that of normal rain
    d) 1000 times that of normal rain

    Answer: d Key 1: C Section: 12

SHORT ANSWER

93. What are the major industrial sources of acid rain?

    Answer: power plants, smelting Key 1: A Section: 18

MULTIPLE CHOICE

94. The two principle sources of acid rain are _____ emissions from power plants and _____ emissions from automobiles and power plants.
    a) sulfur dioxide, ozone
    b) ozone, carbon monoxide
    c) carbon monoxide, nitrogen monoxide
    d) sulfur dioxide, nitrogen monoxide

    Answer: d Key 1: A Section: 12

ESSAY

95. The concentration of lead along heavily traveled roads is often high. Why?

    Answer: Key 1: A Section: 10

TRUE/FALSE

96. Almost all gasoline sold for routine use in the US is lead-free.

    Answer: True Key 1: A Section: 10

MULTIPLE CHOICE

97. Which one of the following IS NOT a property of radon?
    a) unreactive
    b) tasteless
    c) odorless
    d) nonradioactive

    Answer: d Key 1: A Section: 13

98. The ultimate source of radon in the environment is from the radioactive decay of naturally occurring
    a) uranium
    b) plutonium
    c) xenon
    d) carbon

    Answer: a Key 1: C Section: 13

99. Radon is released from soil and rock where it is produced because radon is a
    a) gas
    b) liquid
    c) solid
    d) plasma

    Answer: a Key 1: C Section: 13

100. The major source of all air pollutants in the United States is
    a) industrial emissions
    b) residential emissions
    c) motor vehicle emissions
    d) natural sources

    Answer: c Key 1: A Section: 14

101. The World Health Organization (WHO) rates which pollutant the worst?
    a) carbon monoxide
    b) hydrocarbons
    c) nitrogen oxides
    d) sulfur oxides

    Answer: d Key 1: C Section: 14

102. Which is classified as a "greenhouse gas"?
    a) carbon dioxide
    b) chlorofluorocarbons
    c) methane
    d) all of these

    Answer: d Key 1: C Section: 15

ESSAY

103. What is the "greenhouse effect"?

    Answer: Key 1: C Section: 15

MULTIPLE CHOICE

104. The term "greenhouse effect" is derived from the fact that
    a) greenhouse gases act like the glass in a greenhouse
    b) increasing global temperatures will make the earth a better greenhouse
    c) green things absorb heat energy most efficiently
    d) it was discovered by a scientist living in a green house

    Answer: a Key 1: C Section: 15

105. The unavoidable pollutant is
    a) carbon dioxide
    b) residual heat
    c) nitrogen dioxide
    d) ozone

    Answer: b Key 1: C Section: 16

106. In the removal of pollution, the most expensive fraction of pollution to remove is the
    a) first fraction
    b) middle fractions
    c) last fraction
    d) The cost is constant across all fractions removed

    Answer: c Key 1: A Section: 17

Chapter 13: Water

TRUE/FALSE

1. You can live for weeks without food, but only days without water.

   Answer: True Key 1: C Key 2: I

ESSAY

2. How do the unique properties of water allow for life on Earth?

   Answer: Key 1: C Section: 1

TRUE/FALSE

3. Water is similar to most other substances in its physical and chemical properties.

   Answer: True Key 1: C Section: 1

4. The volume of water increases as it freezes.

   Answer: True Key 1: C Section: 1

FILL-IN-THE-BLANK

5. Ice is _________ (less/more) dense than liquid water.

   Answer: less Key 1: C Section: 1

SHORT ANSWER

6. What are two relatively unique physical properties of water? What impact do these properties have on life on Earth?

   Answer:
   liquid, lower solid density, high heat capacity, high heat of evaporation
   Key 1: A Section: 1

MULTIPLE CHOICE

7. Heat capacity is a measure of the heat required to
   a) expand the volume of a substance
   b) evaporate a substance
   c) freeze a substance
   d) change the temperature of a substance

   Answer: d Key 1: C Section: 1

FILL-IN-THE-BLANK

8. The heat capacity of water is __________ (greater/less) than that of iron.

   Answer: greater Key 1: A Section: 1

9. Water has a relatively ________ heat capacity.

   Answer: high Key 1: C Section: 1

ESSAY

10. Describe how water is capable of moderating the temperature of the Earth.

    Answer: Key 1: C Section: 1

MULTIPLE CHOICE

11. The dramatic temperature changes on the moon between day and night are not seen on the Earth because of what property of water?
    a) excellent solvent
    b) less dense as a solid
    c) high heat capacity
    d) all of the above contribute

    Answer: c Key 1: C Section: 1

12. Heat of vaporization is the amount of heat required to
    a) evaporate a liquid
    b) condense a vapor
    c) melt a solid
    d) evaporate a solid

    Answer: a Key 1: C Section: 1

13. The three dimensional structure of water is
    a) linear
    b) bent
    c) square planar
    d) tetrahedral

    Answer: b Key 1: C Section: 1

14. The climate modifying property of lakes and oceans is because of the water's
    a) density
    b) surface tension
    c) boiling point
    d) high heat of vaporization

    Answer: d Key 1: A Section: 1

15. Water's unique properties, high heat capacity, high density, solid phase less dense than liquid phase can be attibuted to
    a) it's formula, H_2O
    b) the covalent oxygen-hydrogen bonds in the molecule
    c) the shape of the molecule
    d) the polarity of the molecules and hydrogen bonding between molecules

    Answer: d Key 1: C Section: 1

16. The saltiness of the oceans is
    a) decreasing slowly
    b) increasing slowly
    c) increasing rapidly
    d) constant

    Answer: b Key 1: C Section: 2

17. Approximately what fraction of the Earth's surface is covered with water?
    a) 25%
    b) 50%
    c) 75%
    d) 90%

    Answer: c Key 1: A Section: 2

SHORT ANSWER

18. Why is it virtually impossible to find pure water on Earth?

    Answer: water is an excellent solvent Key 1: A Section: 2

MULTIPLE CHOICE

19. What percentage of water on the Earth is seawater, and hence, unfit for drinking?
    a) 2%
    b) 20%
    c) 50%
    d) 98%

    Answer: d Key 1: C Section: 2

20. The majority of freshwater is found in the
    a) surface waters: rivers, lakes, streams
    b) groundwater
    c) polar ice caps
    d) atmosphere

    Answer: c Key 1: A Section: 2

21. The water cycle is driven by the
    a) wind
    b) sun
    c) geothermal energy
    d) tides

    Answer: b Key 1: C Section: 3

ESSAY

22. Describe how the water cycle acts to purify water.

    Answer: Key 1: A Section: 3

MULTIPLE CHOICE

23. The bitter water at Marah, was probably too ______
    a) acidic
    b) basic
    c) muddy
    d) deep

    Answer: b Key 1: A Section: 3

24. It is probable that the tree that Moses threw into the bitter water at Marah was a dead tree with the alcohol groups of cellulose oxidized to give
    a) alcohol groups
    b) esters
    c) carboxylic acid groups
    d) amines

    Answer: c Key 1: A Section: 3

25. The water cycle acts to purify water by
    a) evaporation and condensation
    b) crystallization (freeze-thaw cycle)
    c) filtration
    d) all of these

    Answer: d Key 1: C Section: 3

26. The most serious threat to human health from water supplies is
    a) bacteria
    b) chlorinated hydrocarbons
    c) heavy metals
    d) nitrates

    Answer: a Key 1: A Section: 4

27. It is estimated that biologically contaminated water accounts for what percentage of world disease?
    a) 10%
    b) 25%
    c) 60%
    d) 80%

    Answer: d Key 1: A Section: 4

FILL-IN-THE-BLANK

28. It is estimated that less than _____% of the world's population have access to sufficient clean water.

    Answer: 10 Key 1: A Section: 4

TRUE/FALSE

29. The major use of water in the US is for personal consumption.

    Answer: False Key 1: A Section: 4

MULTIPLE CHOICE

30. According to the World Health Organization's Global Burden of Disease Study, unclean or inadequate water supplies, poor sanitation and poor hygiene kill approximately __________ people worldwide each year.
    a) 3,000,000
    b) 200,000
    c) 1,000,000
    d) 700,000

    Answer: a Key 1: A Section: 4

31. Poor water supplies rank ____ in causes of death.
    a) 1st
    b) 2nd
    c) 4th
    d) 3rd

    Answer: c Key 1: A Section: 4

32. Which of these common human activities contribute to BOD?
    a) dumping lawn clippings in a lake or pond
    b) swimming in a lake or pond
    c) paddling a boat across a lake or pond
    d) fishing in a lake or pond

    Answer: a Key 1: C Section: 4

33. Which of the following human activities contribute to the BOD of a river?
    a) swimming in the river
    b) allowing raw sewage to enter the river
    c) paddling a boat across the river
    d) fishing

    Answer: b Key 1: C Section: 4

34. Algae bloom can be stimulated on a lake or pond by
    a) runoff of fertilizers from crops and lawns
    b) fishing
    c) acid rain
    d) basic rain

    Answer: a Key 1: C Section: 4

35. Hard water contains relatively large concentrations of
    a) magnesium ions
    b) iron ions
    c) calcium ions
    d) one or more of the above ions

    Answer: d Key 1: A Section: 5

36. Biochemical oxygen demand (BOD) is a measure of the amount of
    a) dissolved oxygen in a water sample
    b) dissolved biochemical oxygen in a water sample
    c) oxygen required to degrade organic material in the water
    d) oxygen required by aquatic life in a water sample

    Answer: c Key 1: C Section: 4

37. Aerobic decomposition of organic matter requires
    a) oxygen
    b) nitrogen
    c) carbon dioxide
    d) water

    Answer: a Key 1: C Section: 4

38. Anaerobic degradation of organic material in water systems occurs in the absence of
    a) dissolved oxygen
    b) dissolved nitrogen
    c) nutrients
    d) sunlight

    Answer: a Key 1: C Section: 4

39. As the amount of organic material in a water system increases, the BOD
    a) decreases
    b) remains constant
    c) increases
    d) can not be predicted

    Answer: c Key 1: A Section: 4

40. Which substance is likely to be produced when the dissolved oxygen in a lake is depleted?
    a) methane, CH_4
    b) carbon dioxide, CO_2
    c) phosphate, PO_4^{3-}
    d) bicarbonate, HCO_3^-

    Answer: a Key 1: A Section: 4

41. Which substance is likely to be produced when the dissolved oxygen in a lake is depleted?
    a) ammonia, NH_3
    b) carbon dioxide, CO_2
    c) phosphate, PO_4^{3-}
    d) bicarbonate, HCO_3^-

    Answer: a Key 1: A Section: 4

42. Dissolved oxygen is added to streams and rivers by
    a) aerobic bacteria
    b) waterfalls and rapids
    c) decaying algae
    d) fertilizer runoff

    Answer: b Key 1: A Section: 4

43. Which company's industrial waste water would have a relatively high BOD?
    a) Tasty Tomato Canning Co.
    b) Shameless Stripper Coal Mine
    c) Bullworks Ammonia Company
    d) Spotless Steel Works, Inc.

    Answer: a Key 1: A Section: 4

44. Under aerobic conditions, the carbon in decaying vegetation in a lake ends up primarily as
    a) methane, CH_4
    b) cyanide, CN^-
    c) carbon monoxide, CO
    d) carbon dioxide, CO_2

    Answer: d Key 1: C Section: 4

FILL-IN-THE-BLANK

45. Under aerobic conditions, microorganisms ____________ organic matter; under anaerobic conditions, microorganisms ____________ organic matter.

    Answer: oxidize; reduce Key 1: C Section: 4

46. A stagnant pond has an odor like ammonia. This is a good indication that the BOD of the pond is __________ and that the DO is ________.

    Answer: high; low Key 1: A Section: 4

MULTIPLE CHOICE

47. Algae growth and death in a lake can increase the BOD of the water. This process is called ________.
    a) oxidation
    b) fertilization
    c) eutrophication
    d) regeneration

    Answer: c Key 1: A Section: 4

48. In addition to sewage and other organic contaminants, inorganic chemicals, such as _____ ions from laundry detergents contribute to algae bloom.
    a) phosphate
    b) carbonate
    c) sodium
    d) calcium

    Answer: a Key 1: A Section: 6

49. Along with fertilizers which increases BOD, water is often contaminated by this class of agricultural chemicals.
    a) toxic metal
    b) crude oil
    c) pesticides
    d) radioisotopes

    Answer: c Key 1: A Section: 6

50. Which of the following human activities contribute significantly to increased water pollution?
    a) oil spills
    b) releasing industrial wastes
    c) pouring household chemicals, outdated medicines, etc. down the drain
    d) all of these

    Answer: d Key 1: C Section: 6

ESSAY

51. Once groundwater is contaminated, it is very difficult to purify. Discuss this problem of groundwater sources of water with respect to the water cycle.

    Answer: Key 1: A Section: 7

MULTIPLE CHOICE

52. Which part of the water supply is most isolated from the purifying capacity of the water cycle?
    a) ice caps
    b) groundwater
    c) surface water
    d) oceans

    Answer: b Key 1: A Section: 7

53. Volatile organic chemicals (VOC) make up one category of contaminants in groundwater. Which one of the following **IS NOT** a VOC?
    a) sodium chloride
    b) chloroform
    c) toluene
    d) benzene

    Answer: a Key 1: A Section: 7

FILL-IN-THE-BLANK

54. VOC stands for ______________________________.

    Answer: Volatile Organic Chemical Key 1: A Section: 9

MULTIPLE CHOICE

55. Long term exposure to trace levels of VOCs in water is
    a) absolutely safe
    b) probably safe
    c) definitely hazardous
    d) unknown

    Answer: d Key 1: C Section: 7

56. LUST is an acronym that stands for
    a) Longterm Underground Storage of Toxics
    b) Lowlevel Uranium Storage Tanks
    c) Leaking Underground Storage of Toxics
    d) Leaking Underground Storage Tanks

    Answer: d Key 1: A Section: 7

57. ppm and ppb are
    a) toxic chemicals
    b) chlorinated hydrocarbons
    c) wastewater treatment strategies
    d) concentration units

    Answer: d Key 1: D Section: 7

58. A volatile organic chemical that is widely used as a drycleaning solvent and degreasing compound and is now found in trace amounts in groundwater is
    a) methane
    b) ethylene
    c) acetic acid
    d) trichloroethylene

    Answer: d Key 1: A Section: 7

59. Lakes and streams with limestone rock bottoms are less susceptible to
    a) high levels of BOD
    b) anaerobic organisms
    c) acidification
    d) low DO

    Answer: c Key 1: A Section: 8

60. Lakes and streams with granite rock bottoms are more susceptible to
    a) high levels of BOD
    b) anaerobic organisms
    c) acidification
    d) low DO

    Answer: c Key 1: A Section: 8

61. The metal ion that is found in clays and other minerals that appears to be deadly to young fish is ______.
    a) calcium
    b) magnesium
    c) aluminum
    d) iron

    Answer: c Key 1: A Section: 8

62. Acid rain is made up mainly of two acids. They are:
    a) hydrochloric and acetic
    b) sulfuric and nitric
    c) boric and acetic
    d) phosphoric and carbonic

    Answer: b Key 1: A Section: 8

63. A characteristic of a lake dying from acidification is that the only surviving fish are ______.
    a) old
    b) young
    c) female
    d) male

    Answer: a Key 1: A Section: 8

FILL-IN-THE-BLANK

64. One step to alleviate the problem of acid rain is to remove the _____ from coal before combustion.

    Answer: sulfur Key 1: A Section: 8

MULTIPLE CHOICE

65. Two pollutants which are produced in the manufacture of automobile bumpers and other chrome plated hardware are
    a) SO_2 and NO
    b) CrO_4^{2-} and CN^-
    c) $Cr_2O_7^{2-}$ and N_2O
    d) Cr^{3+} and CNO^-

    Answer: b Key 1: A Section: 9

66. Primary sewage treatment involves
    a) aeration
    b) settling
    c) chemical treatment
    d) all of the above

    Answer: b Key 1: A Section: 10

67. Secondary treatment of sewage involves
    a) filtering and aeration
    b) settling and sludge removal
    c) chlorination
    d) all of the above

    Answer: a Key 1: A Section: 10

ESSAY

68. Describe the activated sludge method of sewage treatment.

    Answer: Key 1: A Section: 10

MULTIPLE CHOICE

69. In secondary treatment of sewage, which removes organic matter?
    a) chlorine
    b) ozone
    c) aluminum sulfate and lime
    d) bacteria

    Answer: d Key 1: A Section: 10

70. One of the potential problems with chlorination of waste water is that it
    a) provides no residual protection
    b) is ineffective against pathogenic bacteria
    c) produces low levels of chlorinated hydrocarbons
    d) is more expensive than other approaches

    Answer: c Key 1: A Section: 10

TRUE/FALSE

71. Each person in the US flushes approximately 50,000 L of drinking quality water down the toilet each year.

    Answer: True Key 1: A Section: 11

MULTIPLE CHOICE

72. One of the advantages of treating sewage effluent with ozone as opposed to chlorine is
    a) O_3 is more effective in killing viruses
    b) O_3 is more effective in killing bacteria
    c) O_3 provides a residual protection against bacteria
    d) O_3 is less expensive

    Answer: a Key 1: A Section: 10

73. Advanced treatment of sewage is required to remove
    a) suspended matter
    b) dissolved organics
    c) nitrates and phosphates
    d) bacteria

    Answer: c Key 1: A Section: 7

74. Carbon filtering of wastewater is an excellent method for the removal of
    a) dissolved ions
    b) organic molecules
    c) nitrates and phosphates
    d) sludge

    Answer: b Key 1: A Section: 14

75. Aeration of drinking water
    a) removes odors
    b) increases dissolved air
    c) improves flavor
    d) does all of the above

    Answer: d Key 1: A Section: 10

76. Fluorides are added to water to
    a) kill bacteria
    b) remove nitrates
    c) neutralize acids
    d) prevent tooth decay

    Answer: d Key 1: A Section: 7

ESSAY

77. Nitrates contaminate many wells in agricultural areas. Why?

    Answer: Key 1: A Section: 7

MULTIPLE CHOICE

78. A major contaminant in well water in many agricultural areas is
    a) nitrates
    b) VOCs
    c) mercury
    d) phosphates

    Answer: a Key 1: A Section: 7

79. Consumption of water with high levels of nitrate is particularly hazardous to
    a) infants
    b) males
    c) females
    d) elderly

    Answer: a Key 1: A Section: 7

80. Which pollutant may cause methemoglobinemia (blue baby syndrome)?
    a) VOCs
    b) iron
    c) carbon monoxide
    d) nitrates

    Answer: d Key 1: A Section: 10

81. Water use is an important aspect of water conservation. For drinking purposes the average adult needs to consume about
    a) 7 L/day
    b) 1.5 L/day
    c) 300 L/day
    d) 13,000 L/day

    Answer: b Key 1: C Section: 12

FILL-IN-THE-BLANK

82. To use clean water is to abuse it. Each of us can do our share by __________ water and ___________ our use of products that require vast amounts of water to make.

    Answer: conserving, minimizing Key 1: C Section: 12

Chapter 14: Energy

TRUE/FALSE

1. The United States has 5% of the world's population and uses 25% of the world's energy.

   Answer: False Key 1: C Key 2: I

MULTIPLE CHOICE

2. The SI unit of energy is the
   a) joule
   b) calorie
   c) gram
   d) watt

   Answer: a Key 1: D Section: 1

3. Approximately what percentage of the total solar radiation that falls upon the Earth is immediately reflected back into space?
   a) 10%
   b) 30%
   c) 60%
   d) 75%

   Answer: b Key 1: C Section: 1

4. Approximately what percentage of solar radiation is used to power the water cycle?
   a) 10%
   b) 25%
   c) 50%
   d) 90%

   Answer: b Key 1: C Section: 1

5. The solar energy absorbing molecules of plants that power photosynthesis are called
   a) carbohydrates
   b) photovoltaics
   c) solarases
   d) chlorophylls

   Answer: d Key 1: D Section: 1

6. When the overall equation for the photosynthesis process is written and balanced, how many molecules of water are required to make one glucose molecule, $C_6H_{12}O_6$?
   a) 1
   b) 3
   c) 6
   d) 12

   Answer: c Key 1: A Section: 1

7. A watt is
   a) 1s/joule
   b) 1 cal/s
   c) 1 joule/s
   d) 1 s/cal

   Answer: c Key 1: A Section: 1

8. How many joules of energy will a stock tank heater rated at 1500 watts use in a 24 hour period?
   a) 1500
   b) 1500 x 24 x 60
   c) 1500 x 3600
   d) 1500 x 24 x 3600

   Answer: d Key 1: A Section: 1

9. The thin film of air, water, and soil in which all life exists is only about 15 km thick and is called the
   a) atmosphere
   b) stratosphere
   c) biosphere
   d) hemisphere

   Answer: c Key 1: A Section: 1

SHORT ANSWER

10. Burning 1 mol of methane to form carbon dioxide and water produces 192 kcal of energy. How much energy is produced when 3 mol of methane is burned?

    Answer: 576 kcal Key 1: A Section: 2

MULTIPLE CHOICE

11. Burning 1 mol of methane in oxygen to form carbon dioxide and water produces 803 kJ of energy. How much energy is produced when 3 mol of methane is burned?
    a) 268 kJ
    b) 803 kJ
    c) 1,606 kJ
    d) 2,409 kJ

    Answer: d Key 1: A Section: 2

FILL-IN-THE-BLANK

12. A student mixes compound A with compound B and notices that a chemical reaction occurs. The temperature of the mixture decreases. The reaction is ___________________________.

    Answer: endothermic Key 1: A Section: 2

MULTIPLE CHOICE

13. The decomposition of 2 mol of water to hydrogen and oxygen requires 137 kcal of energy. The reaction of hydrogen and oxygen to form 2 mol of water
    a) requires 137 kcal
    b) releases 137 kcal
    c) requires more than 137 kcal
    d) releases more than 137 kcal

    Answer: b Key 1: A Section: 2

14. Biological catalysts that mediate nearly all the chemical reactions that take place in living systems are called
    a) esters
    b) enzymes
    c) proteins
    d) amino acids

    Answer: b Key 1: A Section: 2

FILL-IN-THE-BLANK

15. There are several factors that can cause a chemical reaction to proceed faster. One such factor is ____________.

    Answer: temperature Key 1: C Section: 2

16. Raising the temperature of a reaction mixture is the same as increasing the _________ ____________ of the reacting molecules

    Answer: kinetic energy Key 1: C Section: 2

MULTIPLE CHOICE

17. Which of the following will cause the rate of a chemical reaction to speed up?
    a) Temperature
    b) concentration of reactants
    c) catalyst
    d) all of these

    Answer: d Key 1: C Section: 2

18. Burning one mole of propane according to the following reaction: $C_3H_8(g) + 5\ O_2(g)$ x $3\ CO_2 + 4\ H_2O$ liberates 526 kcal of energy. If all of the coefficients are tripled, how much energy will be released?
    a) 526 kcal
    b) 1052 kcal
    c) 1578 kcal
    d) 175.3 kcal

    Answer: c Key 1: A Section: 2

19. The first law of thermodynamics deals with
    a) conservation of mass
    b) conservation of energy
    c) creation of energy
    d) destruction of energy

    Answer: b Key 1: C Section: 3

20. The statement you can't get something for nothing is another way of expressing
    a) the first law of thermodynamics
    b) the second law of thermodynamics
    c) Boyles's law
    d) the third law of thermodynamics

    Answer: a Key 1: A Section: 3

21. Another name for the first law of thermodynamics is
    a) the law of conservation of matter
    b) the law of conservation of energy
    c) the periodic law of the elements
    d) the law of universal gravitation

    Answer: b Key 1: C Section: 3

22. The fact that a heat pump requires energy to move heat from a colder object (the outside of a house) to a hotter object (the inside of the house) is a real life observation of which thermodynamic law?
    a) the first law
    b) the second law
    c) the third law
    d) the fourth law

    Answer: b Key 1: A Section: 4

23. The fact that a refrigerator requires energy to move heat from a colder object (the inside of the refrigerator) to a hotter object (the outside of the refrigerator) is a real life observation of which law of thermodynamics?
    a) first law
    b) second law
    c) third law
    d) fourth law

    Answer: b Key 1: A Section: 4

24. Recycling of aluminum beverage cans is an example of the fact that
    a) increasing entropy is a spontaneous process
    b) increasing entropy is a nonspontaneous process
    c) decreasing entropy is a spontaneous process
    d) decreasing entropy is a nonspontaneous process

    Answer: d Key 1: A Section: 4

FILL-IN-THE-BLANK

25. Recycling of plastics is an example of the fact that __________ (decreasing/increasing) entropy is a __________________ process.

    Answer: decreasing, nonspontaneous Key 1: A Section: 4

MULTIPLE CHOICE

26. Which physical state has the lowest entropy?
    a) solid
    b) liquid
    c) gas
    d) all have the same entropy

    Answer: a Key 1: C Section: 4

27. Which physical state has the greatest entropy?
    a) solid
    b) liquid
    c) gas
    d) all have the same entropy

    Answer: c Key 1: C Section: 4

TRUE/FALSE

28. When a liquid is converted to a gas there is an increase in entropy.

    Answer: True Key 1: A Section: 4

MULTIPLE CHOICE

29. The second law of thermodynamics defines
    a) entropy
    b) energy
    c) heat
    d) temperature

    Answer: a Key 1: D Section: 4

30. Perhaps the first mechanical device used to convert energy into a more useful form was the
    a) steam engine
    b) water wheel
    c) wind mill
    d) nuclear reactor

    Answer: b Key 1: A Section: 5

31. The first fuel was
    a) coal
    b) petroleum
    c) blubber
    d) wood

    Answer: d Key 1: A Section: 5

32. Fuels are _________ forms of matter.
    a) oxidized
    b) reduced
    c) acidic
    d) basic

    Answer: b Key 1: C Section: 5

ESSAY

33. Define a fuel. Give an example. Include a balanced chemical reaction.

Answer: Key 1: C Section: 6

FILL-IN-THE-BLANK

34. Fuels are __________ forms of matter. The energy content of fuels is released by ___________.

Answer: reduced, oxidation Key 1: D Section: 6

MULTIPLE CHOICE

35. More than 50% of the world's petroleum reserves are in the
a) Middle East
b) South America
c) United Kingdom
d) United States

Answer: a Key 1: C Section: 6

TRUE/FALSE

36. At the current rate of consumption and production, U.S. reserves of petroleum will run out sometime in the 21st century.

Answer: True Key 1: A Section: 6

MULTIPLE CHOICE

37. Which one of the following is a nonfuel?
a) H_2
b) CCl_4
c) CH4
d) C_8H_{18}

Answer: b Key 1: A Section: 6

38. The primary element in coal is
a) carbon
b) hydrogen
c) oxygen
d) sulfur

Answer: a Key 1: C Section: 7

39. The highest grade of coal is
    a) anthracite
    b) bituminous
    c) lignite
    d) peat

    Answer: a Key 1: A Section: 7

40. The lowest grade of coal is
    a) anthracite
    b) bituminous
    c) lignite
    d) peat

    Answer: d Key 1: A Section: 7

41. Given the following analysis of coal samples, which is the best fuel?
    a) 95% C, 5% O
    b) 75% C, 25% O
    c) 50% C, 50% O
    d) 25% C, 75% O

    Answer: a Key 1: A Section: 7

ESSAY

42. Is coal being formed today? Is this a solution to our energy concerns?

    Answer: Key 1: C Section: 7

MULTIPLE CHOICE

43. The formation of coal in nature is estimated to take
    a) 100 years
    b) 1000 years
    c) 1 million years
    d) >100 million years

    Answer: d Key 1: C Section: 7

44. Prior to the middle of the 1700s, the major fuel used was
    a) coal
    b) natural gas
    c) petroleum
    d) wood

    Answer: d Key 1: C Section: 7

45. A major inconvenience of coal as a fuel is that it is a(n)
    a) solid
    b) liquid
    c) gas
    d) mixture of all three states

    Answer: a Key 1: A Section: 7

46. The most abundant fossil fuel in the US is
    a) coal
    b) natural gas
    c) petroleum
    d) wood

    Answer: a Key 1: A Section: 7

47. The US is estimated to have approximately what percentage of the world's coal reserves?
    a) 10%
    b) 25%
    c) 40%
    d) 80%

    Answer: c Key 1: A Section: 7

48. Approximately what percentage of US electricity is generated by the burning of coal?
    a) 10%
    b) 30%
    c) 50%
    d) 80%

    Answer: c Key 1: A Section: 7

49. When coal is burned, mineral impurities are converted to
    a) metal oxide gases that go up the smokestack
    b) carbon dioxide and water
    c) metal oxide solids that remain behind as ash
    d) all of the above

    Answer: c Key 1: C Section: 7

50. When coal containing sulfur is burned, the sulfur is converted to
    a) gaseous sulfur oxides that go up the smokestack
    b) liquid sulfur oxides that stay behind as ash
    c) solid sulfur oxides that stay behind as ash
    d) all of the above

    Answer: a Key 1: A Section: 7

51. When coal burns
    a) chemical energy is converted to heat energy
    b) heat energy is created
    c) chemical energy is destroyed
    d) heat energy is converted to electrical energy

    Answer: a Key 1: C Section: 7

52. When coal is heated in the absence of air, the solid left behind is called
    a) coal
    b) coke
    c) coal tar
    d) carbon

    Answer: b Key 1: A Section: 7

TRUE/FALSE

53. Fossil fuels are an important source of chemicals to synthesize other substances.

    Answer: True Key 1: A Section: 7

MULTIPLE CHOICE

54. When coal is heated in the absence of air, the condensed vapor collected during the heating is called
    a) coal
    b) coke
    c) coal tar
    d) carbon

    Answer: c Key 1: A Section: 7

TRUE/FALSE

55. The most inexpensive way of mining coal is strip mining.

    Answer: True Key 1: A Section: 7

56. A disadvantage of strip mining is that it leaves the soil exposed and erosion occurs more readily.

    Answer: True Key 1: A Section: 7

MULTIPLE CHOICE

57. The major component of natural gas is
    a) ethane
    b) methane
    c) propane
    d) butane

    Answer: b Key 1: A Section: 8

58. An advantage of natural gas as a fuel is that it is
    a) more abundant than coal
    b) easy to locate and extract
    c) easy to transport
    d) all of the above

    Answer: c Key 1: A Section: 8

59. Natural gas is mainly
    a) CO_2
    b) CH_4
    c) SO_2
    d) CO and H_2

    Answer: b Key 1: C Section: 8

60. Natural gas burns with a relatively clean flame. Which of the following potential pollutants is produced in significant quantities during the combustion of natural gas in air?
    a) sulfur oxides
    b) nitrogen oxides
    c) metal oxides
    d) all of the above

    Answer: b Key 1: A Section: 8

FILL-IN-THE-BLANK

61. When the ethane and propane components of natural gas are cracked, two new compounds are formed which are essential monomers used in making plastics. These substances are ______________________.

    Answer: ethylene and propylene Key 1: A Section: 8

MULTIPLE CHOICE

62. Petroleum is best described as a(n)
    a) pure substance
    b) compound
    c) simple mixture
    d) complex mixture

    Answer: d Key 1: C Section: 9

63. The main components of petroleum are
    a) hydrocarbons
    b) carbohydrates
    c) fats and oils
    d) ionic compounds

    Answer: a Key 1: C Section: 9

64. Recent evidence indicates that petroleum is derived from
    a) plants
    b) microscopic land animals
    c) microscopic marine animals
    d) decomposition of volcanic ash

    Answer: c Key 1: C Section: 9

65. To make crude petroleum more useful, it must be
    a) distilled
    b) filtered
    c) reduced
    d) washed with water

    Answer: a Key 1: A Section: 9

66. The fraction from the distillation of crude petroleum that is slightly heavier than gasoline is called
    a) kerosene
    b) heating oil
    c) lubricating oil
    d) asphalt

    Answer: a Key 1: A Section: 9

67. The yield of gasoline from crude petroleum can be increased by
    a) catalytic cracking of lighter fractions
    b) catalytic cracking of heavier fractions
    c) simple distillation
    d) vacuum distillation

    Answer: b Key 1: A Section: 9

68. Gasoline is a
    a) compound
    b) pure substance
    c) simple mixture of C_5 - C_{12} hydrocarbons
    d) complex mixture of C_5 - C_{12} hydrocarbons

    Answer: d Key 1: C Section: 9

69. A gasoline with an octane rating of 90 would give the same performance in a standard test engine as a mixture of
    a) 90% isooctane and 10% heptane
    b) 90% heptane and 10% isooctane
    c) 90 parts isooctane and 90 parts heptane
    d) 90 parts isooctane and 90 parts water

    Answer: a Key 1: A Section: 9

70. Pure isooctane would have an octane rating of
    a) 0
    b) 50
    c) 75
    d) 100

    Answer: d Key 1: A Section: 9

71. Pure heptane would have an octane rating of
    a) 0
    b) 50
    c) 75
    d) 100

    Answer: a Key 1: A Section: 9

72. In general, a higher proportion of branched chain hydrocarbons in a gasoline formulation
    a) increases octane rating
    b) decreases octane rating
    c) burns cleaner
    d) burns cooler

    Answer: a Key 1: A Section: 9

73. What metal, when added as a compound, increases octane rating of gasoline?
    a) Pb
    b) Hg
    c) Na
    d) Zn

    Answer: a Key 1: C Section: 9

74. Catalytic reforming is a process for converting
    a) low-octane rated alkanes into high-octane rated aromatics
    b) high-octane rated alkanes into low-octane rated aromatics
    c) low-octane rated alkanes into high-octane rated branched alkanes
    d) high-octane rated alkanes into low-octane rated branched alkanes

    Answer: a Key 1: C Section: 9

75. A compound that has replaced tetraethyllead as an octane booster is
    a) benzene
    b) heptane
    c) isooctane
    d) methyl tert-butyl ether

    Answer: d Key 1: A Section: 9

TRUE/FALSE

76. Oxygen containing additives to gasoline, such as methyl tert-butyl ether or ethanol, improve octane rating and reduce CO emissions in automobile engines.

    Answer: True Key 1: C Section: 9

MULTIPLE CHOICE

77. Which substance is most effective in raising the octane rating of gasoline?
    a) benzene
    b) ethanol
    c) methyl tert-butyl ether
    d) tetraethyllead

    Answer: d Key 1: C Section: 9

78. The heating of large hydrocarbon compounds in the absence of oxygen with a catalyst is called
    a) cracking
    b) catalysis
    c) reforming
    d) flocculation

    Answer: a Key 1: A Section: 9

79. The petroleum fraction with the highest boiling point is
    a) gas
    b) gasoline
    c) kerosene
    d) heating oil

    Answer: d Key 1: A Section: 9

80. The major component of petroleum is (are)
    a) benzene
    b) water
    c) organic compounds of sulfur
    d) hydrocarbons

    Answer: d Key 1: A Section: 9

ESSAY

81. Why is electricity considered a secondary energy source?

    Answer: Key 1: C Section: 10

MULTIPLE CHOICE

82. For most uses, the most convenient form of energy is
    a) chemical
    b) electrical
    c) mechanical
    d) solar

    Answer: b Key 1: C Section: 10

83. In any conversion of energy from one form to another, some of the energy ends up as
    a) entropy
    b) heat
    c) electricity
    d) radioactivity

    Answer: b Key 1: C Section: 10

84. Approximately what percentage of the chemical energy of a fossil fuel electrical power plant is "lost" as heat energy?
    a) 20%
    b) 40%
    c) 60%
    d) 80%

    Answer: c Key 1: A Section: 10

85. The inevitable energy lost as heat in the generation of electrical energy in the most efficient fossil fuel based power plant is a result of
    a) the first law of thermodynamics
    b) the second law of thermodynamics
    c) a poor understanding of energy conversion
    d) designed inefficiencies to increase costs to the consumer

    Answer: b Key 1: A Section: 10

86. At present, what approximate percentage of electricity generated in the US comes from nuclear energy?
    a) 20%
    b) 40%
    c) 60%
    d) 80%

    Answer: a Key 1: A Section: 11

87. Which country leads in percentage of electricity produced by nuclear energy?
    a) Australia
    b) France
    c) Japan
    d) United States

    Answer: b Key 1: A Section: 11

88. Electricity produced from nuclear power is especially important in which part of the U.S.?
    a) Southwest
    b) New England and the Upper Midwest
    c) West
    d) Plains

    Answer: b Key 1: A Section: 11

ESSAY

89. What are two advantages and two disadvantages of nuclear power?

    Answer: Key 1: A Section: 11

MULTIPLE CHOICE

90. Control rods in a nuclear reactor are used to
    a) absorb neutrons and slow down fission
    b) absorb neutrons and speed up fission
    c) release neutrons and slow down fission
    d) release neutrons and speed up fission

    Answer: a Key 1: A Section: 11

ESSAY

91. Discuss the problems of increasing the role of nuclear energy as an energy source.

    Answer: Key 1: A Section: 11

MULTIPLE CHOICE

92. Given the potential benefits and risks associated with nuclear power, the desirability quotient for electrical generation by nuclear power is probably best described as
    a) low
    b) moderate
    c) high
    d) uncertain

    Answer: d Key 1: A Section: 11

93. Which problem do all electric power plants have in common?
    a) excess capacity
    b) release of radioactivity
    c) sulfur dioxide emission
    d) thermal pollution

    Answer: d Key 1: A Section: 11

94. Tailings are the name for
    a) radioactive waste from spent nuclear fuel
    b) radioactive waste produced during the mining of uranium
    c) radioactive coolant water
    d) radioactive ash from coal fired power plants

    Answer: b Key 1: A Section: 11

95. You cannot make a bomb from reactor grade uranium because it
    a) is not radioactive enough
    b) is too well guarded
    c) would explode prematurely
    d) is not enriched enough in uranium-235

    Answer: d Key 1: C Section: 11

96. A breeder reactor converts
    a) nonfissionable U-238 to fissionable U-235
    b) nonfissionable U-238 to fissionable Pu-239
    c) fissionable U-235 to fissionable U-238
    d) fissionable U-235 to fissionable Pu-239

    Answer: b Key 1: C Section: 11

97. Breeder reactors allow for the use of
    a) abundant and naturally occurring U-235 as a nuclear fuel
    b) abundant and naturally occurring U-238 as a nuclear fuel
    c) abundant and naturally occurring Pu-238 as a nuclear fuel
    d) none of the above

    Answer: b Key 1: C Section: 11

98. The principal fuel(s) for nuclear fusion would be
    a) uranium-235 and uranium-238
    b) deuterium and tritium (^{2}H and ^{3}H)
    c) plutonium-238
    d) water

    Answer: b Key 1: C Section: 12

99. Which technology is not used at all today for the production of electricity?
    a) nuclear fusion
    b) nuclear fission
    c) solar cells
    d) geothermal power plants

    Answer: a Key 1: C Section: 12

100. The state of matter characterized by atomic nuclei and free electrons is called a
    a) gas
    b) liquid
    c) solid
    d) plasma

    Answer: d Key 1: D Section: 12

TRUE/FALSE

101. Nuclear fusion is the source of energy that powers the sun.

Answer: True Key 1: A Section: 12

102. Tritium is an isotope of hydrogen with 2 neutrons.

Answer: True Key 1: A Section: 12

MULTIPLE CHOICE

103. What percentage of the electricity produced in the world today comes from nuclear fusion?
a) 0%
b) 10%
c) 25%
d) 40%

Answer: a Key 1: D Section: 12

104. Which of the following statements best describes the status of nuclear fusion as an energy source?
a) Nuclear fusion generates some electrical power today.
b) Nuclear fusion will be a viable source of energy by the year 2000.
c) Nuclear fusion will solve all of our energy problems in the 21st century.
d) Nuclear fusion may help solve our energy problems in the future.

Answer: d Key 1: A Section: 12

105. One of the major difficulties in developing nuclear fusion as a possible source of continuous energy is that temperatures of ______ are needed to initiate fusion reactions.
a) 0 K
b) 300° C
c) 5000° C
d) 50,000,000° C

Answer: d Key 1: A Section: 12

106. Photovoltaic cells convert
a) solar energy into chemical energy
b) solar energy into mechanical energy
c) solar energy into electrical energy
d) solar energy into heat energy

Answer: c Key 1: A Section: 13

107. Most solar cells are composed primarily of
   a) arsenic
   b) boron
   c) carbon
   d) silicon

   Answer: d Key 1: C Section: 13

108. If very pure silicon is doped with a small amount of arsenic, the resulting crystal is called a
   a) solar cell
   b) donor crystal
   c) acceptor crystal
   d) battery

   Answer: b Key 1: C Section: 13

109. If very pure silicon is doped with a small amount of boron, the resulting crystal is called a(n)
   a) solar cell
   b) donor crystal
   c) acceptor crystal
   d) battery

   Answer: c Key 1: A Section: 13

110. The efficiency of current solar cells is approximately
   a) 5%
   b) 10%
   c) 25%
   d) 50%

   Answer: b Key 1: A Section: 13

111. One mechanism for storing solar energy for use at night or cloudy days is to use collected energy to melt salts. The stored energy would be retrieved by
   a) reacting molten salts with water to produce hydrogen gas
   b) allowing salts to solidify to heat steam to drive a turbine
   c) electrolyzing the molten salts
   d) converting molten salts to the gas phase

   Answer: b Key 1: A Section: 13

112. The use of biomass as a solution to all energy needs is limited by
   a) lack of appropriate plants
   b) lack of technology to process and burn biomass
   c) biomass is not renewable
   d) a shortage of land to grow plants for energy consumption

   Answer: d Key 1: C Section: 14

ESSAY

113. Discuss the use of biomass as an energy source. Give two examples.

Answer: Key 1: C Section: 14

MULTIPLE CHOICE

114. The production of biomass as an energy source is an example of the conversion of
a) solar energy to chemical energy
b) solar energy to electrical energy
c) solar energy to mechanical energy
d) solar energy to kinetic energy

Answer: a Key 1: C Section: 14

115. Biomass may be burned directly or chemically converted to a more convenient form (liquid or gas). Which of the following statements is true?
a) The conversion of biomass to a more convenient form improves the overall efficiency of the energy conversion.
b) The conversion of biomass to a more convenient form decreases the overall efficiency of the energy conversion.
c) The conversion of biomass to a more convenient form does not affect the overall efficiency. Energy is conserved!
d) All of the above statements are false.

Answer: b Key 1: A Section: 14

116. The overall efficiency of biomass as a method of harvesting solar energy is approximately
a) 3%
b) 10%
c) 20%
d) 40%

Answer: a Key 1: C Section: 14

117. Which of the following is not powered by the sun?
a) the water cycle
b) the winds
c) geothermal energy
d) biomass production

Answer: c Key 1: C Section: 15

118. Approximately what percentage of electricity generated in the US is hydroelectric?
a) < 1%
b) 10%
c) 25%
d) 40%

Answer: b Key 1: A Section: 15

119. The location of most of the hydroelectric power in the US is in the
a) Northeast
b) Southeast
c) Northwest
d) Midwest

Answer: c Key 1: A Section: 15

120. It is believed that wind power could provide _____ of our energy needs.
a) 5%
b) 10%
c) 25%
d) 50%

Answer: b Key 1: A Section: 15

121. Which of the following alternative energy sources is not intermittent and does not require energy storage?
a) solar cells
b) windmills
c) tides
d) none

Answer: d Key 1: A Section: 15

122. Harnessing the tides for energy production suffers what disadvantage?
a) they are too weak
b) they are too powerful
c) power is available only intermittently
d) they produce a lot of water pollution

Answer: c Key 1: C Section: 15

123. The internal heat from the Earth is due to
a) absorbed solar radiation from the land
b) absorbed solar radiation from the oceans
c) radioactivity and gravitation forces in the Earth's mantle and core
d) mysterious processes not well understood

Answer: c Key 1: A Section: 15

ESSAY

124. What are the limitations of geothermal energy for meeting large scale energy needs?

Answer: Key 1: C Section: 15

MULTIPLE CHOICE

125. Geothermal energy can not meet all of our energy needs because
a) the Earth is not hot enough
b) access to geothermal energy is limited to certain regions
c) geothermal energy is intermittent
d) geothermal sources do not have enough energy to generate electricity

Answer: b Key 1: C Section: 15

126. Liquefaction of coal produces a fuel that
a) increases the energy content of the coal
b) is more conveniently transported
c) contains less hydrogen than coal
d) is mainly methanol

Answer: b Key 1: C Section: 15

127. Hydrogen gas has been proposed as a fuel of the future because
a) it can be obtained cheaply by drilling
b) it can be extracted from seawater with no energy expenditure
c) it is nonflammable
d) it burns to produce water

Answer: d Key 1: C Section: 15

128. A fuel cell is an electrochemical device that
a) produces fuels from water
b) burns gasoline to produce heat
c) converts coal to a gas
d) converts chemical energy directly to electrical energy

Answer: d Key 1: C Section: 15

129. One of the advantages of hydrogen fuel cells as an energy source for space travel is
a) hydrogen is easily generated in space
b) the water produced by the cell can be used for other purposes
c) fuel cells are not limited by second law problems
d) fuel cells produce more energy in the vacuum of space

Answer: b Key 1: C Section: 15

ESSAY

130. Discuss the role of conservation in reducing energy consumption. Where could significant energy savings be made in the US?

     Answer: Key 1: C Section: 16

Chapter 15: Biochemistry

FILL-IN-THE-BLANK

1. The structural unit of living things is the __________.

   Answer: cell Key 1: C Section: 1

2. The largest structure in a cell is usually the __________________.

   Answer: cell nucleus Key 1: C Section: 1

MULTIPLE CHOICE

3. Substructure that distinguish plant and animal cells are
   a) ribosomes
   b) nuclei
   c) mitochondria
   d) chloroplasts

   Answer: d Key 1: A Section: 1

TRUE/FALSE

4. The genetic information of a cell is found in the ribosomes.

   Answer: False Key 1: A Section: 1

MULTIPLE CHOICE

5. In cells, protein synthesis occurs in the
   a) nucleus
   b) mitochondria
   c) ribosomes
   d) cytoplasm

   Answer: c Key 1: A Section: 1

6. In cells, primary energy production occurs in the
   a) mitochondria
   b) nucleus
   c) ribosomes
   d) cell membrane

   Answer: a Key 1: A Section: 1

7. Cell nutrients and waste must pass through the cell
   a) membrane
   b) nucleus
   c) ribosomes
   d) chloroplasts

   Answer: a Key 1: A Section: 1

SHORT ANSWER

8. The major distinguishing feature between plant and animal cells is chloroplast. Discuss this difference.

   Answer: plant cells do photosynthesis Key 1: C Section: 1

MULTIPLE CHOICE

9. Chloroplasts in plants convert
   a) light energy into heat energy
   b) light energy into electrical energy
   c) light energy into chemical energy
   d) heat energy into chemical energy

   Answer: c Key 1: C Section: 1

10. The primary chemical for the storage of energy in plants is
    a) carbohydrate
    b) fat
    c) protein
    d) cellulose

    Answer: a Key 1: C Section: 2

11. The series of chemical reactions that keep living organisms alive is referred to as
    a) anabolism
    b) catabolism
    c) biobolism
    d) metabolism

    Answer: d Key 1: D Section: 2

FILL-IN-THE-BLANK

12. The series of chemical reactions that degrade molecules to provide energy to a living system is called ______________________.

    Answer: catabolism Key 1: D Section: 2

MULTIPLE CHOICE

13. The series of chemical reactions that synthesize molecules for use by a living system is called
    a) anabolism
    b) catabolism
    c) biobolism
    d) metabolism

    Answer: a Key 1: D Section: 2

FILL-IN-THE-BLANK

14. The hydrolysis of sucrose yields glucose and ______.

    Answer: fructose Key 1: A Section: 3

15. The hydrolysis of lactose yields glucose and ______.

    Answer: galactose Key 1: A Section: 3

MULTIPLE CHOICE

16. Which one of the following elements **IS NOT** found in carbohydrates?
    a) carbon
    b) hydrogen
    c) oxygen
    d) nitrogen

    Answer: d Key 1: A Section: 3

17. From an organic chemistry perspective, carbohydrates are polyhydroxy
    a) carboxylic acids
    b) aldehydes and ketones
    c) amines
    d) amino acids

    Answer: b Key 1: A Section: 3

18. Which one of the following is a monosaccharide?
    a) glucose
    b) starch
    c) sucrose
    d) lactose

    Answer: a Key 1: A Section: 3

FILL-IN-THE-BLANK

19. Sucrose and lactose are examples of ____________________.

    Answer: disaccharides Key 1: A Section: 3

ESSAY

20. What is the major structural difference between cellulose and starch?

    Answer: Key 1: A Section: 3

MULTIPLE CHOICE

21. Which of the following serves as dietary fiber?
    a) starch
    b) galactose
    c) cellulose
    d) fructose

    Answer: c Key 1: A Section: 3

22. Which of the following is a polysaccharide?
    a) glucose
    b) fructose
    c) starch
    d) galactose

    Answer: c Key 1: A Section: 3

23. The monomer unit in both starch and cellulose is _____.
    a) glucose
    b) galactose
    c) fructose
    d) sucrose

    Answer: a Key 1: A Section: 3

SHORT ANSWER

24. The glucose units in starch are joined by _____ linkages, while those in cellulose are joined by _____ linkages.

    Answer: alpha, beta Key 1: A Section: 3

MULTIPLE CHOICE

25. Animal starch is called _____.
    a) amylose
    b) amylopectin
    c) cellulose
    d) glycogen

    Answer: d Key 1: D Section: 3

26. The brain's exclusive source of energy is
    a) glucose
    b) sucrose
    c) lactose
    d) maltose

    Answer: a Key 1: A Section: 3

27. An example of a disaccharide is
    a) sucrose
    b) galactose
    c) dextrose
    d) fructose

    Answer: a Key 1: A Section: 3

28. The name carbohydrate reflects
    a) the ratio of carbon to hydrogen in the molecule
    b) the ratio of carbonyl groups to total carbon content
    c) the ratio of carbon to the combined ratio of "hydrogen to oxygen"
    d) the ratio of carbon to oxygen

    Answer: c Key 1: C Section: 3

29. The molecular formula for glucose is
    a) $C_{12}H_6O_6$
    b) $C_6H_{12}O_6$
    c) $C_6H_6O_{12}$
    d) $C_{12}H_{22}O_{11}$

    Answer: b Key 1: A Section: 3

30. Unsaturated fats are often liquids called
    a) hydrogenated fats
    b) oils
    c) triglycerides
    d) glycerol

    Answer: b Key 1: A Section: 4

31. A fatty acid is determined to have 17 carbon atoms. This fatty acid is probably from a
    a) synthetic source
    b) natural source
    c) plant
    d) animal

    Answer: a Key 1: A Section: 4

32. Iodine number is a measure of
    a) the number of iodine atoms in a carbohydrate
    b) the number of iodine atoms in a fat
    c) the number of iodine atoms in a protein
    d) the degree of unsaturation of a fat

    Answer: d Key 1: A Section: 4

FILL-IN-THE-BLANK

33. Cellular constituents that are soluble in low polarity organic solvents are called ______.

    Answer: lipids Key 1: D Section: 4

34. Fats are esters of _______ and glycerol.

    Answer: fatty acids Key 1: D Section: 4

MULTIPLE CHOICE

35. Fats and oils are examples of
    a) ketones
    b) aldehydes
    c) alcohols
    d) esters

    Answer: d Key 1: A Section: 4

36. Fats and oils are differentiated from each other on the basis of their
    a) melting points
    b) densities
    c) glycerol content
    d) boiling points

    Answer: a Key 1: C Section: 4

37. Triglyceride is another term for
    a) cholesterol
    b) protein
    c) blood sugar
    d) fats and oils

    Answer: d   Key 1: D   Section: 4

38. The degree of unsaturation in the side-chain of a fat or an oil is revealed by its
    a) melting point
    b) density
    c) iodine number
    d) pH

    Answer: c   Key 1: A   Section: 4

FILL-IN-THE-BLANK

39. Proteins are composed of long chains of ____________________.

    Answer: amino acids   Key 1: C   Section: 5

MULTIPLE CHOICE

40. Proteins are
    a) polyamides
    b) polyesters
    c) polysaccharides
    d) polyacids

    Answer: a   Key 1: C   Section: 6

FILL-IN-THE-BLANK

41. The bond that holds amino acids together to form the backbone of a protein is called a(n) ____________________ bond.

    Answer: peptide bond   Key 1: A   Section: 6

MULTIPLE CHOICE

42. A relatively small molecule with more than 10 amino acids is called a
    a) polypeptide
    b) protein
    c) polysaccharide
    d) polynucleic acid

    Answer: a   Key 1: A   Section: 6

43. The primary structure of a protein is determined by
    a) the amino acid composition
    b) the order of amino acids in the protein
    c) the hydrogen bonding that gives the protein three dimensional shape
    d) the intertwining of protein molecules to form a "functional" protein

    Answer: b Key 1: C Section: 6

FILL-IN-THE-BLANK

44. The end of the protein molecule with a free carboxyl group is called the ________ end.

    Answer: C-terminal Key 1: A Section: 6

45. The end of the protein molecule with a free amino group is called the________ end.

    Answer: N-terminal Key 1: A Section: 6

ESSAY

46. Discuss the four types of protein structure.

    Answer: Key 1: C Section: 7

MULTIPLE CHOICE

47. The secondary structure of a protein is determined by
    a) the amino acid composition
    b) the order of amino acids in the protein
    c) the hydrogen bonding that gives the protein a three dimensional shape
    d) the intertwining of protein molecules to form a "functional" protein

    Answer: c Key 1: C Section: 7

TRUE/FALSE

48. A salt bridge occurs when the oppositely charged side chains on two amino acids within the same or different protein chains are attracted to each other.

    Answer: True Key 1: A Section: 7

49. The great diversity of proteins is due to the large number of amino acids from which proteins are made.

    Answer: False Key 1: A Section: 7

MULTIPLE CHOICE

50. The helical structure of certain proteins, such as wool, is part of the protein's
    a) primary structure
    b) secondary structure
    c) tertiary structure
    d) quaternary structure

    Answer: b Key 1: C Section: 7

51. The pleated structure of certain proteins, such as silk, is part of the protein's
    a) primary structure
    b) secondary structure
    c) tertiary structure
    d) quaternary structure

    Answer: b Key 1: C Section: 7

ESSAY

52. How do hydrophobic interactions influence the structure of proteins?

    Answer: Key 1: C Section: 7

MULTIPLE CHOICE

53. Disulfide linkages in proteins are due to interactions among one specific amino acid in the primary structure of the protein. This amino acid is
    a) glycine
    b) alanine
    c) cysteine
    d) tyrosine

    Answer: c Key 1: C Section: 7

54. A disulfide linkage in a protein is a(n)
    a) ionic bond between sulfur atoms on different amino acids
    b) covalent bond between sulfur atoms on different amino acids
    c) hydrogen bond between sulfur atoms on different amino acids
    d) hydrophobic interaction between sulfur atoms on different amino acids

    Answer: b Key 1: A Section: 7

55. Certain -R groups attached to amino acids are called "hydrophobic." In the tertiary structure of a protein, hydrophobic groups are generally found
    a) on the interior of the protein structure, shielded from interaction with water molecules
    b) on the exterior of the protein structure, shielded from interaction with water molecules
    c) on the interior of the protein structure, maximizing their interaction with water molecules
    d) on the exterior of the protein structure, maximizing their interaction with water molecules

    Answer: a Key 1: C Section: 7

ESSAY

56. What is a disulfide bond? How does it influence the structure of a protein?

    Answer: Key 1: C Section: 7

FILL-IN-THE-BLANK

57. This peptide produced in the kidneys causes powerful constrictions of blood vessels. It is ___________.

    Answer: angiotensin II Key 1: A Section: 7

MULTIPLE CHOICE

58. Enzymes are
    a) catalysts
    b) structural material
    c) genetic material
    d) nucleic acids

    Answer: a Key 1: D Section: 8

59. In living systems, a specific enzyme generally catalyzes
    a) one specific reaction
    b) a group of similar reactions
    c) many different reactions
    d) all possible reactions

    Answer: a Key 1: C Section: 8

ESSAY

60. Explain in general terms the "lock and key" model of enzyme action. Use the terms substrate and active site in your discussion.

    Answer: Key 1: C Section: 8

MULTIPLE CHOICE

61. The specificity of enzyme catalysis is often described as the
    a) ball and chain mechanism
    b) lock and key mechanism
    c) roller coaster mechanism
    d) kinetic energy mechanism

    Answer: b Key 1: C Section: 8

62. The portion of an enzyme where the substrate "fits" during the reaction is called the
    a) active site
    b) action site
    c) reaction site
    d) substrate site

    Answer: a Key 1: C Section: 8

63. Enzyme activity can be regulated by the cell through the use of _______.
    a) allosteric enzymes
    b) feedback inhibition
    c) zymogens
    d) all of these

    Answer: d Key 1: A Section: 8

64. Clinical analysis of enzymes in blood are used as one means of diagnosing
    a) heart attack
    b) cancer
    c) high blood pressure
    d) stroke

    Answer: a Key 1: A Section: 8

65. The class of compounds that serve as the source of information and control in living systems are
    a) amino acids
    b) carbohydrates
    c) nucleic acids
    d) proteins

    Answer: c Key 1: D Section: 9

66. DNA is found primarily in the cell
    a) nucleus
    b) ribosomes
    c) mitochondria
    d) DNA is found throughout the cell

    Answer: a Key 1: A Section: 9

67. RNA is found primarily in the cell
    a) nucleus
    b) ribosomes
    c) mitochondria
    d) RNA is found throughout the cell

    Answer: d Key 1: C Section: 9

68. The repeating units in both DNA and RNA are called
    a) monomers
    b) nucleic acids
    c) nucleotides
    d) amino acids

    Answer: c Key 1: A Section: 9

69. The sugar in the nucleotides of DNA is
    a) glucose
    b) sucrose
    c) ribose
    d) deoxyribose

    Answer: d Key 1: C Section: 9

70. The sugar in the nucleotides of RNA is
    a) glucose
    b) sucrose
    c) ribose
    d) deoxyribose

    Answer: c Key 1: C Section: 9

71. Nucleotides in nucleic acids are joined by links through the
    a) phosphate groups
    b) base groups
    c) sugar groups
    d) peptide bonds

    Answer: a Key 1: C Section: 9

72. The most important feature that distinguishes one DNA molecule from another (is/are)
    a) the type of phosphate bonds
    b) the type of sugar in each molecule
    c) tthe order of amine attached to the sugar phosphate backbone
    d) all of the above features

    Answer: c Key 1: C Section: 9

FILL-IN-THE-BLANK

73. The genetic information in DNA is carried by _______ different bases.

    Answer: four Key 1: C Section: 9

MULTIPLE CHOICE

74. The information in DNA and RNA is carried by the
    a) phosphate bonds
    b) sugar molecules
    c) length of the nucleic acid chain
    d) base sequence

    Answer: d Key 1: C Section: 9

75. Watson and Crick proposed that DNA exists as a(n)
    a) alpha helix
    b) double helix
    c) beta sheet
    d) pleated sheet

    Answer: b Key 1: A Section: 9

76. Base pairing in DNA occurs through
    a) covalent bonds between complementary bases on nucleic acid chains
    b) hydrogen bonds between complementary bases on nucleic acid chains
    c) salt bonds between complementary bases on nucleic acid chains
    d) an interaction that is not well understood

    Answer: b Key 1: C Section: 9

77. Which one of the following statements comparing DNA and RNA is correct?
    a) DNA exists as a double helix of DNA chains; RNA is single stranded
    b) RNA exists as a double helix of RNA chains; DNA is single stranded
    c) Both DNA and RNA exist as a double helix
    d) Both DNA and RNA are single stranded

    Answer: a Key 1: C Section: 9

78. The hereditary material of all cells is found in the
    a) chromosomes
    b) mitochondria
    c) ribosomes
    d) cytoplasm

    Answer: a Key 1: C Section: 10

79. Human body cells have ________ chromosomes.
    a) 20
    b) 23
    c) 46
    d) 53

    Answer: c Key 1: C Section: 10

80. The first step in protein synthesis in cells is
    a) replication
    b) transcription
    c) translation
    d) destruction

    Answer: b Key 1: A Section: 10

SHORT ANSWER

81. What is the simple evidence that leads to the conclusion that information about the genetic code contained in DNA must be transported out of the cell nucleus?

    Answer: little or no DNA outside of nucleus Key 1: C Section: 10

ESSAY

82. Discuss in very general terms how the genetic code in DNA controls the synthesis of proteins in the cell ribosomes.

    Answer: Key 1: C Section: 10

MULTIPLE CHOICE

83. Transcription is the process by which DNA passes information to
    a) another strand of DNA
    b) transfer RNA
    c) messenger RNA
    d) a new cell

    Answer: c Key 1: C Section: 11

FILL-IN-THE-BLANK

84. The RNA that transports the base sequence information to the ribosomes is called ____________________ RNA or ___RNA.

    Answer: messenger, m Key 1: C Section: 11

MULTIPLE CHOICE

85. Which nucleic acid is involved in translating the base sequence of an RNA molecule into the amino acid sequence of a protein?
    a) DNA
    b) tRNA
    c) mRNA
    d) rRNA

    Answer: b Key 1: C Section: 11

TRUE/FALSE

86. There are 64 codons for 20 amino acids.

    Answer: True Key 1: C Section: 11

MULTIPLE CHOICE

87. Which nucleic acid is involved in the transcription process?
    a) DNA
    b) mRNA
    c) tRNA
    d) rRNA

    Answer: b Key 1: C Section: 11

TRUE/FALSE

88. The genetic code for protein synthesis is known.

    Answer: True Key 1: C Section: 11

MULTIPLE CHOICE

89. Restriction endonucleases are used to chop DNA up into small fragments containing a small number of genes. These fragments are called
    a) RFLPs
    b) RNAs
    c) HDPE
    d) FRMPs

    Answer: a Key 1: C Section: 12

90. Restriction fragment length polymorphisms (RFLPs) are used to
    a) study the primary sequence of proteins
    b) identify complementary bases in DNA
    c) identify persons with genetic diseases
    d) determine codons for specific amino acids

    Answer: c Key 1: C Section: 12

91. The bacterial DNA that is used as the splice receptor in recombinant DNA is called a
    a) plasmid
    b) codon
    c) clones
    d) restrictor

    Answer: a Key 1: A Section: 12

Chapter 16: Food

MULTIPLE CHOICE

1. It is estimated that ______ of adults in the US are overweight.
   a) 10%
   b) 30%
   c) 50%
   d) 75%

   Answer: b Key 1: C Key 2: I

2. What percentage of the human body is water?
   a) ≈10%
   b) ≈25%
   c) ≈50%
   d) ≈70%

   Answer: d Key 1: C Key 2: I

3. Glucose and fructose have the same chemical formula, $C_6H_{12}O_6$. They have different chemical structures. Glucose and fructose are
   a) allotropes
   b) isomers
   c) isotopes
   d) hybrids

   Answer: b Key 1: C Key 2: I

4. Blood sugar is
   a) fructose
   b) glucose
   c) lactose
   d) sucrose

   Answer: b Key 1: D Section: 1

5. Corn syrup is primarily
   a) glucose
   b) fructose
   c) corntose
   d) sucrose

   Answer: a Key 1: A Section: 1

ESSAY

6. High fructose corn syrup is often used to sweeten soft drinks. Discuss briefly the difference between corn syrup and high fructose corn syrup.

   Answer: Key 1: A Section: 1

MULTIPLE CHOICE

7. High fructose corn syrup is produced
   a) from genetically engineered corn that produces more fructose than glucose upon hydrolysis
   b) by processing normal glucose rich corn syrup with an enzyme that converts glucose to fructose
   c) by adding synthetic fructose to normal corn syrup
   d) by a combination of all of the above processes

   Answer: b Key 1: A Section: 1

8. Compared to normal corn syrup, high fructose corn syrup is
   a) sweeter
   b) less sweet
   c) the same sweetness
   d) higher in calories

   Answer: a Key 1: C Section: 1

9. Persons with lactose intolerance
   a) are allergic to lactose
   b) lack the enzyme for the breakdown of lactose
   c) have a deficiency of lactose
   d) have a bitter taste response to lactose

   Answer: b Key 1: C Section: 1

FILL-IN-THE-BLANK

10. Per capita consumption of sugars in the United States per year is approximately ______________ kilograms.

    Answer: 60 Key 1: A Section: 1

ESSAY

11. A significant number of adults suffer from a condition known as lactose intolerance. What is lactose intolerance and why does it occur?

    Answer: Key 1: C Section: 1

MULTIPLE CHOICE

12. Lactose is commonly referred to as
    a) blood sugar
    b) milk sugar
    c) muscle sugar
    d) table sugar

    Answer: b Key 1: D Section: 1

13. Hydrolysis means
    a) broken down by water
    b) broken down by hydrogen
    c) broken down by pressure
    d) broken down by heat

    Answer: a Key 1: D Section: 1

14. When starch is digested, it is hydrolyzed to
    a) fructose
    b) glucose
    c) lactose
    d) sucrose

    Answer: b Key 1: A Section: 1

15. From your body's perspective, glucose is
    a) a fuel
    b) an oxidizing agent
    c) a source of structural material
    d) all of the above

    Answer: a Key 1: C Section: 1

16. Which of the following is not produced during the metabolism of glucose?
    a) energy
    b) carbon dioxide
    c) ammonia
    d) water

    Answer: c Key 1: A Section: 1

17. Complex carbohydrates are essentially polymers of
    a) glucose
    b) amino acids
    c) nucleic acids
    d) cholesterol

    Answer: a Key 1: C Section: 1

18. The body stores a relatively small amount of excess glucose as
    a) cellulose
    b) glycogen
    c) protein
    d) fat

    Answer: b Key 1: C Section: 1

SHORT ANSWER

19. You eat a whole pizza for dinner. You then fall asleep. Discuss what your body does with all of that starch.

    Answer: glucose, glycogen, fat Key 1: C Section: 1

FILL-IN-THE-BLANK

20. The body stores some excess glucose as glycogen in the ______________ and __________________.

    Answer: liver, muscles Key 1: C Section: 1

MULTIPLE CHOICE

21. The body stores most excess glucose as
    a) cellulose
    b) glycogen
    c) protein
    d) fat

    Answer: b Key 1: C Section: 1

22. Animal starch is
    a) glucose
    b) cellulose
    c) glycogen
    d) fat

    Answer: c Key 1: C Section: 1

23. At least what percentage of one's caloric intake should be carbohydrate?
    a) 50%
    b) 65%
    c) 80%
    d) 90%

    Answer: b Key 1: A Section: 1

TRUE/FALSE

24. Complex carbohydrates are better nutrition for humans than simple sugars.

    Answer: True Key 1: A Section: 1

MULTIPLE CHOICE

25. A good source of complex carbohydrates is
    a) sucrose
    b) lactose
    c) cereal grains
    d) beef steak

    Answer: c Key 1: A Section: 1

26. Fats are
    a) esters
    b) ethers
    c) glycerol
    d) cholesterol

    Answer: a Key 1: C Section: 2

27. Most fats are
    a) monoglycerides
    b) diglycerides
    c) triglycerides
    d) polyglycerides

    Answer: c Key 1: A Section: 2

28. In the body, fat serves as a
    a) thermal insulator
    b) protective covering of organs
    c) reserve energy supply
    d) all of the above

    Answer: d Key 1: A Section: 2

29. The first step in the hydrolysis of fats is splitting into fatty acids and
    a) ethanol
    b) glucose
    c) methanol
    d) glycerol

    Answer: d Key 1: A Section: 2

ESSAY

30. What is arteriosclerosis? Why does it often lead to heart attack or stroke?

    Answer: Key 1: A Section: 2

MULTIPLE CHOICE

31. Arteriosclerosis is a condition affecting the
    a) heart
    b) arteries
    c) brain
    d) lungs

    Answer: b Key 1: A Section: 2

32. Saturated fats have
    a) primarily C-C bonds
    b) a large proportion of C=C bonds
    c) one or more C≡C bonds
    d) an odd number of carbon atoms

    Answer: a Key 1: A Section: 2

33. Polyunsaturated fats have
    a) primarily C-C bonds
    b) a large proportion of C=C bonds
    c) one or more C≡C bonds
    d) an odd number of carbon atoms

    Answer: b Key 1: A Section: 2

34. Fats and cholesterol are carried in the blood by association with
    a) hemoglobin
    b) lipids
    c) lipoproteins
    d) glucose

    Answer: c Key 1: C Section: 2

35. Lipoproteins are classified by
    a) density
    b) carbon number
    c) amino acid sequence
    d) iodine number

    Answer: a Key 1: A Section: 2

ESSAY

36. Compare and contrast the roles of LDL and HDL in transporting and processing cholesterol.

    Answer: Key 1: C Section: 2

MULTIPLE CHOICE

37. Low-density lipoproteins are the blood carriers of
    a) triglycerides
    b) oxygen
    c) fatty acids
    d) cholesterol

    Answer: d Key 1: C Section: 2

38. Very low-density lipoproteins are the blood carriers of
    a) triglycerides
    b) oxygen
    c) fatty acids
    d) cholesterol

    Answer: a Key 1: A Section: 2

39. High-density lipoproteins are the blood carriers of
    a) triglycerides
    b) oxygen
    c) fatty acids
    d) cholesterol

    Answer: d Key 1: A Section: 2

40. High-density lipoprotein is often called "good cholesterol" because it
    a) breaks down cholesterol in the bloodstream
    b) delivers cholesterol to the cells for use
    c) carries cholesterol to the lungs where it is oxidized
    d) transports cholesterol to the liver where it is processed and excreted

    Answer: d Key 1: A Section: 2

41. Low-density lipoprotein is often called "bad cholesterol" because it
    a) breaks down cholesterol in the bloodstream
    b) delivers cholesterol to the cells where it may be deposited in arteries
    c) carries cholesterol to the lungs where it is oxidized
    d) transports cholesterol to the liver where it is processed and excreted

    Answer: b Key 1: A Section: 2

42. There is some evidence that exercise increases
    a) HDL
    b) LDL
    c) VLDL
    d) all lipoproteins

    Answer: a Key 1: A Section: 2

SHORT ANSWER

43. A serving of peanut butter contains 204 food calories. The serving contains 9 grams of protein, 16 grams of fat and 6 g of carbohydrate. What percentage of calories comes from fat?
    (1 g fat = 9 kcal) (1 g protein = 4 kcal) (1 g carbohydrate = 4 kcal)

    Answer: 71% Key 1: A Section: 2

MULTIPLE CHOICE

44. A serving of a low fat cream cheese contains 6 g of fat and 3 g of protein. What percentage of calories comes from fat?
    (1 g fat = 9 kcal) (1 g protein = 4 kcal)
    a) 23%
    b) 50%
    c) 73%
    d) 82%

    Answer: d Key 1: A Section: 2

45. One serving of chunk light tuna in water contains 0.5 g of fat. The total food calories in one serving is 60. What percentage of calories come from fat?
    a) <1%
    b) 7.5%
    c) 15%
    d) 75%

    Answer: b Key 1: A Section: 2

46. The class of foods that have the highest caloric value are
    a) carbohydrates
    b) fats
    c) protein
    d) vitamins

    Answer: b Key 1: C Section: 2

47. Some of the fat-laden foods are cream, butter, margarine and ______.
    a) fish
    b) celery
    c) fruit
    d) salad oils

    Answer: d Key 1: A Section: 2

48. The purpose of casein in milk is
    a) as an enzyme
    b) that it stabilizes the emulsion of butterfat in water
    c) as a monosaccharide
    d) as a catalyst

    Answer: b Key 1: C Section: 2

49. It has been shown that Greenlanders who eat a lot of fish have a low risk of heart disease despite the fact that their diet is high in fat and cholesterol. This is probably due to
    a) polyunsaturated fatty acids
    b) taking aspirin
    c) complexing agents
    d) vigorous exercise

    Answer: a Key 1: A Section: 2

TRUE/FALSE

50. Some vegetable oils contain cholesterol and others are cholesterol free.

    Answer: False Key 1: A Section: 2

MULTIPLE CHOICE

51. A 2000 Calorie per day diet should contain not more than _____ grams of fat.
    a) 67
    b) 605
    c) 30
    d) 11

    Answer: a Key 1: A Section: 2

52. A 2000 Calorie per day diet should contain not more than _____ grams of saturated fat.
    a) 67
    b) 22
    c) 33.5
    d) 10

    Answer: b Key 1: A Section: 2

53. Which one of the following is not a fake fat?
    a) cyclamate
    b) Olean
    c) Simplesse
    d) Z-Trim

    Answer: a Key 1: C Section: 2

54. Cholesterol is a
    a) fully saturated triglyceride
    b) highly unsaturated triglyceride
    c) fatty acid
    d) steroidal alcohol

    Answer: d Key 1: D Section: 2

55. Cholesterol does not occur in
    a) coconut oil
    b) butter
    c) beef fat
    d) lard

    Answer: a Key 1: C Section: 2

56. Cholesterol that is present in the blood serum is closely associated with
    a) overactive kidneys
    b) hardening of the arteries
    c) diabetes
    d) osteoperosis

    Answer: b Key 1: C Section: 2

ESSAY

57. Explain why meat is an inefficient source of protein.

    Answer: Key 1: A Section: 3

MULTIPLE CHOICE

58. Proteins are polymers of
    a) glucose
    b) amino acids
    c) nucleic acid
    d) lipids

    Answer: b Key 1: C Section: 3

59. How many essential amino acids are there?
    a) 8
    b) 20
    c) 40
    d) 1000

    Answer: a Key 1: C Section: 3

60. Kwashiorkor is a disease caused by
    a) lack of iodine
    b) iron deficiency
    c) extreme lack of protein and vitamins
    d) sedentary life style

    Answer: c Key 1: C Section: 3

61. Amino acids that are not synthesized by the human body and must be obtained in food sources are called
    a) nucleic acids
    b) carboxylic acids
    c) essential amino acids
    d) vitamins

    Answer: c Key 1: D Section: 3

TRUE/FALSE

62. A total vegetarian diet supplies an adequate amount of everything a human needs to be totally healthy.

    Answer: False Key 1: A Section: 3

MULTIPLE CHOICE

63. The number of different amino acids that combine to form human protein is generally recognized as
    a) 10
    b) 20
    c) 35
    d) 45

    Answer: b Key 1: A Section: 3

64. People who do not eat meat or other animal products can obtain all the essential amino acids most effectively by
    a) taking commercial amino acid supplements
    b) obtaining injections at a hospital or clinic
    c) eating lima beans each day
    d) eating combinations of foods that supply complementary proteins

    Answer: d Key 1: A Section: 3

65. Complete (adequate) protein contains
    a) all the known amino acids
    b) all the amino acids found in human protein
    c) all the essential amino acids
    d) all the amino acids for which U.S. RDAs have been established

    Answer: c Key 1: D Section: 3

66. High quality (better than adequate) protein is a protein that
    a) contains all the amino acids found in human protein
    b) contains all the known amino acids
    c) contains all the essential amino acids in about the same ratio as the occur in human protein
    d) contains all the amino acids in the same sequence as they are found in human protein

    Answer: c Key 1: D Section: 3

67. Chicken eggs are a particularly rich source of
    a) carbohydrates
    b) high quality protein
    c) micronutrients
    d) polyunsaturated acid

    Answer: b Key 1: A Section: 3

68. It is estimated that minerals compose ____ of the mass of the human body.
    a) 1%
    b) 4%
    c) 10%
    d) 20%

    Answer: b Key 1: C Section: 4

69. Iron plays a central role in
    a) protein synthesis
    b) nucleic acid replication
    c) hemoglobin structure and oxygen transport
    d) bones

    Answer: c Key 1: A Section: 4

70. Which class of nutrients in itself does not provide any energy to the human body?
    a) minerals
    b) fats
    c) carbohydrates
    d) proteins

    Answer: a Key 1: C Section: 4

71. How many elements are "essential" to life?
    a) 10
    b) 30
    c) 70
    d) 110

    Answer: b Key 1: C Section: 4

ESSAY

72. The elements essential for life can be classified into four categories: the bulk structural elements; the macrominerals; the trace elements; the ultratrace elements. Phosphorus and sulfur each appear twice in two categories. What are they and why?

    Answer: Key 1: C Section: 4

73. The textbook classifies the elements essential for life into four categories: the bulk structural elements; the macrominerals; the trace elements; the ultratrace elements. What do these categories mean? Give an example of one element in each category.

    Answer: Key 1: C Section: 4

MULTIPLE CHOICE

74. Iodine is an important mineral in the proper functioning of the
    a) brain
    b) thyroid
    c) intestines
    d) heart

    Answer: b Key 1: C Section: 4

ESSAY

75. Sodium chloride is an essential nutrient. What problems are associated with a diet that contains too much sodium chloride?

    Answer: Key 1: A Section: 4

MULTIPLE CHOICE

76. One of the side effects of diuretics is
    a) iron poor blood
    b) potassium depletion
    c) loss of calcium
    d) loss of iodine

    Answer: b Key 1: A Section: 4

ESSAY

77. What are the origins of the word "vitamin"?

    Answer: Key 1: A Section: 5

MULTIPLE CHOICE

78. Vitamins can be grouped into two broad categories:
    a) the B complex and the rest
    b) fat soluble and water soluble
    c) acids and esters
    d) esters and amines

    Answer: b Key 1: C Section: 5

ESSAY

79. What is a vitamin?

    Answer: Key 1: D Section: 5

MULTIPLE CHOICE

80. Fat soluble vitamins are
    a) stored in the body
    b) excreted from the body
    c) rapidly decomposed in the body
    d) less important than water soluble vitamins

    Answer: a Key 1: A Section: 5

81. Water soluble vitamins are
    a) polar
    b) nonpolar
    c) ionic
    d) hydrocarbons

    Answer: a Key 1: A Section: 5

ESSAY

82. Explain why it is more likely that a child will suffer from a deficiency of vitamin A as opposed to an adult.

    Answer: Key 1: A Section: 5

MULTIPLE CHOICE

83. A deficiency of vitamin A may cause
    a) schizophrenia
    b) blindness
    c) cardiac arrest
    d) stroke

    Answer: b Key 1: A Section: 5

84. Which of the following vitamins can cause sickness if taken in too large a quantity?
    a) A
    b) C
    c) B complex
    d) K

    Answer: a Key 1: A Section: 5

85. The fat soluble vitamins are
    a) A,B,C,K
    b) A,C,D,K
    c) A,D,E,K
    d) B,C,D,E

    Answer: c Key 1: C Section: 5

86. A disease or condition that vitamin C is known to cure is
    a) colds
    b) scurvy
    c) cancer
    d) rickets

    Answer: b Key 1: A Section: 5

87. Fiber appears to lower the risk of
    a) lung cancer
    b) liver cancer
    c) stomach cancer
    d) colon cancer

    Answer: d Key 1: A Section: 6

88. Cellulose has many hydroxyl groups. This allows cellulose to
    a) form many hydrogen bonds to water
    b) be easily digested
    c) dissolve in fat tissue
    d) react with a variety of substances

    Answer: a Key 1: A Section: 6

89. A high fiber diet has been linked with the prevention of
    a) diarrhea
    b) colon cancer
    c) aging
    d) the common cold

    Answer: b Key 1: A Section: 6

90. Fiber in the diet
    a) provides quick energy
    b) is readily converted to fat
    c) lowers retention time in the colon
    d) is rich in vitamins

    Answer: c Key 1: A Section: 6

91. Ketosis is a condition that develops during
    a) starvation
    b) overeating
    c) exercise
    d) stress

    Answer: a Key 1: A Section: 7

92. During a fast, your body
    a) cleanses itself of toxic compounds
    b) produces ammonia, acetone, and other waste products
    c) synthesizes more glycogen
    d) converts fat to protein

    Answer: b Key 1: C Section: 7

93. In the late stages of extended starvation or fast, the body uses what as a source of energy?
    a) fat
    b) carbohydrate
    c) glycogen
    d) protein

    Answer: d Key 1: C Section: 7

94. Which does not provide a complete protein?
    a) meat
    b) cheese
    c) eggs
    d) soy protein

    Answer: d Key 1: A Section: 7

95. Processing of foods generally decreases
    a) vitamins
    b) minerals
    c) fiber
    d) all of the above

    Answer: d Key 1: C Section: 7

96. Which additive serves no nutritive function?
    a) KI
    b) $FeCO_3$
    c) vitamin C
    d) FD&C Yellow #5

    Answer: d Key 1: A Section: 8

97. The US government agency charged with keeping our food safe is
    a) EPA
    b) OSHA
    c) FDA
    d) NCAA

    Answer: c Key 1: D Section: 8

98. The GRAS list indicates the generally accepted
    a) carcinogens
    b) essential vitamins
    c) illegal drugs
    d) food additives

    Answer: d Key 1: A Section: 8

SHORT ANSWER

99. Some food additives are listed on the GRAS list. What does the acronym GRAS stand for?

    Answer: generally recognized as safe Key 1: A Section: 8

MULTIPLE CHOICE

100. Vanilla extract and imitation vanilla flavoring differ in that the extract
    a) is purer
    b) is more healthful
    c) contains a greater variety of chemicals
    d) contains fewer carcinogens

    Answer: c Key 1: C Section: 8

101. Benzoic acid serves as a
    a) flavoring
    b) preservative
    c) coloring agent
    d) humectant

    Answer: b Key 1: A Section: 8

102. The addition of nutrients to replace those lost in processing is called
    a) enrichment
    b) fortification
    c) GRAS
    d) incidental addition

    Answer: a Key 1: C Section: 8

103. Potassium iodide is added to table salt to prevent
   a) goiter
   b) caking
   c) oxidation
   d) spoiling

   Answer: a Key 1: A Section: 8

ESSAY

104. Describe the major differences between lemon extract and imitation lemon flavoring.

   Answer: Key 1: A Section: 8

MULTIPLE CHOICE

105. Lemon extract and imitation lemon flavoring differ in that the extract
   a) is purer
   b) is more healthful
   c) contains a greater variety of chemicals
   d) contains fewer carcinogens

   Answer: c Key 1: A Section: 8

106. Table salt is a
   a) flavoring
   b) flavor enhancer
   c) preservative
   d) coloring

   Answer: b Key 1: A Section: 8

107. Which of the following is a synthetic antioxidant?
   a) aflatoxin B_1
   b) vitamin A
   c) BHT
   d) sodium propionate

   Answer: c Key 1: A Section: 8

108. Calcium propionate is added to bread to
   a) prevent oxidation
   b) replace Ca^{2+} lost in processing
   c) retard mold growth
   d) enhance the flavor

   Answer: c Key 1: A Section: 8

109. Which substance is added to foods high in oil and fat to prevent rancidity?
    a) BHT
    b) sodium nitrite
    c) β-carotene
    d) MSG

    Answer: a Key 1: A Section: 8

110. Fats and oils turn rancid by reaction with
    a) carbohydrates
    b) vitamins
    c) oxygen
    d) water

    Answer: c Key 1: C Section: 8

111. Which of the following is a natural antioxidant?
    a) vitamin K
    b) vitamin E
    c) BHT
    d) BHA

    Answer: b Key 1: A Section: 8

112. The yellow-orange color of carrots is due primarily to
    a) chlorophyll
    b) β-carotene
    c) FD&C yellow
    d) BHA

    Answer: b Key 1: A Section: 8

113. Aspartame is a(n)
    a) artificial sweetener
    b) vitamin
    c) protein
    d) monosaccharide

    Answer: a Key 1: A Section: 8

114. The relative sweetness scale uses ____________ as a reference.
    a) aspartame
    b) fructose
    c) glucose
    d) sucrose

    Answer: d Key 1: A Section: 8

FILL-IN-THE-BLANK

115. Aspartame is 160 times as sweet as sucrose. This means that if you use a teaspoon of sugar, you could replace it with ______ teaspoon of aspartame.

Answer: 1/160 Key 1: A Section: 8

SHORT ANSWER

116. What makes a low calorie sweetener low calorie?

Answer: low calorie structures Key 1: C Section: 8

MULTIPLE CHOICE

117. Low calorie sweeteners have
   a) low calorie structures
   b) fewer atoms than natural sweeteners
   c) greater sweet taste per molecule
   d) all of the above

Answer: c Key 1: C Section: 8

118. All are sweet additives except for
   a) corn syrup
   b) saccharin
   c) aspartame
   d) sodium propionate

Answer: d Key 1: A Section: 8

119. An extreme toxin produced by bacteria in improperly canned food is
   a) $NaHCO_3$
   b) botulin
   c) propionic acid
   d) fructose

Answer: b Key 1: A Section: 9

120. Aflatoxin B_1 is a(n)
   a) antioxidant
   b) carcinogen found in moldy peanuts
   c) mold inhibitor
   d) vitamin

Answer: b Key 1: A Section: 9

121. Which fertilizer is also an explosive?
   a) NH_3
   b) NH_4NO_3
   c) KCl
   d) $Ca_3(PO_4)_2$

   Answer: b Key 1: A Section: 12

FILL-IN-THE-BLANK

122. An early source of phosphorus for agriculture was __________.

   Answer: bones Key 1: A Section: 12

MULTIPLE CHOICE

123. An early source of phosphorus for agriculture was
   a) manure
   b) bones
   c) ammonia
   d) all of the above

   Answer: b Key 1: A Section: 12

124. Plants use phosphorus to synthesize
   a) amino acids
   b) nucleic acids
   c) cellulose
   d) starch

   Answer: b Key 1: C Section: 12

125. The amount of phosphorus on the Earth today is __________ than 200 years ago when phosphates were first recognized as an essential plant nutrient.
   a) less
   b) more
   c) about the same
   d) none of the above

   Answer: c Key 1: C Section: 12

126. The conversion of phosphate rock and bone to "superphosphate" was significant because it
   a) increases the phosphorus content of the rock or bones
   b) makes the material more soluble
   c) incorporated phosphorus from the atmosphere
   d) did all of the above

   Answer: b Key 1: A Section: 12

127. Potassium is used by plants in
a) photosynthesis
b) cellulose production
c) protein synthesis
d) a variety of processes not precisely understood at this time

Answer: d Key 1: C Section: 12

128. Uptake of potassium ions from the soil by a plant requires the loss of a hydronium ion from the plant. The soil, therefore, becomes
a) more acidic
b) more basic
c) neutral
d) nitrogen rich

Answer: a Key 1: C Section: 12

129. The usual chemical form of potassium in commercial fertilizers is as
a) elemental potassium, K
b) potassium nitrate, KNO_3
c) potassium chloride, KCl
d) potassium oxide, K_2O

Answer: c Key 1: A Section: 12

130. A 15-10-5 fertilizer has what percentage of N?
a) 15%
b) 10%
c) 5%
d) none of these

Answer: a Key 1: A Section: 12

SHORT ANSWER

131. What does 15-10-5 on a bag of fertilizer mean?

Answer: 15%N, 10%P, 5%K Key 1: A Section: 12

MULTIPLE CHOICE

132. Of the following pesticides and their LD_{50}s (milligrams of pesticide/kg of rat) in rats, which pesticide is the MOST toxic to rats?
a) malathion (1000)
b) lindane (91)
c) nicotine (230)
d) aldicarb (1)

Answer: d Key 1: A Section: 13

TRUE/FALSE

133. As the LD_{50} of a substance decreases, the toxicity of the substance decreases.

Answer: False Key 1: A Section: 13

FILL-IN-THE-BLANK

134. As the LD_{50} of a substance decreases, the toxicity of the substance __________________.

Answer: increases Key 1: A Section: 13

MULTIPLE CHOICE

135. The LD_{50} for aldicarb in rats is 1 mg per kg of body mass. Assuming that the LD_{50} is the same for humans, how much aldicarb would it take to kill a 70 kg farm worker?
a) 1 mg
b) 70 mg
c) 100 mg
d) 745 mg

Answer: b Key 1: A Section: 13

136. DDT is concentrated in living organisms because it is
a) water soluble
b) fat soluble
c) synthetic
d) synthesized in the liver

Answer: b Key 1: C Section: 13

137. DDT is particularly harmful to birds because it
a) interferes with eyesight
b) interferes with calcium metabolism and egg production
c) is fat soluble
d) is water soluble

Answer: b Key 1: A Section: 13

ESSAY

138. Explain the biological magnification of DDT and its impact on animal life.

Answer: Key 1: C Section: 13

MULTIPLE CHOICE

139. Biological magnification of DDT is a result of its
   a) fat solubility
   b) water solubility
   c) chemical reactivity
   d) widespread use

   Answer: a Key 1: C Section: 13

140. In 1957, Clear Lake in California was sprayed with DDT such that the water contained 0.02 PPM of DDT. After a period of time, fish in the lake were found to have DDT levels as high as 2000 PPM. This is an example of
   a) biological magnification of DDT
   b) species resistance to DDT
   c) natural decomposition of DDT
   d) species tolerance of DDT

   Answer: a Key 1: A Section: 13

141. In 1957, Clear Lake in California was sprayed with DDT such that the water contained 0.02 PPM of DDT. After a period of time, large fish in the lake were found to have DDT levels as high as 2000 PPM. Which of the following animals would be predicted to have DDT levels > 2000 PPM?
   a) algae
   b) hummingbirds
   c) small fish
   d) eagles

   Answer: d Key 1: A Section: 13

142. A phosphorus containing pesticide is
   a) DDT
   b) parathion
   c) lead arsenate
   d) pyrethrins

   Answer: b Key 1: C Section: 13

143. Organophosphorus pesticides are generally less ________ than DDT.
   a) potent
   b) insect resistant
   c) persistent
   d) fat soluble

   Answer: c Key 1: A Section: 13

144. Which is classified as a narrow spectrum pesticide?
   a) DDT
   b) organophosphorus pesticides
   c) carbamates
   d) lead arsenate

   Answer: c Key 1: A Section: 13

145. Carbaryl is one type of carbamate pesticide. A major problem associated with carbaryl is
   a) persistence in the environment
   b) toxicity towards honey bees
   c) broad range of action
   d) interference with egg production in birds

   Answer: b Key 1: A Section: 13

146. A worker at an experimental agricultural station spills a substance on her lab coat. The next morning her lab coat is covered with sex crazed moths. The spilled substance was probably
   a) parathion
   b) fertilizer
   c) DDT
   d) pheromone

   Answer: d Key 1: C Section: 13

147. Pheromones are
   a) chemical substances excreted by insects
   b) a class of organophosphorus pesticides
   c) natural insecticides produced by plants
   d) human sex hormones

   Answer: a Key 1: C Section: 13

148. Insects are attracted to a piece of sticky paper in great numbers. The paper has probably been treated with
   a) DDT
   b) pheromone
   c) plutonium
   d) parathion

   Answer: b Key 1: A Section: 13

149. An experimental pesticide with a very specific action, that is harmless to humans and other animals, and completely biodegradable, is
a) DDT
b) parathion
c) carbamates
d) viral pesticides

Answer: d Key 1: A Section: 14

150. Juvenile hormones are chemicals
a) that speed up the maturation of insects
b) that slow down the maturation of insects
c) that halt maturation of insects
d) that kill juvenile insects before they mature

Answer: c Key 1: C Section: 14

151. Dioxin is a chemical contaminant produced during the manufacture of
a) 2,4,5 - T
b) DDT
c) paraquat
d) PCB

Answer: a Key 1: C Section: 15

152. Which is the herbicide among the insecticides?
a) atrazine
b) carbaryl
c) nicotine
d) parathion

Answer: a Key 1: C Section: 15

153. Paraquat is an example of a _______________ herbicide.
a) narrow spectrum
b) broad spectrum
c) pre-emergent
d) postemergent

Answer: c Key 1: A Section: 15

154. The largest consumer of petroleum among all industries is
a) agriculture
b) steel production
c) automobile manufacturing
d) food processing

Answer: a Key 1: A Section: 16

155. In a modern society, approximately what percentage of energy is used to produce food?
  a) 10%
  b) 30%
  c) 50%
  d) 75%

  Answer: a Key 1: C Section: 16

156. The ultimate solution to the Malthusian dilemma is
  a) ever increasing food production
  b) population control
  c) better fertilizers and pesticides
  d) organic farming

  Answer: b Key 1: A Section: 17

Chapter 17: Household Chemicals

MULTIPLE CHOICE

1. One of the major problems with the use of household chemicals is
   a) they are toxic
   b) consumers often fail to read directions and warnings
   c) they do not perform well
   d) all of the above

   Answer: b Key 1: C Key 2: I

2. The majority of household chemicals are
   a) detergents and cleaners
   b) solvents
   c) lawn and garden products
   d) paints

   Answer: a Key 1: A Key 2: I

3. Perhaps the first cleaners were
   a) detergents
   b) lye based soaps
   c) saponins
   d) plant ashes

   Answer: d Key 1: A Section: 1

4. Plant ashes react with water to form
   a) acidic solutions
   b) alkaline solutions
   c) detergents
   d) soaps

   Answer: b Key 1: A Section: 1

5. The substance with the formula
   $CH_3CH_2CH_2CH_2CH_2CH_2CH_2CH_2CH_2CH_2CH_2CH_2COOH$
   a) is a soap
   b) is a hydrocarbon
   c) is a detergent
   d) is a fatty acid

   Answer: d Key 1: C Section: 2

6. Soap is
   a) a glycerol ester
   b) a salt of a fatty acid
   c) sodium carbonate
   d) trisodium phosphate

   Answer: b Key 1: C Section: 2

7. Animal fats and vegetable oil can be converted to soaps by reaction with
   a) sodium hydroxide
   b) sodium bicarbonate
   c) sodium hypochlorite
   d) sodium phosphate

   Answer: a Key 1: A Section: 2

8. Floating soaps are
   a) composed of short chain fatty acids
   b) composed of branched chain fatty acids
   c) blown with air during processing
   d) detergents

   Answer: c Key 1: A Section: 2

9. The molecule shown below is a

$$CH_3CH_2CH_2CH_2CH_2CH_2CH_2CH_2CH_2CH_2CH_2CH_2CH_2CH_2CH_2\overset{\overset{O}{||}}{C} - O^-Na^+$$

   a) fat
   b) fatty acid
   c) soap
   d) detergent

   Answer: c Key 1: C Section: 2

ESSAY

10. Describe how the structure of a soap molecule makes it an effective cleaning agent in water.

    Answer: Key 1: C Section: 2

MULTIPLE CHOICE

11. In cleaning, soap acts as a(n) ____________ between "dirt" and water.
    a) catalyst
    b) chemical reactant
    c) emulsifier
    d) insulator

    Answer: c Key 1: C Section: 2

12. In acidic solutions, soaps are converted to
    a) salts
    b) fatty acids
    c) detergents
    d) esters

    Answer: b Key 1: A Section: 2

13. In hard water, soaps are converted to
    a) insoluble salts
    b) fatty acids
    c) detergents
    d) esters

    Answer: a Key 1: A Section: 2

14. An advantage of potassium soaps is that they are ______ than sodium soaps.
    a) softer
    b) harder
    c) more neutral
    d) stronger

    Answer: a Key 1: A Section: 2

15. Bathtub ring is caused by
    a) the action of bleach with water
    b) precipitation of soap by "hard" metal ions
    c) rust formation from iron in the water
    d) soap and water cause a ringing sound in the ears

    Answer: b Key 1: A Section: 2

16. Washing soda is
    a) sodium hydroxide
    b) sodium carbonate
    c) trisodium phosphate
    d) sodium chloride

    Answer: b Key 1: A Section: 2

17. Water softeners
    a) remove hard ions
    b) destroy hard ions
    c) modify hard ions
    d) all of the above

    Answer: a Key 1: A Section: 2

18. The molecule shown below is a

$$CH_3CH_2CH_2CH_2CH_2CH_2CH_2CH_2CH_2CH_2CH_2CH_2OSO_2^- \ Na^+$$

(the S bears two double-bonded O atoms, drawn above and below)

a) soap
b) detergent
c) fatty acid
d) polymer

Answer: b Key 1: C Section: 3

19. A problem with ABS detergents is that they
a) are toxic
b) do not degrade readily
c) contain phosphates
d) are less effective in hard water

Answer: b Key 1: C Section: 3

ESSAY

20. What are ABS detergents? Why were they banned?

Answer: Key 1: C Section: 3

MULTIPLE CHOICE

21. An advantage of LAS detergents over ABS detergents is
a) effectiveness in hard water
b) nonpetroleum based
c) biodegradable
d) they lack phosphates

Answer: c Key 1: C Section: 3

22. Detergents are better cleaners than soaps in
a) hard water
b) soft water
c) alkaline water
d) all of the above

Answer: a Key 1: A Section: 3

23. Which water softener "ties up" calcium ions and keeps them in solution?
    a) sodium carbonate
    b) sodium phosphate
    c) fatty acids
    d) zeolites

    Answer: d Key 1: A Section: 4

24. Substances added to surfactants to increase their detergency are
    a) bleaches
    b) builders
    c) emulsifiers
    d) enzymes

    Answer: b Key 1: A Section: 4

25. Optical brighteners are often added to
    a) detergents
    b) toothpastes
    c) cosmetics
    d) all of the above

    Answer: d Key 1: C Section: 4

26. Optical brighteners work by
    a) absorbing visible light and emitting invisible UV light
    b) absorbing invisible UV light and emitting visible light
    c) spontaneously emitting visible light when they attach to clothing fibers
    d) spontaneously emitting invisible UV light when they attach to clothing fibers

    Answer: b Key 1: C Section: 4

ESSAY

27. What is an optical brightener and how does it work?

    Answer: Key 1: C Section: 4

MULTIPLE CHOICE

28. Soaps are
    a) anionic surfactants
    b) cationic surfactants
    c) nonionic surfactants
    d) neutral surfactants

    Answer: a Key 1: C Section: 5

ESSAY

29. How do automatic dishwashing detergents differ from detergents used for the hand washing of dishes?

    Answer: Key 1: A Section: 5

MULTIPLE CHOICE

30. Automatic dishwashing detergents are
    a) similar to detergents for hand washing
    b) relatively strong bases
    c) relatively strong acids
    d) safe for hand washing of dishes

    Answer: b Key 1: A Section: 5

31. Which of the following forms a strongly caustic solution when mixed with water?
    a) automatic dishwashing detergent
    b) liquid dishwashing detergent
    c) liquid clothing detergent
    d) bath soap

    Answer: a Key 1: A Section: 5

32. Cationic surfactants are not good detergents but are used mainly for their ______ action.
    a) foaming
    b) lively
    c) germicidal
    d) bleaching

    Answer: c Key 1: A Section: 6

33. Quaternary salts with two long carbon chains and two smaller chains on the nitrogen are used as
    a) bleaches
    b) analgesics
    c) fabric softeners
    d) weed killers

    Answer: c Key 1: A Section: 6

34. Bleaches are
    a) oxidizing agents
    b) reducing agents
    c) brighteners
    d) detergents

    Answer: a Key 1: C Section: 7

35. The active ingredient in chlorine laundry bleaches is
    a) chlorine, Cl_2
    b) sodium hypochlorite, NaOCl
    c) sodium chloride, NaCl
    d) a mixture of CFCs

    Answer: b Key 1: A Section: 7

ESSAY

36. Why is mixing chlorine containing bleaches with other cleaners dangerous?

    Answer: Key 1: A Section: 7

MULTIPLE CHOICE

37. The active ingredient in oxygen bleaches is
    a) NaOCl
    b) $NaBO_2 \cdot H_2O_2$
    c) O_2
    d) Na_3PO_4

    Answer: b Key 1: A Section: 7

SHORT ANSWER

38. What happens when chlorine bleaches are used on polyester fabrics?

    Answer: yellowing Key 1: A Section: 7

MULTIPLE CHOICE

39. Why are perborate bleaches better for white, resin treated, polyester-cotton fabrics than chlorine bleaches?
    a) chlorine bleaches release a toxic gas when in contact with this type of fabric
    b) chlorine bleaches ruin the fabric
    c) oxygen bleaches are cheaper
    d) the fabric lasts longer

    Answer: d Key 1: A Section: 7

40. Most all-purpose cleaners are
    a) acids
    b) bases
    c) neutral
    d) oxidizing agents

    Answer: b Key 1: C Section: 8

41. Baking soda is an effective
    a) automatic dishwashing detergent
    b) disinfectant
    c) abrasive
    d) laundry detergent

    Answer: c Key 1: A Section: 8

ESSAY

42. Why are toilet bowl cleaners usually acids?

    Answer: Key 1: A Section: 9

MULTIPLE CHOICE

43. The abrasive in commercial powdered cleansers is often
    a) silica
    b) baking soda
    c) carbide
    d) diamond dust

    Answer: a Key 1: A Section: 9

44. The principal hazard of organic solvents in the home is that most are
    a) flammable
    b) toxic
    c) carcinogenic
    d) mutagenic

    Answer: a Key 1: C Section: 10

FILL-IN-THE-BLANK

45. The universal pigment used in paint today is ____________________.

    Answer: TiO_2 Key 1: A Section: 11

46. The three basic ingredients of a paint are __________, __________ and ______________.

    Answer: solvent, binder, pigment Key 1: A Section: 11

SHORT ANSWER

47. What is the difference between paraffin and other waxes?

Answer:
Paraffin is made up of hydrocarbons. Waxes are esters of long chain alcohols with fatty acids.

Key 1: A Section: 12

MULTIPLE CHOICE

48. Which one of the following IS NOT considered a cosmetic?
a) soap
b) toothpaste
c) facial cream
d) hair spray

Answer: a Key 1: A Section: 13

49. Which generally does not need to be proven safe and effective before marketing?
a) cosmetic
b) drug
c) food additive
d) all must be proven safe and effective

Answer: a Key 1: A Section: 13

50. Which IS NOT a cosmetic?
a) antiperspirant
b) lipstick
c) perfume
d) shampoo

Answer: a Key 1: A Section: 13

51. The oil secreted by glands in the skin is called
a) sweat
b) sebum
c) musk
d) resin

Answer: b Key 1: D Section: 13

ESSAY

52. What is the difference between a skin cream and a skin lotion?

    Answer: Key 1: D Section: 13

MULTIPLE CHOICE

53. A cosmetic that is a suspension of oil in water is called a(n)
    a) cream
    b) lotion
    c) sunscreen
    d) wax

    Answer: b Key 1: D Section: 13

54. A cosmetic that is a suspension of water in oil is called a(n)
    a) cream
    b) lotion
    c) sunscreen
    d) wax

    Answer: a Key 1: D Section: 13

55. The ideal moisture content of skin is approximately
    a) 1%
    b) 10%
    c) 50%
    d) 70%

    Answer: b Key 1: A Section: 13

56. The outer layer of skin is called the
    a) exoskin
    b) episkin
    c) epidermis
    d) exodermis

    Answer: c Key 1: C Section: 13

57. Baby oil is the same as
    a) mineral oil
    b) whale oil
    c) soybean oil
    d) peanut oil

    Answer: a Key 1: A Section: 13

58. Emollients are
    a) artificial skin
    b) skin plasticizers
    c) skin coatings
    d) skin catalysts

    Answer: c Key 1: A Section: 13

59. Skin moisturizers
    a) add moisture to skin
    b) prevent loss of moisture from skin
    c) cause skin to produce more water
    d) do all of the above

    Answer: b Key 1: A Section: 13

60. Sunscreens contain chemicals that
    a) absorb shorter wavelength UV radiation
    b) absorb longer wavelength UV radiation
    c) inhibit melanin production in the skin
    d) promote melanin production in skin

    Answer: a Key 1: C Section: 13

ESSAY

61. How do sunscreens protect the skin from harmful radiation?

    Answer: Key 1: C Section: 13

MULTIPLE CHOICE

62. Exposure of skin to UV radiation causes
    a) melanin production
    b) increased risk of skin cancer
    c) premature aging of skin
    d) all of the above

    Answer: d Key 1: C Section: 13

63. Skin cream and lipsticks have approximately the same basic composition. What is added to lipsticks to make them more firm?
    a) wax
    b) cellulose
    c) petroleum jelly
    d) abrasive

    Answer: a Key 1: A Section: 13

64. A major problem with eye makeups is
    a) bacterial contamination after extended use
    b) color fading
    c) allergic reactions
    d) all of the above

    Answer: a Key 1: A   Section: 13

65. White eye shadow is "colored" with titanium dioxide or
    a) lampblack
    b) chromic oxide
    c) lead sulfide
    d) zinc oxide

    Answer: d Key 1: A   Section: 13

66. Deodorants act by
    a) breaking down odorous chemicals as they are produced
    b) destroying odor causing bacteria
    c) producing enzymes
    d) reacting with sweat glands to stop perspiration

    Answer: b Key 1: C   Section: 13

67. The active ingredient in almost all antiperspirants is
    a) aluminum chlorohydrate
    b) ethanol
    c) ethylene oxide
    d) aluminum oxide

    Answer: a Key 1: A   Section: 13

68. Astringents are used primarily in
    a) perfumes
    b) lipsticks
    c) antiperspirants
    d) hair spray

    Answer: c Key 1: A   Section: 13

69. Aluminum chlorohydrates are useful as
    a) antiperspirants
    b) hair colorings
    c) toothpaste abrasives
    d) uv blocking agents

    Answer: a Key 1: A   Section: 13

70. The layer of skin that contains sweat glands and hair follicles.
    a) apocrine
    b) dermis
    c) epidermis
    d) eccrine

    Answer: b Key 1: A Section: 13

71. The layer of skin whose moisture content determines whether our skin feels moist and soft or dry and flaky is the
    a) apocrine
    b) dermis
    c) epidermis
    d) eccrine

    Answer: c Key 1: A Section: 13

72. Detergents and abrasives are the major active ingredients in
    a) colognes
    b) shampoos
    c) skin creams
    d) toothpastes

    Answer: d Key 1: A Section: 14

73. Which substance strengthens tooth enamel?
    a) fluoride
    b) abrasive
    c) plaque
    d) protein

    Answer: a Key 1: C Section: 14

74. The principal material of tooth enamel is
    a) fluoride
    b) collagen
    c) hydroxyapatite
    d) protein

    Answer: c Key 1: C Section: 14

75. The following is a list of ingredients in a familiar product: water, glycerin, hydrated silica, alumina, cellulose gum, sodium lauryl sulfate, wintergreen flavoring, sodium benzoate, titanium dioxide, sodium saccharin. The product is
    a) ice cream
    b) industrial abrasive
    c) lipstick
    d) toothpaste

    Answer: d Key 1: A Section: 14

76. The essential ingredients in toothpastes are
    a) abrasive and detergent
    b) abrasive and fluoride
    c) detergent and tartar control
    d) detergent and fluoride

    Answer: a Key 1: A Section: 14

77. In toothpaste, the most important function of the abrasive is to
    a) remove food particles lodged between the teeth and gums
    b) produce a shiny gloss on the teeth
    c) cause a reaction between detergent and fluorides in the toothpaste
    d) remove the polysaccharide film known as plaque

    Answer: d Key 1: C Section: 14

78. Probably the oldest and most widely used cosmetics are
    a) toothpastes
    b) deodorants
    c) perfumes
    d) shampoos

    Answer: c Key 1: C Section: 15

79. The top note of a perfume
    a) is the most volatile component
    b) is the least volatile component
    c) has the most pleasenat odor
    d) has the least pleasenat odor

    Answer: a Key 1: C Section: 15

ESSAY

80. Explain why disagreeable odors like musk and civetone are used in the formulation of perfumes.

    Answer: Key 1: C Section: 15

MULTIPLE CHOICE

81. A substance added to perfume to balance the flowery odors is
    a) middle note
    b) solvent
    c) musk
    d) top note

    Answer: c Key 1: C Section: 15

82. Perfumes are
    a) pure substances
    b) compounds
    c) simple mixtures of compounds
    d) complex mixtures of compounds

    Answer: d Key 1: C Section: 15

83. What substance is added to aftershave lotions to provide a cooling effect?
    a) acetone
    b) menthol
    c) ethanol
    d) methanol

    Answer: b Key 1: A Section: 15

84. A perfume's fragrance is just a bit too sweet and flowerly. The perfume chemist might add some
    a) menthol
    b) more top note
    c) skatole
    d) ethanol

    Answer: c Key 1: C Section: 15

85. Colognes are
    a) similar to aftershaves
    b) diluted perfumes
    c) perfumes derived from natural products only
    d) totally synthetic perfumes

    Answer: b Key 1: A Section: 15

86. The substance left out of most hypoallergenic cosmetics is
    a) hydrogen peroxide
    b) oil
    c) perfume
    d) salt

    Answer: c Key 1: A Section: 15

87. Colognes are about ____% as strong as perfumes.
    a) 1
    b) 5
    c) 50
    d) 10

    Answer: d Key 1: A Section: 15

88. Colognes differ from perfumes largely in that colognes
    a) are prepared from less expensive organic fragrances
    b) contain impurities not found in perfumes
    c) oxidize more rapidly than perfumes
    d) are dilute versions of perfumes

    Answer: d Key 1: D Section: 15

89. Which of the following cosmetics contain the least amount of fragrant compounds?
    a) perfumes
    b) colognes
    c) aftershave lotions
    d) none of these, they contain the same amount

    Answer: c Key 1: A Section: 15

90. Hair is composed of
    a) carbohydrate
    b) protein
    c) fat
    d) nucleic acid

    Answer: b Key 1: C Section: 16

91. Relative to skin protein, hair protein has more
    a) amino acids
    b) disulfide bonds
    c) hydrogen bonds
    d) amide bonds

    Answer: b Key 1: C Section: 16

92. The only necessary ingredient in shampoo is
    a) water
    b) conditioner
    c) fragrance
    d) detergent

    Answer: d Key 1: C Section: 16

93. The pH of hair is
    a) greater than 7
    b) equal to 7
    c) slightly less than 7
    d) much less than 7

    Answer: c Key 1: C Section: 16

94. Wet hair is softer because water disrupts
    a) disulfide bonds
    b) hydrogen bonds
    c) peptide bonds
    d) all of the above

    Answer: b Key 1: A Section: 16

95. If you wish to make a shampoo formulation that helps "fix split ends" you would probably add some
    a) additional detergent
    b) astringent
    c) protein
    d) pH balance

    Answer: c Key 1: C Section: 16

96. The brown pigment in hair is called
    a) melanin
    b) phaeomelanin
    c) chlorophyll
    d) ∉-carotene

    Answer: a Key 1: A Section: 16

97. The red-brown pigment in hair is called
    a) melanin
    b) phaeomelanin
    c) chlorophyll
    d) ∉-carotene

    Answer: b Key 1: C Section: 16

98. People with brunette hair have lots of
    a) melanin
    b) phaeomelanin
    c) chlorophyll
    d) none of these

    Answer: a Key 1: A Section: 16

99. People with red hair have lots of
    a) melanin
    b) phaeomelanin
    c) chlorophyll
    d) none of these

    Answer: b Key 1: A Section: 16

100. What chemical compound is used to bleach hair?
   a) hydrogen peroxide
   b) sodium hypochlorite
   c) melanin
   d) thioglycolic acid

   Answer: a Key 1: A Section: 16

FILL-IN-THE-BLANK

101. People with blonde hair have __________ pigment in their hair.

   Answer: very little Key 1: A Section: 16

MULTIPLE CHOICE

102. People with blonde hair have __________ pigment(s) in their hair.
   a) very little
   b) melanin
   c) phaeomelanin
   d) melanin & phaeomelin

   Answer: a Key 1: A Section: 16

103. Hair is most efficiently "permanently" dyed by
   a) soaking hair in the colored dye
   b) adding colorless reactants that react in the hair to form the desired color
   c) using water soluble dyes
   d) none of the above

   Answer: b Key 1: A Section: 16

104. There is evidence that some hair dyes may be carcinogenic. Because hair dyes are classified as cosmetics, the FDA cannot
   a) ban them without sufficient proof of harm
   b) approve them without sufficient proof of safety
   c) approve them without sufficient carcinogenic testing
   d) ban them

   Answer: a Key 1: C Section: 16

105. Hair colorings that hide grey hair
   a) have chemistry similar to other hair dyes
   b) contain lead compounds that react with hair to form black lead sulfide
   c) are dilute solutions of black paint
   d) react with hair to reform melanin and phaeomelanin

   Answer: b Key 1: A Section: 16

106. The first step in hair curling is to add thioglycolic acid. This causes
a) hair protein to hydrolyze into amino acids
b) disulfide bonds to break
c) new disulfide bonds to form
d) cysteine to be added to the amino acid sequence

Answer: b Key 1: A Section: 16

107. The last step in hair curling is to roll the hair on curlers and treat the rolled hair with hydrogen peroxide (neutralizer). This causes
a) new disulfide bonds to form
b) old disulfide bonds to break
c) amino acids to reform into a new sequence
d) cysteines to be inserted into the primary structure

Answer: a Key 1: A Section: 16

108. The substances in hair sprays and mousses that hold hair in place are
a) emollients
b) resins
c) oxidizing agents
d) waxes

Answer: b Key 1: A Section: 16

109. Minoxidil was first used as a drug for treating high blood pressure, it is now used for
a) bleaching hair
b) growing hair
c) curling hair
d) dying hair

Answer: b Key 1: A Section: 16

110. The protein that forms the stand of hair is
a) cortex
b) cuticle
c) follicle
d) keratin

Answer: d Key 1: A Section: 16

111. Wet wave hair is held together largely by
a) amide links
b) hydrogen bonds
c) sulfur-sulfur bonds
d) ionic bonds

Answer: b Key 1: A Section: 16

112. The color of human hair depends partly on the ratio of
    a) cortex to cuticle
    b) melanin to phaeomelanin
    c) cystine to cysteine
    d) sebum to lanolin

    Answer: b   Key 1: C   Section: 16

113. Permanent waves are held together largely by the sulfur-sulfur bonds of
    a) cysteine
    b) cystine
    c) cytosine
    d) thioglycolic acid

    Answer: b   Key 1: A   Section: 16

TRUE/FALSE

114. In purchasing a shampoo or laundry detergent it is always best to buy the most expensive product.

    Answer: False   Key 1: A   Section: 17

115. Most cosmetics are made from very expensive ingredients.

    Answer: False   Key 1: A   Section: 17

Chapter 18: Fitness and Health

FILL-IN-THE-BLANK

1. The recommended maximum percentage of calories from fat in one's diet is _____%; in the typical American diet, _____% comes from fat.

   Answer: 25%; 34% Key 1: A Section: 1

MULTIPLE CHOICE

2. An athlete's pre-game meal should consist mainly of
   a) carbohydrates
   b) fat
   c) protein
   d) vitamins

   Answer: a Key 1: C Section: 1

3. The base of the food guide pyramid contains items like
   a) meat
   b) bread and pasta
   c) fruit
   d) vegetables

   Answer: b Key 1: A Section: 1

4. The top section of the food guide pyramid contains items like
   a) fat
   b) vegetables
   c) fruit
   d) bread

   Answer: a Key 1: A Section: 1

TRUE/FALSE

5. It is healthier to eat too much than too little.

   Answer: False Key 1: C Section: 1

MULTIPLE CHOICE

6. It is recommended that our diets contain no more than
   a) 50% calories from fats
   b) 25% calories from fats
   c) 10% calories from fats
   d) 45% calories from fats

   Answer: b Key 1: C Section: 1

7. A down-side of a high protein diet is that
   a) more toxic wastes are produced during digestion
   b) it produces more calories than a high carbohydrate diet
   c) it produces more calories than a high fat diet
   d) it is digested faster than other food groups

   Answer: a   Key 1: C   Section: 1

8. Recent research shows that for persons on high protein diets
   a) weight gains are faster
   b) weight loss is more difficult
   c) if protein is from red meat, colon cancer risk increases
   d) all of these are true

   Answer: d   Key 1: C   Section: 1

9. Muscles are built by
   a) eating diets high in carbohydrates
   b) eating diets high in protein
   c) eating diets high in fats
   d) exercising

   Answer: d   Key 1: C   Section: 1

10. The RDA values for vitamins and nutrients are set by
    a) the FDA
    b) FD&C
    c) Food and Nutrition Board of the U. S. NAS
    d) each of the state governments

    Answer: c   Key 1: A   Section: 2

11. The general recommendation for vitamin consumption by most members of the scientific community is
    a) to take high doses of vitamin supplements daily
    b) to eat a well balanced diet
    c) to take high doses of water soluble vitamins
    d) make sure your vitamin supplements are enriched with iron and zinc

    Answer: b   Key 1: C   Section: 2

12. To which of the following vitamins is a vegetarian who, is not on vitamin supplements, likely to show a deficiency?
    a) B_{12}
    b) A
    c) B_6
    d) E

    Answer: a   Key 1: C   Section: 2

13. Heat strokes resulting from physical exertion occur when the body's heat regulatory system fails. This condition is likely to occur when
    a) there is a vitamin deficiency
    b) the body is dehydrated
    c) the sodium ion level in body fluids is low
    d) one has overeaten

    Answer: b Key 1: C Section: 3

ESSAY

14. What is set point theory? What impact does it have on dieting and weight loss?

    Answer: Key 1: C Section: 4

MULTIPLE CHOICE

15. Set point theory involves
    a) the prediction of optimum muscle composition based on diet
    b) the determination of your optimum percentage of body fat for your age and weight
    c) the manner in which hunger sensation is controlled by the hypothalmus
    d) the manner in which protein is produced relative to the level of exercise

    Answer: c Key 1: C Section: 4

16. On any diet that restricts carbohydrate intake,
    a) only fat is lost
    b) fat and protein are lost
    c) only protein is lost
    d) only glycogen is lost

    Answer: b Key 1: A Section: 4

17. On a weight-loss diet without exercise about ____ of the weight lost is muscle.
    a) 65%
    b) 34%
    c) 11%
    d) 0%

    Answer: c Key 1: A Section: 4

TRUE/FALSE

18. A person who diets many times and regains the weight has a more difficult time losing weight the next time he/she diets.

    Answer: True Key 1: A Section: 4

MULTIPLE CHOICE

19. The number of dieters who lose weight and then gain it back is approximately
    a) 1%
    b) 10%
    c) 50%
    d) 90%

    Answer: d Key 1: A Section: 4

ESSAY

20. The Law of Conservation of Mass applies to dieting, too. Explain.

    Answer: Key 1: A Section: 4

MULTIPLE CHOICE

21. A pound of fat has an energy content of 3500 kcal. Walking a mile uses about 100 kcal. How many miles must you walk to lose a pound of fat?
    a) 3500
    b) 350
    c) 35
    d) 3.5

    Answer: c Key 1: A Section: 4

FILL-IN-THE-BLANK

22. The only way to lose weight is to increase ____________ and/or decrease ________________.

    Answer: activity, calories Key 1: C Section: 5

23. Loss of fat during any weight loss program that does not include an exercise program is accompanied by a loss of ________________.

    Answer: muscle Key 1: C Section: 5

MULTIPLE CHOICE

24. If you ordinarily expend 1700 kcal/day and you diet at 1500 kcal/day, how long will it take to lose 1.0 pound of fat? (1.0 lb of adipose fat is 3500 kcal)
    a) 35 days
    b) 15 days
    c) 17.5 days
    d) 2.33 days

    Answer: c Key 1: A Section: 5

TRUE/FALSE

25. A benefit of exercise is that the metabolic rate is increased during the exercise and it continues at an elevated level for several hours after the exercise is completed.

    Answer: True Key 1: A Section: 5

MULTIPLE CHOICE

26. What is the body mass index (BMI) of a person who is 6 ft tall and weighs 205 pounds?
    a) 28
    b) 2.9
    c) 4000
    d) .35

    Answer: a Key 1: A Section: 6

27. The body mass index (BMI) is determined by which of the following physical quantities?
    a) mass
    b) weight and height
    c) density and height
    d) height

    Answer: b Key 1: C Section: 6

28. The body mass index is used to measure one's level of
    a) fatness
    b) hydration
    c) stamina
    d) hunger

    Answer: a Key 1: C Section: 6

29. Which of the following is not commonly known to be a vitamin deficiency disease?
    a) beriberi
    b) cancer
    c) scurvy
    d) pellagra

    Answer: b Key 1: A Section: 2

TRUE/FALSE

30. Unlike humans, most animals synthesize their own ascorbic acid.

    Answer: True Key 1: A Section: 2

31. The human body does not synthesize vitamin C.

    Answer: True Key 1: A Section: 2

MULTIPLE CHOICE

32. Which vitamin is sometimes called the "antisterility" vitamin?
    a) Vitamin A
    b) Vitamin B complex
    c) Vitamin D
    d) Vitamin E

    Answer: d Key 1: A Section: 2

33. Which vitamin is sometimes called the "antiaging" vitamin?
    a) Vitamin A
    b) Vitamin B complex
    c) Vitamin D
    d) Vitamin E

    Answer: d Key 1: A Section: 2

FILL-IN-THE-BLANK

34. Vitamin C and E are considered to be possible anticarcinogens because both are ______________________.

    Answer: antioxidants Key 1: A Section: 2

MULTIPLE CHOICE

35. Which vegetable shows evidence of having anticancer activity?
    a) cabbage
    b) corn
    c) potatoes
    d) peas

    Answer: a Key 1: A Section: 2

36. Which of the following vitamins is not found in plants?
    a) B_6
    b) A
    c) B_{12}
    d) B_3

    Answer: c Key 1: A Section: 2

37. Vitamin D is a steroid-type vitamin that offers protection against
    a) beriberi
    b) scurvy
    c) pellagra
    d) rickets

    Answer: d Key 1: A Section: 2

TRUE/FALSE

38. There are no consequences that result from taking more than the RDA of vitamin D.

    Answer: False Key 1: A Section: 2

MULTIPLE CHOICE

39. The best thing to drink to replenish lost body fluids after exercise is
    a) salt water
    b) water
    c) beer
    d) Gatorade

    Answer: b Key 1: C Section: 3

40. The major component of body sweat is
    a) sodium chloride
    b) potassium chloride
    c) calcium chloride
    d) water

    Answer: d Key 1: C Section: 3

41. What hormone signals the kidneys to conserve water?
    a) antidiuretic hormone (ADH)
    b) insulin
    c) norepinephrine
    d) progesterone

    Answer: a Key 1: C Section: 3

42. A smoker's breathing is less efficient because of ____ in the smoke.
    a) NaCl
    b) Fe
    c) CO_2
    d) CO

    Answer: d Key 1: A Section: 10

43. The immediate source of energy for muscle action is
    a) glucose
    b) glycogen
    c) ATP
    d) fatty acids

    Answer: c Key 1: A Section: 7

44. Once ATP is depleted, the next available energy is from
    a) glucose
    b) glycogen
    c) fats
    d) protein

    Answer: b Key 1: A Section: 7

FILL-IN-THE-BLANK

45. If sufficient oxygen is available to muscles during energy conversion, the by-products of energy production are water and ________________.

    Answer: carbon dioxide Key 1: A Section: 7

MULTIPLE CHOICE

46. If insufficient oxygen is available to muscles during energy conversion, the by-products of energy production are water and
    a) pyruvic acid
    b) lactic acid
    c) carbon dioxide
    d) ATP

    Answer: b Key 1: A Section: 7

47. If sufficient oxygen is available to muscles during energy conversion, the by-products of energy production are water and
    a) pyruvic acid
    b) lactic acid
    c) carbon dioxide
    d) ATP

    Answer: c Key 1: A Section: 7

48. Which substance serves as stored energy in muscle?
    a) glycogen
    b) glucose
    c) ATP
    d) protein

    Answer: a Key 1: C Section: 7

49. An oxygen debt is incurred when a person is engaged in
    a) aerobic exercise
    b) anaerobic exercise
    c) electrolytic depletion
    d) overeating

    Answer: b Key 1: A Section: 7

50. During the last stages of a marathon (26 miles) the body's principal source of energy is
    a) ATP
    b) glycogen
    c) fat
    d) protein

    Answer: c Key 1: A Section: 7

51. The protein directly responsible for muscle contraction is
    a) collagen
    b) actomyosin
    c) keratin
    d) hemoglobin

    Answer: b Key 1: C Section: 7

ESSAY

52. Compare the energy and muscle processes involved in running a sprint and running a marathon.

    Answer: Key 1: A Section: 7

MULTIPLE CHOICE

53. Respiratory capacity of muscle is increased by
    a) light exercise
    b) endurance exercise
    c) weight lifting
    d) eating more protein

    Answer: b Key 1: A Section: 7

54. Which activity is aided by a large proportion of fast-twitch muscles?
    a) lifting a 100 kg weight
    b) swimming 1.5 km
    c) a 6 day bicycle race
    d) running 50 km

    Answer: a Key 1: A Section: 7

55. The albatross (a sea bird) can fly for days on end. Its breast muscle would have a high proportion of
    a) fat
    b) glycogen
    c) lactic acid
    d) slow-twitch muscle

    Answer: d Key 1: A Section: 7

56. Which activity would be aided by a large proportion of slow-twitch muscles?
    a) lifting a 300 lb weight
    b) hitting a home run
    c) slam dunking a basketball
    d) swimming 2.5 km

    Answer: d Key 1: A Section: 7

57. The protein that stores and transports oxygen in muscle is
    a) hemoglobin
    b) myoglobin
    c) glycogen
    d) ATP

    Answer: b Key 1: A Section: 7

58. Muscles are built through
    a) eating a protein rich diet
    b) taking an amino acid supplement
    c) megavitamin and mineral supplements
    d) exercise

    Answer: d Key 1: C Section: 7

59. The drug most commonly used by athletes and others to relieve pain is
    a) aspirin
    b) cocaine
    c) codeine
    d) methyl salicylate

    Answer: a Key 1: A Section: 8

FILL-IN-THE-BLANK

60. Methyl salicylate is used as a rub-on type drug for sore muscles. It is an ______________________.

    Answer: analgesic Key 1: A Section: 8

MULTIPLE CHOICE

61. Anabolic steroids
    a) enhance the buildup of muscle tissue
    b) reduce inflammation
    c) increase testicular mass
    d) increase sexual potency

    Answer: a Key 1: C Section: 8

62. Athletic performance can best be improved by
    a) anabolic steroids
    b) electrolyte replacement fluids
    c) blood doping
    d) practice

    Answer: d Key 1: A Section: 8

63. You bike 50 km. Though tired, you feel great because your brain has synthesized some
    a) amphetamine
    b) endorphins
    c) glucose
    d) morphine

    Answer: b Key 1: A Section: 9

64. The major feature of Gore-Tex fabric is
    a) durability
    b) good looks
    c) permeable to water vapor but not water liquid
    d) permeable to heat but not to cold

    Answer: c Key 1: A Section: 11

65. Most sport materials are
    a) cotton
    b) wool
    c) other natural polymers
    d) synthetic polymers

    Answer: d Key 1: A Section: 11

ESSAY

66. Use pole vaulting as an example of how the chemistry of sports materials has enhanced athletic performance.

    Answer: Key 1: A Section: 11

Chapter 19: Drugs

ESSAY

1. The term "chemotherapy" has been around for over 90 years. What are its origins and what does it mean?

   Answer: Key 1: A Key 2: I

MULTIPLE CHOICE

2. Studies seem to indicate that small daily doses of aspirin lowers the risk of
   a) heart attack
   b) cold
   c) cancer
   d) all of the above

   Answer: a Key 1: A Section: 1

3. The evidence that aspirin may lower risk of stroke and heart attack seems to be related to its
   a) antipyretic properties
   b) analgesic properties
   c) anti-inflammatory properties
   d) anti-coagulant properties

   Answer: d Key 1: A Section: 1

4. Prolonged use of aspirin may lead to
   a) mental disorders
   b) gastrointestinal problems
   c) joint swelling
   d) liver damage

   Answer: b Key 1: A Section: 1

5. Buffered aspirin contains
   a) less acidic aspirin
   b) aspirin and an antacid
   c) aspirin and a pH buffer
   d) the compound bufferin

   Answer: b Key 1: A Section: 1

TRUE/FALSE

6. The use of aspirin to treat children's fevers has a strong link to the onset of Reye's syndrome.

   Answer: True Key 1: A Section: 1

7. Different brands of aspirin contain different types of aspirin.

   Answer: False Key 1: A Section: 1

ESSAY

8. What are two limitations of aspirin as a drug?

   Answer: Key 1: A Section: 1

9. The store brand aspirin costs less than the name brand. What is the difference between the two brands?

   Answer: Key 1: A Section: 1

MULTIPLE CHOICE

10. The difference between different brands of aspirin is
    a) effectiveness
    b) composition
    c) purity
    d) price

    Answer: d Key 1: A Section: 1

11. Studies indicate that small daily doses of aspirin lowers the risk of
    a) cold
    b) cancer
    c) stroke
    d) all of the above

    Answer: c Key 1: A Section: 1

FILL-IN-THE-BLANK

12. Acetaminophen does not provide ____________________ activity.

    Answer: anti-inflammatory Key 1: C Section: 1

MULTIPLE CHOICE

13. Which is not part of APC pain relievers?
    a) acetaminophen
    b) aspirin
    c) caffeine
    d) phenacetin

    Answer: a Key 1: D Section: 1

14. You want a pain reliever "stronger than aspirin." You get it by
    a) taking Excedrin
    b) taking Anacin
    c) taking Advil
    d) obtaining a prescription

    Answer: d Key 1: A Section: 1

15. Evidence indicates that this compound counteracts the ability of aspirin to reduce fever.
    a) acetaminophen
    b) ethanol
    c) prostaglandins
    d) caffeine

    Answer: d Key 1: A Section: 1

16. A "nonaspirin pain reliever" usually means
    a) acetaminophen
    b) Anacin
    c) Excedrin
    d) caffeine

    Answer: a Key 1: A Section: 1

17. The fact that acetominophen is prescribed more frequently in hospitals than aspirin is probably due to the fact that acetaminophen is not
    a) anticoagulant
    b) antipyretic
    c) anti-inflammatory
    d) synthetic

    Answer: a Key 1: A Section: 1

18. The most common over-the-counter pain reliever, after aspirin, is
    a) acetaminophen
    b) caffeine
    c) phenacetin
    d) ibuprofen

    Answer: a Key 1: A Section: 1

19. Persons who are sensitive to the acidity of aspirin or who are allergic to aspirin will probably have similar problems with
    a) acetaminophen
    b) ibuprofen
    c) phenacetin
    d) caffeine

    Answer: b Key 1: A Section: 1

FILL-IN-THE-BLANK

20. An antipyretic is a drug that relieves ________________.

    Answer: fever Key 1: D Section: 1

MULTIPLE CHOICE

21. An antipyretic is a drug that relieves
    a) fever
    b) inflammation
    c) pain
    d) sleeplessness

    Answer: a Key 1: D Section: 1

22. After dental surgery, the physician usually recommends acetaminophen rather than aspirin for relief of pain because
    a) acetaminophen is less expensive
    b) acetaminophen is more effective for relief of pain
    c) acetaminophen is more effective for reduction of inflammation
    d) aspirin promotes bleeding

    Answer: d Key 1: A Section: 1

TRUE/FALSE

23. There is no cure or prevention for the common cold.

    Answer: True Key 1: A Section: 2

MULTIPLE CHOICE

24. The only expectorant that the FDA panel has approved to be safe and effective is
    a) ephedrine
    b) codeine
    c) cocaine
    d) guaifenesin

    Answer: d Key 1: A Section: 2

25. According to the author of the text, which of the following is the best treatment for the common cold?
    a) chicken soup
    b) antitussives
    c) expectorants
    d) nasal decongestants

    Answer: a Key 1: A Section: 2

26. Antihistamines are chemicals that
    a) cure colds
    b) relieve some of the symptoms of allergies and colds
    c) relieve aches and pains associated with colds and flu
    d) relieve fevers

    Answer: b Key 1: D Section: 2

27. A side effect of many antihistamines is
    a) sleeplessness
    b) drowsiness
    c) irritability
    d) sneezing and runny nose

    Answer: b Key 1: A Section: 2

28. A substance that causes an allergic reaction triggers the release of a class of substances known as
    a) allergens
    b) antibodies
    c) antigens
    d) histamines

    Answer: d Key 1: A Section: 2

ESSAY

29. Compare the leading causes of death in the U.S. in 1900 and 1992. Is there a significant difference? Why?

    Answer: Key 1: C Section: 3

MULTIPLE CHOICE

30. In 1900, the leading cause of death in the U.S. was
    a) heart disease
    b) infectious diseases
    c) cancer
    d) accidents

    Answer: b Key 1: C Section: 3

31. The first antibacterial drugs were
    a) sulfa drugs
    b) tetracyclines
    c) penicillin
    d) cephalosporins

    Answer: a Key 1: A Section: 3

32. In 1900, half of the top ten causes of death in the U.S. were related to
    a) heart disease
    b) infections
    c) cancer
    d) accidents

    Answer: b Key 1: C Section: 3

33. In 1995, the leading cause of death in the U.S. was
    a) heart disease
    b) infectious disease
    c) cancer
    d) accidents

    Answer: a Key 1: C Section: 3

34. One of the first antibacterial drugs was
    a) penicillin
    b) ephedrine
    c) sulfanilamide
    d) iodine

    Answer: c Key 1: A Section: 3

35. One of the disadvantages of sulfa drugs is
    a) damage to the kidneys
    b) damage to the brain
    c) that they cause euphoria
    d) damage to the liver

    Answer: a Key 1: A Section: 3

TRUE/FALSE

36. There are no problems associated with wide spread use of antibiotics.

    Answer: False Key 1: A Section: 4

MULTIPLE CHOICE

37. Which antibacterial drug interferes with the formation of cell walls in bacteria?
    a) sulfa drugs
    b) penicillin
    c) tetracyclines
    d) PABA

    Answer: b Key 1: C Section: 4

38. Compounds related to penicillins are
    a) cephalosporins
    b) sulfanilamide
    c) tetracyclines
    d) antihistamines

    Answer: a Key 1: A Section: 4

39. Tetracyclines bind to bacterial ribosomes and inhibit bacterial
    a) energy conversion
    b) cell membrane formation
    c) DNA replication in the cell nucleus
    d) protein synthesis

    Answer: d Key 1: A Section: 5

ESSAY

40. Describe what is meant by a broad spectrum antibiotic.

    Answer: Key 1: A Section: 5

FILL-IN-THE-BLANK

41. AIDS stands for ____.

    Answer: Acquired Immune Deficiency Syndrome Key 1: A Section: 6

MULTIPLE CHOICE

42. Acquired immune deficiency syndrome (AIDS) is a
    a) bacterial infection
    b) viral infection
    c) mutagenic disease
    d) genetically inherited disease

    Answer: b Key 1: A Section: 6

43. HIV is the virus that causes
    a) AIDS
    b) herpes
    c) chickenpox
    d) smallpox

    Answer: a Key 1: D Section: 6

44. AZT is a drug to treat
    a) AIDS
    b) influenza
    c) chickenpox
    d) herpes

    Answer: a Key 1: A Section: 6

45. The genetic material of a virus is
    a) always DNA
    b) either DNA or RNA
    c) always RNA
    d) none of the above

    Answer: b Key 1: A Section: 6

46. Viruses are usually composed of combinations of
    a) carbohydrates and nucleic acids
    b) protein and nucleic acid
    c) fats and proteins
    d) protein and carbohydrate

    Answer: b Key 1: C Section: 6

47. In infected cells, DNA viruses directly
    a) interfere with DNA replication
    b) interfere with cell membrane construction
    c) interfere with protein synthesis
    d) interfere with all of the above cell processes

    Answer: a Key 1: C Section: 6

48. Retroviruses are
    a) RNA viruses that synthesize DNA
    b) RNA viruses that interfere directly with protein synthesis
    c) DNA viruses that synthesize RNA
    d) DNA viruses that interfere directly with protein synthesis

    Answer: a Key 1: C Section: 6

49. In infected cells, RNA viruses directly
    a) interfere with DNA replication
    b) interfere with cell membrane construction
    c) interfere with protein synthesis
    d) interfere with all of the above cell processes

    Answer: c Key 1: C Section: 6

FILL-IN-THE-BLANK

50. Antimetabolites are a class of anticancer agents that interfere with __________________________.

    Answer: DNA synthesis Key 1: A Section: 7

MULTIPLE CHOICE

51. One class of cancer drugs is antimetabolites. These compounds interfere with
    a) DNA synthesis
    b) energy conversion
    c) protein synthesis
    d) cell membrane production

    Answer: a Key 1: A Section: 7

52. Some nitrogen mustards that were originally developed as chemical warfare agents are used in the treatment of
    a) arthritis
    b) viruses
    c) cancer
    d) AIDS

    Answer: c Key 1: A Section: 7

53. Nitrogen mustards are used as effective anticancer agents against certain cancers. Nitrogen mustards are also carcinogens. From the perspective of a cancer patient, the DQ of nitrogen mustard treatment is
    a) low
    b) moderate
    c) high
    d) uncertain

    Answer: d Key 1: A Section: 7

54. Nitrogen mustards have been proven particularly effective against which type of cancer?
    a) leukemia
    b) lung cancer
    c) ovarian cancer
    d) skin cancer

    Answer: d Key 1: A Section: 7

55. The most widely used anticancer drug is Cisplatin. Cisplatin is a(n)
a) antimetabolite agent
b) alkylating agent
c) radioactive agent
d) light induced agent

Answer: a Key 1: D Section: 7

56. The nitrogen mustards are effective agents against some forms of cancer. They act by donating ______ groups to compounds of biological importance.
a) carboxyl
b) amine
c) chlorine
d) alkyl

Answer: d Key 1: A Section: 7

57. The nitrogen mustard of choice as an anticancer agent is
a) HN_1
b) HN_2
c) Cytoxan
d) H

Answer: c Key 1: A Section: 7

58. The overall death rate from cancer in the United States declined 2.6% from 1991 to 1995 after decades of increases. The decrease is probably due to
a) better anticancer agents
b) vaccines
c) a decline in cigarette smoking
d) less stress

Answer: c Key 1: A Section: 7

FILL-IN-THE-BLANK

59. Hormones are produced by the ________________ system.

Answer: endocrine Key 1: D Section: 8

60. $PGF_{2\alpha}$ is a ________________ that is used to induce the release of many ova from a prize cow in cattle breeding.

Answer: prostaglandin Key 1: C Section: 8

61. An important class of hormone mediators are the ________________.

Answer: prostaglandins Key 1: C Section: 8

MULTIPLE CHOICE

62. Hormones are produced by the
    a) digestive system
    b) reproductive system
    c) endocrine system
    d) central nervous system

    Answer: c Key 1: C Section: 8

63. A class of molecules that work at very low concentrations in mediating hormonal activity have been studied and used to treat a variety of problems, including blood pressure, heart disease, and asthma. This group of compounds are known as
    a) hormones
    b) prostaglandins
    c) fatty acids
    d) nucleic acids

    Answer: b Key 1: A Section: 8

64. Cholesterol is an example of
    a) a steroid with very specific hormonal activity
    b) a steroid with very general hormonal activity
    c) a steroid with reproductive hormonal activity
    d) a steroid with no known hormonal activity

    Answer: d Key 1: C Section: 9

65. Cortisone is a steroid produced by the adrenal gland. It has been isolated and used to treat
    a) AIDS
    b) cancer
    c) arthritis
    d) high blood pressure

    Answer: c Key 1: A Section: 9

66. The female sex hormones that control the development of female characteristics are called
    a) androgens
    b) estrogens
    c) estradiol
    d) progesterone

    Answer: b Key 1: D Section: 9

67. Male sex hormones are produced in the
    a) brain
    b) adrenal gland
    c) testes
    d) pancreas

    Answer: c Key 1: D Section: 9

68. The female sex hormone that is particularly important during pregnancy is
    a) androgens
    b) estrogens
    c) estradiol
    d) progesterone

    Answer: d Key 1: C Section: 9

69. Compounds that have the same skeletal, four-ring structure are
    a) ketones
    b) steroids
    c) sugars
    d) champhors

    Answer: b Key 1: A Section: 9

70. The general name for the male sex hormones is
    a) androgens
    b) estrogens
    c) progesterones
    d) testosterones

    Answer: a Key 1: D Section: 9

FILL-IN-THE-BLANK

71. Compounds that mimic the behavior of progesterone are called ____________________.

    Answer: progestins Key 1: D Section: 10

MULTIPLE CHOICE

72. Female birth control drugs attempt to mimic the structure and properties of
    a) androgens
    b) estrogens
    c) estradiol
    d) progesterone

    Answer: d Key 1: C Section: 10

73. Diethylstilbestrol (DES), a synthetic female hormone, has been used as
    a) a drug to maintain pregnancy
    b) a drug to induce abortion
    c) a growth promoter in cattle and poultry
    d) all of the above

    Answer: d Key 1: A Section: 10

74. RU-486 is a drug that blocks the action of progesterone and
    a) prevents pregnancy
    b) ends pregnancy
    c) promotes pregnancy
    d) prevents bleeding during pregnancy

    Answer: b Key 1: A Section: 10

75. In 1990, the FDA approved a new contraceptive device for use in the US. The device was
    a) a male contraceptive pill
    b) a progesterone like drug implant device
    c) a once a year injection for females
    d) RU-486

    Answer: b Key 1: A Section: 10

76. The first commercially available female contraceptive drug was produced in
    a) 1935
    b) 1950
    c) 1960
    d) 1975

    Answer: c Key 1: A Section: 10

77. DES has been banned as an additive in cattle feed because it
    a) is a carcinogen
    b) was ineffective
    c) is poisonous
    d) causes allergic reactions

    Answer: a Key 1: A Section: 10

FILL-IN-THE-BLANK

78. Drugs that affect the human mind are called ____________________________ drugs.

    Answer: psychotropic Key 1: C Section: 11

MULTIPLE CHOICE

79. An illegal drug that is classified as a "mindbender" or hallucinogen is
    a) cocaine
    b) opium
    c) marijuana
    d) ethanol

    Answer: c Key 1: A Section: 11

ESSAY

80. Discuss the impact of ethanol abuse on society.

    Answer: Key 1: A Section: 12

MULTIPLE CHOICE

81. The most abused drug is
    a) amphetamine
    b) cocaine
    c) ethanol
    d) barbiturate

    Answer: c Key 1: A Section: 12

82. The first successful general anesthetic was
    a) diethyl ether
    b) nitrous oxide
    c) nitrogen
    d) chloroform

    Answer: a Key 1: C Section: 13

83. Chloroform is
    a) CCl_4
    b) $CHCl_3$
    c) CH_2Cl_2
    d) CH_3Cl

    Answer: b Key 1: A Section: 13

84. Most gaseous and volatile liquid organics produce some
    a) analgesic action
    b) anesthetic action
    c) hallucinogenic action
    d) stimulant action

    Answer: b Key 1: A Section: 13

85. The anesthetic (or intoxicating) dose of most volatile organics like chloroform is very close to the
    a) lethal dose
    b) stimulant dose
    c) therapeutic dose
    d) hallucinogenic dose

    Answer: a Key 1: A Section: 13

86. The first successful local anesthetic was
    a) amphetamine
    b) cocaine
    c) diethyl ether
    d) novacaine

    Answer: b Key 1: A Section: 13

87. Halothane ($CF_3CHBrCl$) has which advantage over anesthetics such as cyclopropane and diethyl ether ($CH_3CH_2OCH_2CH_3$)? It
    a) is more potent
    b) is quicker acting
    c) is completely safe
    d) is nonflammable

    Answer: d Key 1: A Section: 13

88. Phencyclidine (PCP) is a
    a) narcotic
    b) local anesthetic
    c) dissociative anesthetic
    d) stimulant

    Answer: c Key 1: A Section: 13

89. It is speculated that the reason users of PCP often experience "flashbacks" is that PCP is
    a) stored in the brain
    b) decomposed slowly
    c) fat soluble
    d) water soluble

    Answer: c Key 1: A Section: 13

90. Barbiturates are
    a) analgesics
    b) depressants
    c) stimulants
    d) hallucinogens

    Answer: b Key 1: C Section: 14

91. In small doses, barbiturates act as
    a) stimulants
    b) sedatives
    c) sleep-inducers
    d) poisons

    Answer: b Key 1: A Section: 14

92. An acquaintance takes a few alcoholic drinks after taking some barbiturates that have already made him appear drunk. Your acquaintance will most likely
    a) sober up at once
    b) stay drunk for days
    c) have a hangover in the morning
    d) die

    Answer: d Key 1: A Section: 14

93. The interaction of two drugs to give an effect markedly greater than either alone is called
    a) addiction
    b) activation
    c) stimulation
    d) synergism

    Answer: d Key 1: D Section: 14

94. Which one of the following is strictly a synthetic drug?
    a) phenobarbital
    b) endorphin
    c) morphine
    d) THC

    Answer: a Key 1: A Section: 14

95. In the last century, this natural product was a common ingredient in many "patent medicines."
    a) acetaminophen
    b) novacaine
    c) LSD
    d) opium

    Answer: d Key 1: A Section: 15

96. "Soldier's disease" after the US Civil War was
    a) dysentary
    b) infection
    c) blindness
    d) morphine addiction

    Answer: d Key 1: A Section: 15

97. Codeine is usually produced as a
    a) completely synthetic drug
    b) slight chemical modification of cocaine
    c) slight chemical modification of morphine
    d) slight chemical modification of opium

    Answer: c Key 1: A Section: 15

ESSAY

98. What are the three components of addiction?

    Answer: Key 1: A Section: 15

MULTIPLE CHOICE

99. Heroin is an easy to prepare derivative of
    a) morphine
    b) codeine
    c) cocaine
    d) phenobarbital

    Answer: a Key 1: A Section: 15

ESSAY

100. The frequency of heroin overdose among heroin addicts fluctuates significantly over time. Health officials believe this is related to the quality of the drug on the street. Explain and comment.

     Answer: Key 1: A Section: 15

MULTIPLE CHOICE

101. The frequency of heroin overdose among heroin addicts is probably the result of
     a) decreasing tolerance to the drug
     b) variable quality control among heroin suppliers
     c) synergistic effects with alcohol
     d) reuse of hypodermic needles

     Answer: b Key 1: A Section: 15

102. Which compound was originally proposed as a "cure" for morphine addiction?
   a) codeine
   b) heroin
   c) cocaine
   d) aspirin

   Answer: b Key 1: A Section: 16

103. Methadone, an addictive narcotic, is used as a treatment for
   a) schizophrenia
   b) high blood pressure
   c) depression
   d) heroin addiction

   Answer: d Key 1: A Section: 16

104. Drugs that block the action of other substances are called
   a) agonists
   b) antagonists
   c) addictives
   d) analgesics

   Answer: b Key 1: C Section: 16

105. Heroin antagonists are effective at
   a) speeding up the breakdown of heroin
   b) chemically modifying heroin to make it less narcotic
   c) enhancing the euphoria associated with heroin
   d) blocking the binding of heroin to receptors in the brain

   Answer: d Key 1: C Section: 16

106. The discovery of opiate receptors in human brains led to the discovery of
   a) amphetamines
   b) barbiturates
   c) endorphins
   d) LSD

   Answer: c Key 1: C Section: 17

107. Endorphins appear to be the body's own
   a) analgesics
   b) antipyretics
   c) anti-inflammatories
   d) anticoagulants

   Answer: a Key 1: A Section: 17

108. Endorphins are composed of
a) morphinelike molecules
b) amino acids
c) glucose
d) nucleic acids

Answer: b Key 1: C Section: 17

109. There is some evidence that __________ are produced by humans during acupuncture.
a) acetaminophen molecules
b) endorphin molecules
c) aspirin molecules
d) all of the above

Answer: b Key 1: A Section: 17

110. Nerve cells are called
a) photons
b) neurons
c) neutrons
d) muons

Answer: b Key 1: C Section: 18

111. The fluid filled gaps that separate individual neurons are called
a) gaps
b) axons
c) dendrites
d) synapses

Answer: d Key 1: C Section: 18

112. Chemicals that transmit nerve impulses from neuron to neuron are called
a) neurons
b) nerve chemicals
c) amphetamines
d) neurotransmitters

Answer: d Key 1: A Section: 18

113. The common name of epinephrine is
a) androgen
b) amphetamine
c) adrenaline
d) codeine

Answer: c Key 1: A Section: 19

114. Abnormal levels of what neurotransmitter(s) is believed to be involved in depression and other mental illness?
a) serotonin
b) norepinephrine
c) epinephrine
d) serotonin and norepinephrine

Answer: d Key 1: C Section: 19

115. Norepinephrine agonists
a) destroy norepinephrine
b) mimic norepinephrine
c) block neural receptor sites for norepinephrine
d) all of the above

Answer: b Key 1: A Section: 19

116. Norepinephrine antagonists
a) destroy norepinephrine
b) mimic norepinephrine
c) block neural receptor sites for norepinephrine
d) all of the above

Answer: c Key 1: A Section: 19

117. Serotonin is produced in the body from the amino acid
a) alanine
b) glycine
c) histidine
d) trytophan

Answer: d Key 1: A Section: 19

118. Dopa is an intermediate in the synthesis of norepinephrine from tyrosine. Dopa has been used successfully in the treatment of
a) Parkinson's disease
b) Lou Gehrig's disease
c) Alzheimer's disease
d) AIDS

Answer: a Key 1: A Section: 19

119. What neurotransmitter is considered as possibly being involved in the feeling of "love"?
a) adrenaline
b) testosterone
c) phenylethylamine (PEA)
d) norepinephrine

Answer: c Key 1: A Section: 19

ESSAY

120. How may diet be related to the levels of serotonin and norepinephrine in the brain?

Answer: Key 1: A Section: 19

MULTIPLE CHOICE

121. Which of the following toxic gases is not a chemical messenger?
a) H_2S
b) HCN
c) NO
d) CO

Answer: b Key 1: A Section: 19

122. The amphetamines are structurally similar to
a) neurotransmitters
b) narcotics
c) hormones
d) prostaglandins

Answer: a Key 1: C Section: 21

123. Phenylpropanolamine is a widely used over-the-counter
a) analgesic
b) appetite suppressant
c) sleeping pill
d) cold medication

Answer: b Key 1: C Section: 21

124. Amphetamines are
a) stimulants
b) depressants
c) narcotics
d) endorphins

Answer: a Key 1: C Section: 21

125. Amphetamines are
a) amides
b) amines
c) ethers
d) esters

Answer: b Key 1: C Section: 21

126. Caffeine is a mild
   a) depressant
   b) narcotic
   c) stimulant
   d) neurotransmitter

   Answer: c Key 1: C   Section: 21

127. Nicotine
   a) is a mild stimulant
   b) is present in tobacco
   c) is widely used as an insecticide
   d) all of the above

   Answer: d Key 1: C   Section: 21

128. Cocaine is a local anesthetic and a powerful
   a) barbiturate
   b) narcotic
   c) amphetamine
   d) stimulant

   Answer: d Key 1: C   Section: 21

129. Crack cocaine is
   a) the hydrochloride salt of cocaine
   b) the free base form of cocaine
   c) a more potent derivative of cocaine
   d) synthetic cocaine

   Answer: b Key 1: C   Section: 21

130. Cocaine blocks the uptake of ____________ by nerve cells.
   a) dopamine
   b) epinephrine
   c) norepinephrine
   d) serotonin

   Answer: a Key 1: C   Section: 21

131. LSD is a(n)
   a) amphetamine
   b) barbiturate
   c) hallucinogen
   d) narcotic

   Answer: c Key 1: C   Section: 22

132. The physiological properties of LSD were
    a) predicted from its structure
    b) designed into the molecule by Albert Hoffman
    c) discovered in a chemical laboratory serendipitously
    d) all of the above

    Answer: c Key 1: C Section: 22

133. LSD is derived from a natural product found in
    a) opium
    b) rye fungus
    c) cow manure
    d) certain mushrooms

    Answer: b Key 1: C Section: 22

134. The principal active ingredient in marijuana is
    a) LSD
    b) PEA
    c) PCP
    d) THC

    Answer: d Key 1: C Section: 23

135. THC remains in the body for several days after ingestion because it is
    a) water soluble
    b) fat soluble
    c) produced in the body
    d) not excreted

    Answer: b Key 1: C Section: 23

Chapter 20: Poisons

FILL-IN-THE-BLANK

1. Toxicology is the study of ______________.

   Answer: poisons Key 1: A Key 2: I

TRUE/FALSE

2. Herbicides and insecticides are the only poisons to be found in a garden.

   Answer: False Key 1: A Section: 1

MULTIPLE CHOICE

3. Which of the following common kitchen chemicals are toxic at certain concentration or under certain biological conditions?
   a) table salt
   b) cane sugar
   c) baking soda
   d) all of these

   Answer: d Key 1: C Section: 1

4. In previous discussions the toxicity of drain cleaners, oven cleaners, and toilet bowl cleaners was discussed. All of these common household chemicals are
   a) metabolic poisons
   b) corrosive poisons
   c) mutagenic poisons
   d) carcinogenic poisons

   Answer: b Key 1: A Section: 1

SHORT ANSWER

5. List two common chemicals used in cleaning that are toxic and that will produce another toxin when mixed.

   Answer: Laundry or chlorine bleach and ammonia. Key 1: C Section: 1

6. Name one commonly cultivated potted plant grown indoors that is very poisonous.

   Answer: The philodendron. Key 1: C Section: 1

MULTIPLE CHOICE

7. The active ingredient in which of the following is a corrosive poison?
   a) rubbing alcohol
   b) drain cleaners
   c) dishwashing liquids
   d) fabric softeners

   Answer: b Key 1: A Section: 1

8. Which is a corrosive poison?
   a) carbon monoxide
   b) cyanide
   c) nicotine
   d) sulfuric acid

   Answer: d Key 1: A Section: 2

9. Oxidizing agents, like ozone, are classified as
   a) blood agents
   b) nerve poisons
   c) corrosive poisons
   d) carcinogens

   Answer: c Key 1: C Section: 2

10. Many oxidizing agents "poison" by
   a) deactivating enzymes
   b) hydrolyzing proteins
   c) breaking down carbohydrates
   d) reacting with water

   Answer: a Key 1: A Section: 2

11. Strong acids and bases are damaging to living cells because even in dilute solutions they
   a) are oxidizing agents
   b) are reducing agents
   c) catalyze the hydrolysis of proteins
   d) form dangerous peroxides

   Answer: c Key 1: A Section: 2

SHORT ANSWER

12. What type of damage do all corrosive poisons cause to living tissue?

   Answer:
   Corrosives cause the breakdown of peptide bonds, destroying proteins and their functions.

   Key 1: A Section: 2

MULTIPLE CHOICE

13. Which of the following is a corrosive poison?
    a) Sulfuric acid
    b) vinegar
    c) table salt
    d) sugar

    Answer: a Key 1: A Section: 2

14. Which of the following corrosive toxins is also called an oxidizing agent?
    a) nitric acid
    b) hydrochloric acid
    c) sodium hydroxide (lye)
    d) ozone

    Answer: d Key 1: C Section: 2

15. Inhaling which of the following components of air pollution can cause corrosive damage to the tissue of the lungs?
    a) SO_3
    b) NO_2
    c) ClO_3
    d) any of these

    Answer: d Key 1: C Section: 2

16. Which is a blood agent poison?
    a) nitrate
    b) cyanide
    c) nicotine
    d) sulfuric acid

    Answer: a Key 1: A Section: 3

17. Cyanide poisons by
    a) blocking oxygen transport by hemoglobin
    b) reacting with lung tissue
    c) deactivating glucose oxidation enzymes
    d) blocking cell protein synthesis

    Answer: c Key 1: C Section: 3

18. There is some speculation among cosmological chemists (chemists who study the origin of chemicals!) that ______ was the building block for nucleotides and amino acids.
a) CH_4
b) HCN
c) NH_3
d) Hg

Answer: b Key 1: C Section: 3

19. The average fatal dose of cyanide is
a) 1 to 2 g
b) 50 to 60 mg
c) 1 to 2 g
d) 10 to 20 g

Answer: b Key 1: A Section: 3

20. The treatment for cyanide poisoning is
a) sodium sulfate
b) potassium chloride
c) hydrogen chloride
d) sodium thiosulfate

Answer: d Key 1: A Section: 3

21. Which compound was used as a poison by ranchers to kill predators, and was later banned because of its impact on eagles?
a) NaCN
b) fluoroacetic acid
c) Cd
d) DDT

Answer: b Key 1: A Section: 4

22. Iron (as Fe^+) is
a) toxic at all concentrations
b) safe at all concentrations
c) toxic at high concentrations, essential at low concentration
d) toxic at high concentration, not known to be essential

Answer: c Key 1: C Section: 5

23. Pb (as Pb^+) is
a) toxic at all concentrations
b) safe at all concentrations
c) toxic at high concentrations, essential at low concentration
d) toxic at high concentration, not known to be essential

Answer: d Key 1: C Section: 5

24. Which of these IS NOT considered a heavy metal?
    a) Ca
    b) Cd
    c) Ag
    d) Hg

    Answer: a Key 1: A Section: 5

25. Which of these IS NOT considered a heavy metal?
    a) Pb
    b) Cd
    c) Al
    d) Hg

    Answer: c Key 1: A Section: 5

26. The antidote for mercury poisoning is
    a) thiosulfate
    b) atropine
    c) BAL
    d) EDTA

    Answer: c Key 1: A Section: 5

27. The human body can eliminate half of a dose of mercury poisoning in ____ days.
    a) 1
    b) 100
    c) 70
    d) 365

    Answer: c Key 1: A Section: 5

28. Arsenic compounds are poisons because they
    a) deactivate enzymes
    b) catalyze the hydrolysis of proteins
    c) are reducing agents
    d) deplete calcium from the bones

    Answer: a Key 1: A Section: 5

29. The antidote for mercury poisoning, BAL, acts by
    a) precipitating mercury
    b) reducing Hg^{2+} to Hg
    c) oxidizing Hg to Hg^{2+}
    d) complexing the mercury

    Answer: d Key 1: A Section: 5

30. Lead is used in
    a) batteries
    b) some gasolines
    c) plumbing fixtures
    d) all of the above

    Answer: d Key 1: A Section: 5

31. Lead poisoning affects the
    a) digestive system
    b) endocrine system
    c) reproductive system
    d) central nervous system

    Answer: d Key 1: C Section: 5

32. The number of children suffering from lead poisoning each year is
    a) less than one hundred
    b) several thousand
    c) several hundred
    d) more than one million

    Answer: b Key 1: A Section: 5

33. Cadmium poisons by
    a) promoting loss of calcium from bone
    b) deactivating enzymes
    c) hydrolyzing proteins
    d) destroying cell membranes

    Answer: a Key 1: C Section: 5

34. The cause of itai-itai, the "ouch-ouch" disease is
    a) cadmium
    b) copper
    c) mercury
    d) lead

    Answer: a Key 1: C Section: 5

FILL-IN-THE-BLANK

35. People with Alzheimer's disease are deficient in ________.

    Answer: acetylase Key 1: A Section: 6

MULTIPLE CHOICE

36. Botulin, the most deadly poison known, is
    a) organophosphorus pesticide
    b) a nerve gas for chemical warfare
    c) formed in improperly canned food by anaerobic bacteria
    d) a chlorinated hydrocarbon

    Answer: c Key 1: A Section: 6

37. Curare, the blow dart poison of Amazonian Indians, disrupts the acetylcholine cycle by blocking
    a) receptors
    b) the release of acetylcholine
    c) the breakdown of acetylcholine
    d) the formation of acetylcholine

    Answer: a Key 1: A Section: 6

38. The antidote for poisoning by organophosphorus nerve poisons is
    a) atropine
    b) EDTA
    c) thiosulfate
    d) BAL

    Answer: a Key 1: A Section: 6

39. Which of the following will make the most effective poison for rats and mice?
    a) aspirin, LD_{50} = 1.5 g/kg
    b) acetaminophen, LD_{50} = 0.34 g/kg
    c) nicotine, LD_{50} = 0.23 g/kg
    d) caffeine, LD_{50} = 0.13 g/kg

    Answer: d Key 1: C Section: 6

40. The organ most used for the detoxification of poisons in the human body is the
    a) liver
    b) pancreas
    c) stomach
    d) thyroid

    Answer: a Key 1: A Section: 8

FILL-IN-THE-BLANK

41. The system of liver enzymes that helps to detoxify poisons is called ______________________.

    Answer: P-450 Key 1: A Section: 8

MULTIPLE CHOICE

42. Most detoxification of poisons in the body occurs via
    a) combination with chemicals other than oxygen
    b) oxidation
    c) reduction
    d) direct excretion

    Answer: b Key 1: A Section: 8

43. Generally, alcohols and other foreign substances are detoxified in the
    a) stomach
    b) kidneys
    c) liver
    d) intestine

    Answer: c Key 1: A Section: 8

44. The antidote for methyl alcohol poisoning is
    a) propyl alcohol
    b) salt
    c) ethyl alcohol
    d) iron sulfate

    Answer: c Key 1: A Section: 8

ESSAY

45. What is LD_{50}? Use the following compounds and their LD_{50}s to explain.
    Caffeine: LD_{50} = 0.13 g/kg mice
    Sodium Cyanide: LD_{50} = 15 mg/kg (estimated)

    Answer: Key 1: A Section: 7

MULTIPLE CHOICE

46. The known cause of approximately 40% of all cancers is
    a) asbestos
    b) cigarette smoking
    c) saccharin
    d) trichloroethylene

    Answer: b Key 1: C Section: 9

47. The carcinogenic hydrocarbons produced during the incomplete burning of organic materials are known as
    a) aromatic hydrocarbons
    b) benzene
    c) polyaromatic hydrocarbons
    d) all of the above

    Answer: c Key 1: C Section: 9

48. Which class of compounds is thought to be possibly anticarcinogenic?
    a) oxidizing agents
    b) steroids
    c) teratogens
    d) antioxidants

    Answer: d Key 1: A Section: 9

TRUE/FALSE

49. Only synthetic chemicals have been found to be carcinogenic.

    Answer: False Key 1: C Section: 9

MULTIPLE CHOICE

50. The simplest and least expensive method for testing for possible carcinogenic activity is
    a) the Ames test
    b) animal testing
    c) epidemiological studies
    d) human testing

    Answer: a Key 1: A Section: 10

51. The Ames test is used to screen for
    a) all potential poisons
    b) heavy metal poisons
    c) mutagens and potential carcinogens
    d) carcinogens

    Answer: c Key 1: A Section: 10

52. The study of the behavior of a specific population and cancer incidence is an example of _________ testing for carcinogenic activity.
    a) Ames
    b) animal
    c) epidemiological
    d) human

    Answer: c Key 1: C Section: 10

53. Substances that cause birth defects are called
    a) carcinogens
    b) mutagens
    c) androgens
    d) teratogens

    Answer: d Key 1: C Section: 11

54. A well known teratogen is
    a) thalidomide
    b) botulin
    c) cyanide
    d) arsenic

    Answer: a Key 1: A Section: 11

55. Which would be classified as a reactive waste?
    a) sodium metal
    b) sodium chloride
    c) sodium bromide
    d) aluminum metal

    Answer: a Key 1: A Section: 12

56. The best way to dispose of a flammable waste is
    a) process through a wastewater treatment plant
    b) bury in a landfill
    c) burn in an incinerator
    d) store in a sealed barrel

    Answer: c Key 1: A Section: 12

57. The best way to handle hazardous wastes is
    a) to bury them
    b) to incinerate them
    c) to chemically modify them
    d) to avoid producing them

    Answer: d Key 1: C Section: 12